HELPING FAMILIES
Through the Church

A book of practical guidance
for pastors, members of church boards,
workers with children, young people,
and adults.

HELPING FAMILIES
Through the Church

A SYMPOSIUM ON FAMILY LIFE EDUCATION

Edited by OSCAR E. FEUCHT

CONCORDIA PUBLISHING HOUSE, Saint Louis

Prepared under the auspices of
the Family Life Committee
of the Board for Parish Education

———————————————————

Copyright 1957 by
Concordia Publishing House
St. Louis, Missouri
Library of Congress Catalog Card No. 56-12708

Manufactured in the United States of America

Dedicated to
Christian fathers and mothers,
to whom we owe so much, and to
all Christian workers interested
in strengthening the homes of today.

Foreword

THE CHRISTIAN CHURCH joins many others in talking about the family today, because the family, any family in our world, feels the force and impact of a great many difficulties. Not every family, not even every Christian family, can resist and triumph over them.

The church knows itself to be surrounded, beset, and invaded by the forces of the devil, the world, and the flesh. These forces invade the life not merely of the church, but also of its component individuals and families. These forces are versatile and often attractive; their objective is the weakening, the disintegration or replacement, the secularization and profaning of the Christian family.

HELPING FAMILIES is designed to do just what the words say. It brings an array of resources, tried and tested on the battle line of the kingdom of God versus the kingdom of Satan, for the direct use of families and for the purposeful use of those who with Christian family members everywhere look for the godly assistance needed to be and do, believe and live, worship and work — "as being heirs together of the grace of life" (1 Peter 3: 7).

"Heirs together of the grace of life." The Christian family does not come into being casually or continue accidentally; it is a valid aspect of the relationship between people in and through the love of God in Christ.

"Heirs together of the grace of life." The Christian family as part of God's order of life for men and women, for boys and girls, is the natural, basic unit of resistance to demonic authority, directly felt or indirectly manifested in the claims and gains of any would-be totalitarian or omnicompetent state. The Christian family sees all authority in reference to Christ the Lord, the Source of all authority.

"Heirs together of the grace of life." The Christian family in and under the Gospel of Christ puts sex and its powerful drives into proper and wholesome perspective, adorns and sanctifies this great gift of God through the divine means of grace, and uses it with other fruits of saving faith for personal and general welfare and to the praise and glory of the Heavenly Father who gives it.

"Heirs together of the grace of life." Reduced to the ultimate, helping families must mean, for the church and church people, recognizing readily, accepting faithfully, and using thankfully the manifold helping gifts of the Spirit of God. When also such families fail, as fail they will, the failure, stark and real, is human failure. But in Christ Jesus there is the offer and the guarantee of forgiveness and a fresh start: daily repentance, daily forgiveness, and heavenly strength for the new day.

"Heirs together of the grace of life." The Christian family is not overwhelmed or overlooked; but it can be and wants to be a living and united witness to its own members, to the Christian fellowship and communion, and to its neighborhood and community, to the common yet unique actualities and possibilities of the power and grace of God.

WALTER F. WOLBRECHT, *Chairman*
FAMILY LIFE COMMITTEE
The Lutheran Church — Missouri Synod

Preface

THE PRACTICAL APPROACH to families outlined in this book should not be confused with new twentieth-century activism in the church. It is a normal part of the church's ministry. It is teaching that is more than verbalism and memorization. It is preaching that gets down to concrete applications in the basic unit of the church and society. It is pastoral work that extends beyond pious wishes and attacks the real causes. It is working with youth and adult groups, but it is the kind that goes beyond the "silver tea" and the "speaker with an interesting subject." It asks for a ministry greater than celebrations, observances, and holding meetings.

Helping families is not an expression of what has been called "the social gospel." It is the Gospel of God's love in Christ reflected and applied in our love. It is the functional side of sound Biblical theology. It asks for a faith that works by love — and the Bible teaches no other kind. The ministry of our Lord was carried into homes. The first applications in the practical parts of Paul's letters are to households. The Protestant church teaches the priesthood of all believers — and the priest is to function first in his own home.

Family life education can develop into mere social action for the good of the community. Even then it must be respected. But Christian family life education is interested not primarily in developing the *morally good* family but, by the grace of God, in making the *Christian* family. Its base and starting point as well as its drive and motivation is the love of Christ. It is only one expression (but a major expression) of the new creatures we are, when Christ comes to live in our hearts. Where Christ is, the home will be a workshop of the Holy Spirit, and parents and children will be His workmanship.

These chapters had their inception at a Family Life Workshop set up by the Board for Parish Education of The Lutheran Church — Missouri Synod. It was held at Concordia Teachers College, River Forest, Illinois, in the summer of 1949. Those who attended, and others who read the digest of that significant meeting, asked for the original lectures. But at that time we were not ready for a book. It took five more years of practical experience on the part of the board's Family Life Committee, much testing and evaluating of needs, a subsequent workshop at Concordia Seminary, St. Louis, in 1955, and ten regional training workshops to help develop depth and breadth in the program.

In a special sense these chapters are the product of the Board for Parish Education's Family Life Committee, which has in a comparatively few years developed a program both comprehensive and Christian.

This book is a symposium. Each writer treated his subject without seeing any other chapters. This accounts for some overlapping and re-emphasis of salient points. The editor begs your indulgence. He wished, however, to let each chapter stand alone, so that the busy church worker interested in only one phase of family life work could get adequate help in an adequate context from a single chapter. Many chapters, while similar, complement one another admirably. By way of example we point to chapters 14, 15, and 16, dealing with parent education.

We are indebted, first of all, to the writers of these chapters:

Richard R. Caemmerer, Ph. D., head of the Department of Practical Theology, Concordia Seminary, St. Louis, Mo.

Theo. J. C. Kuehnert, Litt. D., for many years professor at Concordia Teachers College, River Forest, Ill.

Paul W. Jacobs of Milwaukee, Wis., formerly with the Wheat Ridge (Colo.) Foundation, and now with the Social Welfare Department of the State of Wisconsin.

Arnold C. Mueller, D. D., head editor of Sunday school materials, The Lutheran Church — Missouri Synod, St. Louis, Mo.

Erdmann W. Frenk, Ph. D., pastor of Saint Peter's Lutheran Church, Joliet, Ill.

Arthur L. Miller, Ph. D., executive secretary of the Board for Parish Education, The Lutheran Church — Missouri Synod, St. Louis, Mo.

E. H. Ruprecht, parish school teacher, Immanuel Lutheran Church, Valparaiso, Ind.

Martin P. Simon, Ph. D., editor of *The Christian Parent Magazine*, Highland, Ill.

Otto A. Geiseman, Th. D., pastor of Grace Lutheran Church, Oak Park, Ill.

Marjorie Stolzenburg, M. A., case worker for The Lutheran Child Welfare Association, Addison, Ill.

Edgar F. Witte, M. A., executive secretary of Associated Lutheran Charities, of Chicago, Ill.

John P. Uhlig, pastor of Emmanuel Lutheran Church, Fresno, Calif.

Remus C. Rein, executive secretary of the Central Illinois District of The Lutheran Church — Missouri Synod, Decatur, Ill.

Arnold F. Meyer, executive secretary of the Colorado District of The Lutheran Church — Missouri Synod, Denver, Colo.

Walter F. Wolbrecht, D. D., executive secretary of the Board for Higher Education, The Lutheran Church — Missouri Synod, and chairman of the Family Life Committee, St. Louis, Mo.

We also acknowledge with deep gratitude the services of those who read the entire manuscript and made many helpful suggestions, namely, Dr. Walter F. Wolbrecht, Dr. Theo. J. C. Kuehnert, and Prof. Walter A. Juergensen of Concordia Teachers College, Seward, Nebr., all of whom are now teaching, or have taught, courses on marriage and the family; Prof. Arthur E. Graf of Concordia Seminary, Springfield, Ill., and Prof. Harry Gordon Coiner of Concordia Seminary, St. Louis, Mo., both teaching pastoral theology.

Many others helped directly and indirectly to make this book a reality. The men and women who, as participants in the workshops, gave many new insights; Dr. W. H. Reals, co-chairman of the Committee on Gerontology, Washington University, St. Louis, Mo., who reviewed the chapter on "The Aging Family"; and the many authors and publishers who so kindly gave permission for quotations from their works.

Helping Families is intended to serve especially the parish pastor, the Christian teacher, the director of religious education, the active laymen and women is the local church who work with children, young people, and adults, as they inaugurate and strengthen family life education. If it also serves all those who are taking leadership courses for volunteer or full-time church work, and students preparing for the ministry in seminaries and students at teachers colleges, the authors and the editor will feel amply repaid.

With the prayer that this volume might glorify the heavenly Father, of whom the whole family in heaven and earth is named (Eph. 3:14), this volume is sent forth.

In Jesus' Name,

OSCAR E. FEUCHT, *Editor*
Secretary of Adult Education
and of the Family Life Committee

St. Louis, Mo.
August 3, 1956

Contents

Part III. The Church and Family Guidance

Contents

Part IV. Family Counseling

Part V. Helping Families

Part VI. Materials for Family Life Education

PART I
The Christian Family

Chapter 1

The Human Family in God's Design

Richard R. Caemmerer

A BOOK ABOUT THE FAMILY should prove interesting to a great many people; for the great majority of them are in families, or have been, or hope to be. Furthermore, human beings don't have, or at least shouldn't have, their families like the animals. They should do a good deal of thinking about their families. Their young take a long time to grow up. Human parents and their children need a great deal of help to adjust to one another. The problems of finding food and shelter are getting to be more complicated day by day. It takes good thinking to make a good family.

Right from the start, however, we want to realize that a Being more than human has thoughts and plans for the human family. That Being is God. God designed men to live in families. God has a plan and program which families are to carry out.

God's plans and ideals for the family are amply set forth in God's Book, the Bible. If we want to embark on a fruitful program of helping families, we shall do well to review God's plans and intentions for the family as He reveals them in His Book. The Bible sets forth these plans, and it portrays families in action as they try to realize these plans.

1. God's Plan for Families

If you want to take God into your thinking about the family, begin by realizing that God made us. You miss the most helpful approach to life and families if you leave God out (Gen. 1:26, 27, 28; 2:18, 23, 24; Matt. 5:27, 28, 31, 32).

The Family Gives and Sustains Physical Life. When God created everything from nothing, He manifestly performed a great miracle. Just as miraculous is God's plan to hand on life from one living thing to the next. "Be fruitful and multiply" — that is as wonderful a word of power as "Let there be . . ."

God made man with special care. He joined the man and his helpmate ("a helper fit for him," RSV) together in a union that was to have priority over every other in their lives. In marriage they were to be one, not simply in acts of sexual intimacy but in an enduring companionship. God wanted this human pair, and every pair that would succeed them, to bring forth children, to live together with one another in households, and to care for one another so that each new generation might mature according to His plan (Gen. 2:18-24; Pss. 127 and 128).

The Family Should Give and Sustain the Life of God. The first human pair fell away from God. Therewith, as a reminder of their sad state without God, childbirth and breadwinning would become burdensome, and physical death would ever threaten physical life (Gen. 3:16-19). For man had forfeited the one ingredient of life that makes for success in carrying out God's plan, and that is God Himself (Gen. 2:7, 17). As men beget children and mothers bear them, they hand on only physical life (Ps. 51:5; John 3:5). Sin had separated the creature from his Creator. The cleavage from God is not, however, for man to bridge.

Before He ever made the world, God also planned to bring His life back to spiritually dead man. That plan was carried out in His Son Jesus Christ. Hence, the very first human pair received the promise of His help (Gen. 3:15). God sent His Son into the world to give life to men again and to restore the broken relations (John 3:1-16; 10:10; 2 Cor. 5:14-21). So God enrolled the family into His plan for restoring His own life in men. Husband and wife were to answer more than physical hunger in each other; they were to minister to each other's life in God through Christ. Human parents were to be responsible not merely for physical life and nurture, but for nurture of the life from God in Christ (Eph. 5:22—6:4). Our Savior wanted the tiniest child to have the life of God. He was, and is, Himself the Source of that life (Mark 10:13-16).

God Designs Families. The Bible sets down the characteristic for the family that meets God's design. In these characteristics there is one common trait: the family is to be permanent. It is to be an institution that provides a stable setting for the lives of children and adults, that holds people together in unbreakable ties.

1) Marriage is to be *permanent* (Matt. 19: 3-9; 1 Cor. 7: 10-15). Human beings are not simply to mate like the animals but are to enter into a permanent union that holds up against every shock until God Himself signals its end through death. The structure of the family has this on its cornerstone: "What God hath joined together let not man put asunder."

2) Husbands and wives, parents and children, are to be bound together by Christian *love* (Eph. 5: 1, 2). This word implies not simply affection, "being in love." But it is the divine word for an attitude of the inner self by which one person becomes responsible for another (even as God holds Himself responsible) and by which he makes the other person a concern higher than himself (Matt. 5: 43-48; Phil. 2: 1-15). The physical side of marriage thus becomes more than the stilling of sexual hunger, namely, care for the other person (1 Cor. 7: 1-5). Marriage becomes a concern for spiritual life (Eph. 5: 21-33). Love is an attitude in parents which makes them willing to sacrifice themselves for the spiritual growth of their children (Rom. 12: 1, 2; Eph. 6: 3, 4). Love causes children to honor parents, not because of their authority or power but because of the relation in which they stand to parents under God and because God provides for them through parents (Eph. 5: 1, 2; 1 Tim. 5: 1-8).

3) Families are *continuously to draw upon God for physical and spiritual life.* More important than housekeeping and care for the body is the provision for the life of the spirit through Jesus Christ (Luke 10: 38-42). First in the plan of God is His part in the lives of those who care for one another in the family. Members of the family are to remind one another of the part that God plays. They are to reach out to God for His provisions for the body and the spirit (Ps. 107:32-43; 128:1; Proverbs, e. g., 3: 11-26; Luke 11: 1-13).

2. Families and God's Plan

In addition to principles, the Bible gives us case studies of families — of some that followed the plan of God, of others that failed. Hence the Scriptures are helpful, from beginning to end, with suggestions for carrying out God's plan for the family. Throughout the Scriptures we read not simply accounts of family life but also a diagnosis of that life as lived with or without God.

The Early Age. From Creation on, families were of obvious importance. The patriarchs before and after the Flood lived and handed on their experience from one generation to another. Eve hoped at once to bear the Son who, according to the promise, would break the bondage of Satan; yet her first son became a murderer and the ancestor of a line that exalted the physical at the expense of the spiritual (Gen. 4). That accent on the physical led to a deterioration of life and necessitated a new start for the race (Gen. 6:1-5). Noah and his sons and their wives were a closely knit family circle conscious of the love of God and faithful in worship. With them God began a new world (Gen. 8:20-22; 9:1-17).

The Patriarchs. The patriarchs set the pattern of living for the chosen people of the Old Testament. Basic in that pattern was the family, how it made its living, handed on its property, cared for the marriage of its children, and, above all, looked to the fulfillment of the promise that One of their line should be the Blessing to the world (Gen. 12:3; 15:1 ff.; 17:4, 8, 9; 49:22 to 26). Abraham's chief trials of faith centered about the Descendant (Gen. 16—18; 21; 22). In God's design the families of the patriarchs were to be kept clean from contamination by godless people (Gen. 13:12; 14; 19; 26; 32; 33; 34). In the strong portraits painted of the patriarchs stand out the love for children (Gen. 35; 46) and the veneration for parents (Gen. 45:3-19).

Israel and Its Code. Old Testament people looked upon a scene — the deliverance of Israel from bondage; and the rite which led them annually to contemplate that evidence of God's love was the Passover, a family festival (Ex. 11 and 12). God Himself guided Israel out of Egypt and through the wilderness to the Holy Land. God's laws gave special attention to the solidarity of the family: honor to parents (Ex. 20:12; 21:17; Lev. 20:9); penalties for fornication and adultery (Ex. 22:16; Lev. 20:10 ff.; Deut. 22:13-30); purity of the marriage stock (Ex. 34:15, 16; Num. 31; Deut. 7); forbidden degrees of marriage (Lev. 18); inheritance of daughters (Num. 36); divorce (Deut. 24:1-5). The mountain peak to which the people of the New Testament look for proof of the love of God is Calvary, and the rite which emphasizes it is the Sacrament of Christ's body and blood.

Under the Levitical Code the unit of government was the tribe, with its constituent "families," or clans, and households. The heads of the tribal houses were the ruling princes (Num. 7: 2 ff.). The genealogies were scrupulously preserved (cf. Num. 1; 2; 26; Ezra; Matt. 1; Luke 3). The household became the one agency for religious instruction (Deut. 6: 1-9, 20-25; 11: 18-25).

Judges and Kings. Joshua set up a pattern for life in the Promised Land with the pious example of a household that served God (Joshua 24: 15). Soon came the unhappy years, however, of idolatry accompanied by some of the saddest degeneration of family life reported in the Bible (Judges 19; 21). Yet in the midst of these dark years are rays of filial piety (Ruth) and maternal devotion (Hannah, 1 Sam. 1 and 2).

The age of the kings begins with a noble family portrait, that of Jesse and his sons (1 Sam. 16 and 17). David, however, though blessed with gifts of prophecy and song, succumbed to polygamy and adultery and had to flee from his son Absalom, toward whom he had been so indulgent. His family was defiled by incest and violence (2 Sam. 13; 15; 18). Solomon, son of David and Bathsheba, was a man of peace. He exalted wisdom and praised marriage and the family (1 Kings 3: 9 ff.; Prov. 5: 18; 17: 1 ff.; 15: 20; 18: 22; 23: 24; 30; 31); yet, he, too, practiced polygamy with pagans (1 Kings 3: 1 ff.; 11). Among the unhappy rulers of Israel, Ahab and Jezebel stand out as the most evil pair in the Bible (2 Kings 9; 10).

The Exile and the Return. A long line of prophets warned a rebellious and idolatrous Israel and Judah against the wrath of God. In this rebellion the family had deteriorated as a training ground for godliness (e. g., Jer. 9: 14; Amos 2: 4). That downfall of the family was at the same time a potent reminder to seek God again (Micah 7: 6, 7).

When Jerusalem was rebuilt after the Exile, Ezra reproached the people for mating with pagans and admonished them to purify their line (Ezra 9 and 10; Neh. 12: 43).

The Book of Esther gives a stirring demonstration of a woman steadfast in her devotion to God, to her pious uncle, and to her royal husband.

Our Lord Jesus Christ. Turning to the books of the New Testament, the first picture is that of a family. Joseph, a Galilean carpenter, takes a young woman to wife though she was with child by One other than he. The child, he is told, is the Son of the Highest. In order to complete His plan for the salvation of the world, God sends His Son, and He sends Him into a human family as a human baby, subject to parents, nurtured by their care, maturing in their household (Matt. 1 and 2; Luke 1 and 2).

The Lord Jesus taught a kinship that was higher than that of blood (Matt. 12:48 ff.). Yet His most complete definition of God whom He came to reveal is Father (Luke 11:2-13). His most beloved parable likens the love of God for the sinner and the obligation of the older Christian to the weaker to relations in the family (Luke 15:11-32). His first miracle is performed at a wedding (John 2:1 ff.). A favorite retreat was a simple household at Bethany (Luke 10:38-42; John 11; 12:1-11). On the cross He provided for His mother's security and made her the responsibility of the disciple whom He loved (John 19:26).

The Church and the Apostles. The family remained central in the transition from the Old to the New Testament. No longer was the accent on genealogy. That had served its purpose (Eph. 2; Rom. 4 and 9). Even more strongly the family was prized as the nurturing ground for the Christian faith through the Gospel and the Sacrament. The first church worshiped and celebrated the Sacrament in the homes of its members (Acts 2:46; 5:42; 12:12). The first churches were probably the households of the first converts (Acts 16:15; Rom. 16:5; 1 Cor. 16:19; Col. 4:15; Philemon 2). Hence, as the apostles describe the worship of the first church, we get a description of the piety within the households of the first Christians (Eph. 5:19, 20; Phil. 4:4-9; Col. 3:12-17).

Some of the apostles were men with families (1 Cor. 9:5). St. Paul felt that for his person and business the unmarried state was preferable, but he honored marriage for others (1 Cor. 7:7 ff.; 1 Tim. 4:3). He urged Christian spouses of Gentiles to remain in their union and to sanctify the other spouse (1 Cor. 7:13 ff.). He made wholesome family life one of the means of witness for pastors and deacons (1 Tim. 3:1-13; Titus 1:5-7). He stressed hospitality as a virtue of all Christians (Titus 1:8; 1 Tim. 3:2; 5:10; Rom. 12; 13). Peter joined in these emphases (1 Peter 4).

Writing to Christians dispersed among the Gentiles, he was most careful to describe the virtues within the family circle as a potent witness toward unbelievers (1 Peter 3). Touching is the picture of the elect lady in 2 John who preserved the faith and love of her family against attack by deceivers.

God planned the family. He made it the keystone in human living. It launches human beings into the world; it starts them out on their journey of life; it protects them in mind and body in their first perilous years and helps to develop in them the personality which they will have for life. Above all, the family is God's instrument to insert into people the life which they do not have by physical birth, the life which God Himself must give through His Spirit and because of Jesus Christ.

This is a grand design, a large order. But God has given adequate means to carry out His design. In His Word He has given chart and blueprint for the family, precepts and counsel, records of successful and unsuccessful families. But more — He has given the fuel for running this complex mechanism and helping it to do its job, namely, His Spirit. The supply of that fuel can be replenished ever anew through the Word of Christ. So every Christian family becomes a new record of God at work, and a new unit in His plan for revealing Himself to others as their Father and enrolling them through Christ in His eternal family.

DISCUSSION QUESTIONS

1. What basic principles of marriage and family-living do you find in the first ten chapters of Genesis?
2. What positive patterns for family life do you find in the lives of Abraham, Isaac, and Jacob? What negative patterns or incidents?
3. What laws and regulations did God give for the protection of the family in the Old Testament?
4. What influence did royal families have on the life of Israel in the light of the books of Samuel, Kings, Chronicles?
5. List and discuss the ministry of Jesus in households as contrasted to appearances in public places.
6. How would you characterize the Christian family in the early church on the basis of the Book of Acts?
7. Which are the chief references in Paul's writings to marriage, husband-wife relationships, family relations?
8. Discuss Paul's teaching in the light of family life trends in America today.

Chapter 2

The Nature of the Christian Home

Oscar E. Feucht

USUALLY PEOPLE ANSWER THE QUESTION "When is a home Christian?" by saying, "When certain conditions are fulfilled, and certain practices have been adopted." They are thinking of such things as saying grace at meals, having family prayers, and reading the Bible. Others will say, "When the family is affiliated with a Christian church."

No one will deny that these practices are important. Yet all these things can be done in such a routine fashion as to be only "surface symptoms" or "mere traditions." They can be counterfeit coin instead of genuine identification marks. We must not make the mistake of identifying the means of religion with the ends. The Christian home is more than Bible on the table, some religious pictures, and routine table prayers.

On the other hand, we believe that where the means of grace are employed, there the Holy Spirit is at work. That means that where father, mother, and children seek the Lord in His Word, where He is found, there faith is quickened, and Christian love is awakened.

We must also ask ourselves, "What does it mean to be Christian?" There are churches and individuals who define Christianity as merely "following Jesus Christ." They define it as a life lived after the pattern which Jesus set in His own life. But is this reducing Christianity to a "works religion" when essentially it is a faith-life? Being a Christian starts with the new birth. The end result is a whole philosophy and life that is the outgrowth of the Spirit working in our hearts. The Holy

Spirit works repentance and saving faith. He also causes faith to work in our lives, transforming us by God's grace into new creatures (2 Cor. 5:17). It is this definition of "Christian" which this book accepts as fundamental.

In writing about the Christian home there is danger that we become too rigid, that is, that we set down a group of practices and demand outward conformity with a sort of "legal code." This is not evangelical Christianity. One can also describe home situations which are so ideal that comparatively few families can attain them. This could be discouraging. Rather we intend to name those elements which we consider essentially Christian, and to urge all families by the grace of God to grow up with respect to those elements as God does His work in the heart and in the home. Christian families are not perfect. None will attain fully the ideals toward which they strive. But all of them are working day by day to please God. God, who dwells in them, enables them to grow stronger in Christ.

We shall consider the following characteristics of the Christian Home: A common faith in Jesus, a Christian conception of marriage, a Christian attitude toward parenthood, Christian teaching and guidance, Christian harmony and right relations, accepting God's values and God's will, a Christian atmosphere.

1. A Common Faith in Jesus the Savior

A family, like an individual person, can be morally good, can provide well for its members, and can practice good citizenship without being religious in the Christian sense of the word. It can be religious in many ways, according to the customs of a completely non-Christian cult, with much display of reverence, without being Christian. The family is Christian when its members sincerely accept Jesus Christ as the Savior from sin and desire to live as persons who are "in Christ."

The essence of the Christian religion is salvation by God's grace abundantly revealed in the life, suffering, and vicarious death of Jesus Christ and in His resurrection (1 Cor. 15:1-4). When people have faith in Christ, they are Christians (John 6:68, 69; John 20:31). Actually then a Christian home is one where real Christians live, those in whose hearts the Holy Spirit has wrought conviction of sin and has awakened faith in the complete atonement made by Christ for all people. A Christian is

a Christ-man or a Christ-woman, one in whom Christ has come
to live, not for a moment, not for a day, but always. Christian
faith is rooted and grounded in Christ and expresses itself in
love toward God and man (Ephesians 3 and 4; Galatians 5).

Faith in Christ permeates the whole life. It is more than
intellectual acceptance. It involves the heart's assent and daily
trust. That is why the Apostle Paul calls it the "obedience" of
faith (Rom. 1:5). This kind of faith transforms us. It leads
to a life *in* Christ, a life *with* Christ, a life *for* Christ.

When two people who have such a faith marry and establish
a home, that home will be a Christian home. There God comes
to dwell. Christ is the daily Companion and Guest. His kingdom comes, and His will is done.

Prof. Paul H. Vieth of Yale University gives us a good definition of a Christian home: "A man and a woman, who have
been saved by grace through faith in Jesus Christ, enter into
permanent union in Christian marriage, in the consciousness
that it is God's will for them and with the purpose so to live
their common life together and with their children that they
may grow in the knowledge, understanding and love of God
through Christ."[1] Faith in Jesus, the Savior, is the first essential
mark of the Christian family.

2. A Christian Conception of Marriage

God made man and woman for each other. Their bodies,
their minds, and their temperaments are to complement one
another. The love of husband and wife is as normal as eating,
sleeping, working, playing. Normal sexual relations between
husband and wife belong to God's order of creation. The Scriptures teach that marriage includes the marriage bed (Heb. 13:4)
and that sexual intercourse is not only a blessed privilege but
a conjugal right (1 Cor. 7:1-3, RSV). Sex as planned by God is
good and intended for good. It is man's misuse of sex that has
resulted in evil and much unhappiness and trouble. But from
the beginning it was not so. Nor is sex as planned by God to be
considered "sinful," "unclean," or, when properly used, "harmful." Reformers, ascetics, and purists have distorted God's teachings and have done great harm to marriage itself. Sex is God's

---

[1] Used by permission.

own plan for man's happiness and for the fulfillment of one of man's purposes on earth. Let marriage be held in honor by all!

Christians accept three purposes of marriage as intended by God for all mankind: (1) In marriage God provides a deep and lasting companionship between husband and wife, for their mutual enrichment, happiness, and welfare (Gen. 2:20-24). (2) The second purpose is "the management of the dynamic and explosive function of sex in such a way that it may serve rather than disrupt human cultures"[2] (Gen. 2:24; Heb. 13:4; 1 Cor. 7:2-5, 9. (3) The third purpose of marriage is to bring children into the world and to provide adequately for their care (body, mind, soul) (Gen. 1:27, 28; Pss. 127, 128; Prov. 22:6). The Bible does not teach that marriage (and sexual union) is only for the procreation of children.

Along with these three purposes we must recognize three distinctly Christian principles that characterize the Christian view of marriage. First, marriage is intended by God to be and remain monogamous. Christ answered the Pharisees thus: "He who made them from the beginning made them male and female, and said, For this reason shall a man leave his father and mother and be joined to his wife, and these TWO shall become ONE. So they are no longer TWO but ONE" (Matt. 19:4, 5, RSV). Secondly, Christian marriage demands fidelity on the part of both husband and wife. God has given us a single standard of morality and has given us one of His commandments for the purpose of guarding the sacredness of the union and warding off promiscuity. Both fornication and adultery are condemned. This is not true of all cultures or of all religions. Thirdly, Christian marriage is *for life,* and the bond is not to be dissolved. "What therefore God hath joined together, let not man put asunder" (Matt. 19:7). Indeed the realities of dealing with sin-hardened man have made for some exceptions. But it is clearly God's will that marriage once consummated is not to be disrupted. Therefore the phrase "till death us do part" belongs in the Christian marriage ceremony.

The physical, mental, and spiritual aspects of marriage have been compared to a house having a foundation, living quarters, and a roof. The *foundation* of marriage "lies in the physical,

---

2 David Mace in *The Christian Family in Changing East Asia,* p. 55.

because it is sex that gives to marriage its unique and exclusive character and makes it different from all other human relationships." [3] This is the "becoming one flesh" of which the Scriptures speak. When adjustments fail here, the whole house is likely to fall into ruins.

The *living quarters* of a house may be compared to the daily give-and-take of interpersonal relationships. There is a constant meeting of man and wife as persons — with their strengths and their weaknesses. They co-operate as partners in the same enterprise. They must, at the same time, continue to be lovers. They must complement each other. The man and the woman have different roles. In marriage we have the closest and the most demanding of all human relationships.

The *roof* of a marriage is that higher bond which we call philosophy of life. It comes from the couple's sense of values, and the Christian faith supplies this spiritual cement. Husband and wife work, and serve each other, side by side. What is more, they are to be partners in a spiritual quest. They are to build each other up in the Christian faith and to encourage each other in the achievement of God-pleasing goals. Many a husband has been guided into fuller Christian discipleship by the life and testimony of the wife, and many a wife has been guided by the husband. Mace puts it well when he says: "The married couple can climb the ladder to heaven together better than either can climb alone." [4] On the other hand, it often happens that a bad marriage results in spiritual as well as moral degeneration.

Successful marriage is vital not only for the husband and wife but also for their children. It is in marriage that many of the fine qualities of the home have their origin. When husband and wife live in daily understanding and appreciation of each other, and are themselves well-adjusted persons, their mutual affection and tenderness overflow into the lives of their children and even into the community and the church. By their own proper Christian understanding of marriage and by their achievement of happiness they create the ideal climate in which children thrive.

---

[3] Mace in *The Christian Family in Changing East Asia,* p. 57.

[4] Mace in *The Christian Family in Changing East Asia,* p. 59.

3. A Christian Attitude toward Parenthood

The desire for children is both natural and normal. God has planned it that way. Not only does man have love for woman, but both man and woman have a deep desire for offspring made in their own image, as they co-operate with God in the continuation of creation. Children, to Christian couples, are indeed a blessed gift of God and, having been given by God, are held in trust and looked upon as "belonging to God" (Ps. 127:3).

In having children man and woman come to a point of fulfillment. For that purpose God made them male and female. In the birth of their children their marriage comes to a high point of achievement, not only in the eyes of God but also in the eyes of man.

The coming of children provides opportunity for spiritual growth for husband and wife, since now they assume greater responsibilities by teaching and training their offspring to be useful, fruit-bearing Christians, and good citizens. While Christian spouses will always help each other to be spiritually growing persons, they will intensify such teaching by recapturing the great spiritual truths of their religion in the very process of passing on these truths to their children and helping their young people discover for themselves the richness of God's Word, God's grace, and God's house (Deut. 6:5-9).

In a Christian home children will be welcomed. "Be fruitful and multiply" is the will of God for a Christian marriage. Husband and wife will not in selfishness close the door to little ones. The children God gives will be carried in prayer before God's throne of grace, will be guided to Christ; they will be trained with a flexible program that adjusts itself to changing needs, with a discipline that leads from parental control to self-control to God-control.

Christian parents regard parenthood as their highest vocation. They give to the world sons and daughters who will imbue the next generation with a genuine reverence for God and a clear testimony to the Gospel, thus perpetuating the Church of Jesus Christ (Psalm 78). God can say of the Christian father of today what He said about Abraham: "I know him that he will command his children and his household after him, and they shall keep the way of the Lord, to do justice and judgment; that the

Lord may bring unto Abraham that which he hath spoken of him" (Gen. 18:19).

At the persent time the number of children in American families is on the increase. This indicates a healthy attitude toward larger families.

4. Christian Teaching and Guidance

Directly and indirectly every home teaches some kind of philosophy of life — good or bad. The Christian home does not merely "tolerate" Christianity, nor does it delegate teaching to the church and the school. Instead, it recognizes that the home is the foremost school, and that the family should give to its members not only the mere facts of faith but also some of the warmth and glow of personal testimony and experience.

Religion should not be taught apart from life. Nor is it to be restricted to one day a week. It belongs to the activities of every normal day, as parents share the great truths of God with their children and by their own example demonstrate the godly life.

Christian homes teach six essentials of the Christian faith and life:

Christian parents give their children a sense of security by explaining and illustrating from life *God's love and care*. Life is insecure in any age. Every person needs to have faith in the providence of God and His loving care. This is eloquently taught in the history of God's people in the Old Testament and in the psalms. Trust in God gives a security which no old age pension or social security can provide. Nor can insurance policies purchase it. Above all, the very personal love of God, as demonstrated in the gift of Jesus, is the birthright of every child.

Every child needs moral values that come from a proper *sense of right and wrong* as taught by means of the Ten Commandments. God has established a Law which is above every other law. No individual, community, or civilization can ignore God's Law without punishment. God's commandments are for our protection and good. Without them society has no solid foundation, and every man is a law to himself. Without a knowledge of God's Law the child will not fully know what it means to sin and offend God. People who follow God's commandments are blessed in many ways.

Every child also needs a solid foundation on which to build

life. This comes with an understanding of the Bible as the *Word of God.* Without the truths of the Holy Scriptures life will shift with every wind and has no solid foundations. Every thinking person asks: What can a person believe? What is certain and sure? On what foundation shall I build the house of my life? The Bible is that sound, well-tried foundation and authority. It answers the basic questions of life, equips us to meet life's crises, and gives the noblest conception of man as well as the sure comfort and hope of the Gospel of Jesus Christ.

Every child also needs the *skills of worship* — guidance in hearing, reading, and understanding the Scriptures, the means by which God still speaks to man today. Christian parents will teach their children to pray, that is, how to praise and thank God, how to confess sins to God, how to pray for their own needs and the needs of others. Every new generation needs to discover for itself the art of Bible reading and Bible interpretation, the art of worship, and the art of living by the Word of God.

But the greatest thing Christian parents can do is to lead every child to the *way of forgiveness.* That Way is Jesus Christ Himself. Every person sins in words, thoughts, and deeds. Every person has a conscience that rises up in self-accusation. It can be relieved only with a forgiveness that is certain. This can be found only in the free salvation of Jesus Christ. It calms our fears, removes our guilt, and gives us the assurance that we are God's children again. Without forgiveness the child is prepared neither for this life nor for eternity.

Christian parents will also want to relate each child to the *Holy Christian Church,* the Body of Christ, into which it has been baptized. Worship with the visible congregation of believers is necessary as an expression of a common faith and for the feeding of the soul. It is jointly with the Christian congregation that a believer carries out his Christian mission. Every Christian needs this inward growth and this outward expression of faith. Without it Christian faith dies.

The teaching of these essentials will not be delegated by Christian parents to the church alone. To do its part, the family will have regular family worship, personal, family, and table prayers; it will give help with church school lessons and will supply Christian literature. But it will teach as much or more

by Christian example and by spiritual conversation that uses the
everyday incidents of living to bear witness to God and His
goodness. Christianity is caught as well as taught. Parents must
themselves be genuine Christian persons; to be effective teachers
of their children, they must grow in grace and knowledge.

5. Christian Harmony and Right Relations

The family is God's design. He called it into being. He
created Adam and Eve. He supplied their first earth-home in
beautiful Eden. God also provided for good order in the home.
He gave to the home a head, the man. Together with authority
He gave responsibility. But this authority was to be exercised
in love (Ephesians 5; Col. 3:18, 19). Women are charged to
love their husbands and their children, and to be discreet, chaste,
keepers at home (Titus 2:4, 5). The husband is to give honor
to his wife, to maintain a relationship that bespeaks the equality
of both under grace and the joint inheritance of both in Christ
(1 Peter 3:2, 7). The love of Christ for His church — nothing
less — is to be the pattern of the love of husbands. Harmony,
not quarreling and bitterness, is to be cultivated (Eph. 4:32; Col.
3:12-21; 1 Cor. 13).

In the Christian home there is respect for the individual,
from the newborn babe to the aged grandmother. The New
Testament in many ways teaches the dignity and worth of the
human being. To God every person is precious. Jesus exclaims:
"Of how much more value is a man than a sheep!" Each child
is different and needs different treatment. Each person in the
family has his own personality needs. In the Christian home
no one rides roughshod over the desires and needs of another.
Both self-respect and respect for others are Christian traits.
The purpose is to help each person (husband, wife, each child)
unfold and grow, developing the talents God has given, growing
up into Christ in all things, becoming a well-adjusted Christian
adult ready to assume the responsibilities of life.

Good cheer and a radiant spirit should be a natural by-product of living under the grace of God and having a truly thankful
heart. The Christian home should reflect joy and happiness,
because it is in the nature of Christians to "sing a new song"
to the Lord each day. Good humor is not only in order but

a grace to be cultivated. Humor supplies a healing touch to the sore spots of life.

In modern homes thermostats control the room temperature. Every home also needs temperament control. Emotions out of control wreck many marriages, disturb family relations, injure children for life. Christian virtues need to be practiced first in the home. Emotional maturity needs cultivation. Christian families will pray for the gifts of the Spirit: "love, joy, patience, kindness, goodness, faithfulness, gentleness, self-control" (Gal. 5: 22-24). Jesus could be both gentle and firm. Christians will endeavor to be like Him.

Christian families will strive for such goals as harmony and peace (Matt. 5: 9; 1 Cor. 1: 10), friendliness and hospitality (Prov. 18: 24; Heb. 13: 2; Rom. 16), courtesy and respectfulness toward others (Eph. 6: 2, 3; 1 Peter 2: 17), industry and reliability (Prov. 12: 11; 1 Tim. 5: 8), service rather than selfishness (Matt. 20: 26). Sincere concern for one another in good family relationships is the fountain of good will toward all men and of all good citizenship. The whole world is sorely in need of human relations that are Christian.

6. Accepting God's Values and God's Will

The Christian family is differentiated from the "secular" family because it has an entirely different view of life itself. It allows God to determine what comes first. It uses His scale of values in putting a price tag on all things. It will, of course, not do this prefectly and always consistently; but it strives to look at money, houses, cars, clothes, recreation, entertainment, food and drink, social contacts and human associations, vocations, the arts and sciences, just as Jesus would evaluate them. "What is a man profited if he shall gain the whole world and lose his own soul?" (Matt. 16: 26). It is in this "Christian sense of values" that a man and woman reveal whether at heart Christianity is to them a philosophy of life or only a group of intellectually accepted beliefs that do not concern daily living.

Christians have one major goal for their lives: "to glorify God and to enjoy Him forever." They live not only by reason but by faith in Jesus Christ, as Paul says: "The life I now live in the flesh I live by the faith of the Son of God who loved me and gave Himself for me" (Gal. 2: 20; 2 Cor. 5: 14, 15). Life is

looked upon as a stewardship for which man is accountable to
God. It is to be invested for the fullest development of every
God-bestowed gift, endowment, and opportunity.

Prof. Paul Vieth puts it well: "Christians measure success
in terms of achievement in God-centered lives and Christ-like
character, rather than in material possessions. They live . . . in
the spirit of Christian love which sees God as a third Person
in every human contact and which transcends the merely con-
ventional human obligations. . . . In humble thanksgiving for
the joy which the guiding presence of Christ in their midst has
brought them, they accept and express in practical ways a concern for all people." [5]

Christians approach life differently in still another way. They
live daily under the providence of God and in Christian resigna-
tion to God's will in all things. They recognize that the wisdom
of God, the Ruler of the universe, is greater than the wisdom
of men. And it is precisely this, together with the assurance of
being in God's grace through Christ, that enables them to meet
life's crises with bouyancy, courage, and an inner strength which
only God can supply (Rom. 8).

7. A Christian Atmosphere

The spirit of a home can be utterly "worldly," or it can be
highly "spiritual and Christian." And there are many degrees
in between. A strongly Christian home has a spirit about it that
is soon noticeable. It is more than "religious." It is deeper than
routine talk of "the church" and congregational affairs. It reflects
the presence of Jesus Christ in the hearts of the members of the
family. Where Christ is truly present, there one finds security,
peace, hope, and a joyous outlook on life.

Such a home is a haven where fears and anxieties melt away,
where problems are worked out, where eternal values are kept
in mind. Birthdays and holidays are celebrated with more than
food and drink. A favorite psalm, a great Christian hymn, the
carols of Christmas and the alleluias of Easter are but natural;
for here is a family that has accepted the words of Paul: "Let
the Word of Christ dwell among you richly, teaching and admon-

---

[5] Used by permission.

ishing one another in psalms and hymns and spiritual songs, singing with grace in your hearts to the Lord" (Col. 3:16).

Good atmosphere in the home is composed of many parts — respect for parents and for children, a sense of fellowship and family unity, freedom for proper self-expression, sympathy, good counsel, hospitality, mutual confidence. These things give children and adults a sense of security and make home a true refuge.

But its chief ingredients are trust, love, affection. The love of husband and wife will overflow into the love for each child according to his need. Christian love is more than human affection. It gets its motives and its patterns of action from Christ.

"Love is very patient, very kind, knows no jealousy, makes no parade, gives itself no airs, is never rude, never selfish, never irritated, never resentful" (1 Cor. 13:4, 5, Moffat's translation). Love is the cardinal Christian virtue, and the very pinnacle of the Christian spirit toward which Christians strive.

The power of love in the home cannot be overestimated. Evelyn Duvall says: "When you feel loved, accepted, appreciated, and closely related, you can feel yourself lifted up to the challenge that is presented."[6] That is why psychologists tell us that as a rule there is no juvenile delinquency where there is a capacity to give and to receive love.

> The family is like a book,
>   The children are the leaves,
> The parents are the cover
>   Which full protection gives.
> *Love* is the golden clasp
>   That binds it all in one.
> Oh, break it not, lest all the leaves
>   Be scattered — and be gone.

These are the marks of the Christian home.

This is the ideal of the Christian family. No family will fully achieve this ideal. And many families will only approach it in a small degree. Nevertheless let us thank God for every approach toward the ideal which may be made, and let us ask Him to bless Christian homes in every effort to achieve such goals.

Every Christian pastor has seen homes that have made great strides toward the family pattern here described. Therefore the answer to the question "Can it be done?" is "It has been done!"

---

[6] Mace in *The Christian Family in Changing East Asia,* p. 62.

Yet it does not come without struggle, nor without flaws and some failures. Every family has its moments of tension, even of friction. Every family has its problems and its temporary setbacks as it rubs against the hard facts and ways of life. And yet we *are* equal to this cherished pattern of living — not in our own strength but in the power of Christ, who dwells in us, and in the power of the Holy Spirit, who transforms us.

DISCUSSION QUESTIONS

1. Why is it dangerous to confuse means with ends in describing the nature of the Christian home?
2. Why is an intellectual acceptance of Christ and the mere verbalization of faith in a creed not an adequate description of Christian discipleship?
3. What are the three purposes of marriage? What are the three Christian principles of marriage? What do you consider a Christian interpretation of sex?
4. Make a list of the blessings that come to a home through children. How do children and their care contribute to the growth of parents?
5. Why must direct and indirect Christian teaching be given in the home as well as in the church and school? Give an example of each type.
6. What do you believe is God's purpose in establishing "good order in the household"? In what ways does the home contribute to the socialization of the child?
7. How can the values of husband and wife who are members of the same church nevertheless differ considerably? Give an example.
8. Just what contributes to a Christian home atmosphere?

SELECTED REFERENCES

The Bible.

The Christian Parent. Highland, Ill.

The Christian Home. Abingdon. May, 1947 issue.

The Christian Family in Changing East Asia. International Missionary Council and the Philippine Federation of Christian Churches. 1955.

Orr, William W. *Seven Rules for a Happy Christian Home.* Scripture Press.

The Christian Family in the Modern World. Lutheran Education Association Yearbook.

Feucht, O. E. *Building the Christian Home,* Concordia Publishing House.

Chapter 3

A Christian Family Standard

Oscar E. Feucht

WE HAVE CREEDS in which churches express their beliefs. These serve as a standard and have helped to preserve fundamental Christianity for hundreds of years. In World War II it was the Confessional Church of Germany that rose in the defense of fundamental rights and divinely established truths.

When the White House Children's Charter (1930) was set up, it was hailed with enthusiasm and set the sights of parents and educators toward their goals with fresh vision and zeal.

Similarly, the Christian home needs a banner under which it can rally its noblest impulses and respond to the church's call for families that live their religion.

1. A Family's Charter

There are great Christian values and practices that belong to the heritage of the Christian family. They deserve not only to be preserved but to be championed, especially in an age in which in some parts of the world the family has fallen apart and has almost completely lost its religious significance. To help preserve these values, a number of church bodies have prepared Christian home charters.

In a general workshop on Christian Family Life, held in the summer of 1949 at Concordia Teachers College, River Forest, Ill., some forty-nine churchmen, mostly pastors, undertook as one of their tasks the drawing up of such a family charter. This task became the special assignment of seven persons (five parish pastors, a Christian mother, and a seminary professor). At the conclusion of the workshop this committee brought in a ten-point statement with a commentary and referred its report to the Board for Parish Education for further refinement. In the revision two more statements were added, one on work and one on play, since they were considered worthy of separate mention. In this manner the twelve-point statement given below was developed. It first appeared in tract form and was the basis of the 1951 Christian Family Week Observance in The Lutheran Church — Missouri Synod. Since that time the tract has had wide distribution.

"A STANDARD FOR THE CHRISTIAN FAMILY"

GOD Made Us a Family

+   +   +

We Need One Another
We Love One Another
We Forgive One Another

+   +   +

We Work Together
We Play Together
We Worship Together

+   +   +

Together We Use God's Word
Together We Grow in Christ
Together We Love All Men
Together We Serve Our God
Together We Hope for Heaven

+   +   +

These Are Our Hopes and Ideals
Help Us Attain Them, O God
Through Jesus Christ, Our Lord.

2. The Standard Interpreted

God Made Us a Family

We acknowledge that God ordained marriage for the welfare of man and woman, and as the means for continuing the human family. As husband and wife we chose each other and asked God to bless our marriage, which must be kept sacred and unbroken. We also acknowledge children as precious gifts of God and regard them as a sacred trust. We pledge ourselves to live together as a family in a manner pleasing to our heavenly Father.

We Need One Another

We acknowledge the God-established family as providing the ideal environment in which man and woman and their children can best supply one another's needs and find their fullest development and their highest happiness. We pledge ourselves to live for one another in mutual encouragement and helpfulness.

We Love One Another

We acknowledge mutual love and true devotion one to another as the will of God and as a basic human need. We shall constantly endeavor to foster attitudes and expressions of love between husband and wife, children and parents. In good days and in evil days, in strength and in weakness, the love of Christ shall be our pattern.

We Forgive One Another

We acknowledge the boundless grace of God, who for Christ's sake daily forgives all sins to all believers and gives them the peace of a good conscience. As He forgave us, so we seek pardon from each member of the family whom we have offended and pledge ourselves to extend complete pardon where we have been wronged.

We Work Together

We acknowledge that God has ordained work as the means of supplying our daily needs and that family ties are strengthened by planning and working together. We pledge ourselves to employ our minds and our hands in useful labor and to co-operate in providing for the physical welfare of our family.

We Play Together

We acknowledge the wise provision of God for companionship and recreation as a means for refreshing body and mind. We pledge ourselves to take time to be with one another, to join in recreational activities, and to plan our leisure in the interest of family happiness and unity.

We Worship Together

We acknowledge the worship of God through Christ as a sacred privilege and responsibility and as the effective means of bringing us closer to God and to one another. We pledge ourselves to gather in Christ's name in the family circle and in the Christian congregation, that God may speak to us and that we may speak to Him.

Together We Use God's Word

We acknowledge the Bible as the divine means of bestowing, increasing, and directing faith, as the necessary food for our souls, and as the certain guide for our lives. We pledge ourselves to read and study the Holy Scriptures together and to apply them to our varied needs and problems.

Together We Grow in Christ

We acknowledge that Christ dwells in the hearts of all true believers and by His Holy Spirit causes them to grow in Christian faith, in spiritual understanding, and in godly living. We pledge ourselves to aid one another in the development of Christian personalities and in the practice of Christian virtues.

Together We Love All Men

We acknowledge that in our attitudes and behavior toward our fellow men we should follow our Lord's example. We pledge ourselves to make our family a wholesome influence in the community so that our friends may be served, our enemies won, the righteous fortified, and unbelievers led to praise our Father in heaven.

Together We Serve Our God

We acknowledge that all that we are and have — our life and our time, our talents and possessions — is a trust from God; that all is to be used for His glory and the good of men — in the home, in the Christian congregation, and wherever opportunity presents itself.

Together We Hope for Heaven

We acknowledge that by faith in Christ heaven is even now our possession. We pledge ourselves to live for God and not to center our affections on the things of this world. We commit ourselves to the guidance of the Holy Spirit and pray that our family may in God's own time be united with the whole family of God in our eternal home.

3. The Practical Use of Such a Standard

We should like to indicate briefly five possible uses of this standard: for worship, in parent education, in evangelism, in family counseling, and as a family measuring device.

In Worship. — Connected with appropriate Scripture selections from the Old and New Testaments this standard makes an interesting set of home devotions for a two-week period where there is resourceful leadership on the part of a father or mother. Members of the family, particularly young people and older children, should get much from the resultant discussions, which should be an integral part of such family worship. Suitable hymns may be selected and read or sung.

In a church service dealing with the home the standard may be used alongside a litany for the Christian home;[1] for instance, during Christian Family Week. The unison reading by the congregation will add something significant to the service. It can be reproduced in the Sunday church bulletin or can be read from the front page of the tract[2] which contains the standard. Similarly, it can be used effectively on family nights at church, and it is most fitting as part of a home dedication service.

In Parent Education. — In 1953 the Family Standard became the basis of a series of eight discussion topics for parents appearing under the title *Making Home Life Christian.*[3] All twelve points are developed in this study booklet. This study shows how rich the standard can be when applied in life situations and in the hands of a Christian educator or parent. Here is enough material for a whole quarter's study in a Bible class for adults. A parent-teacher group will find that it offers enough material for an eight-month activity year. Fathers in the men's club of the local church and mothers and wives in the women's group will likewise find it a resource for a worthwhile educational program. It also serves as a home-study course for Christian parents.

---

[1] Feucht, *Building the Christian Home.*

[2] *Our Family.*

[3] Parent Guidance Series No. 2. Concordia Publishing House.

In Evangelism. — One Christian family in your community is worth a dozen sermons. In presenting the values which the church has to offer nothing speaks louder and more effectively than the faith and fortitude, the happiness and achievements, of a Christian family. In pressing the claims of the church on the unchurched, the appeal for a Christian home should not be over-looked. Whatever other appeals and invitations are used in winning others to Christ, the call to make the home Christian is both legitimate and effective. *Our Family,* the tract containing the Christian Family Standard, may be part of the equipment which you give to those making evangelism calls. Christian teachers will want to leave it with parents as they visit the homes of their pupils. Pastors and parish workers will find in it a helpful ally in pastoral as well as in missionary calling.

In Family Counseling. — The Christian Family Standard can also take its place beside other materials used in preparing young people for marriage and family living. It helps them answer the question "Just what is a Christian family?" In the youth group it can serve as the basis of a topic discussion, or for a series of discussions with pertinent visual aids.[4] The main emphasis of this standard is on day-to-day living with brothers and sisters and parents.

Similarly, the pastor can use this standard when he does private counseling with persons about to be married. It is something to give to bride and groom as they set out on their first weeks together. Families having trouble are turning more and more to the church for help. Often they diagnose their own troubles. The Christian Family Standard can help them see that marriages and families fail because people fail — fail to live by the standards God has given us.

As a Measuring Device. — At a recent family workshop a District director of education chose as his project "A Rating Scale for the Practical Use of the Christian Family Standard." By breaking down each of the twelve points of the standard he arrived at fifty-eight items on which families might check themselves.[5] Much good would come to the church and the home if

---

4 See selected Audio Visual Aids, at the end of this book.

5 For a similar device see *Self-Analysis Chart for the Home* (CPH) and the seven marks of the Christian Home developed in the preceding chapter.

once a year — perhaps during Christian Family Week — the families were shown how to use such a measuring device and were encouraged in the sermon to develop along the lines of the Christian Family Standard.

DISCUSSION QUESTIONS

1. Discuss the individual family council idea and its values for the family.
2. How can we get more families actually to talk about spiritual things in the home? How can we get them to face and solve problems instead of postponing solutions to another day?
3. What are the possibilities of serving families with a parent guidance tract rack in your church vestibule? What tracts would you order to stock such a tract rack?
4. Which of the five practical uses of the Family Standard could be used in your church at this time? During the next five years?

SELECTED REFERENCES

Feucht, Oscar E. *Building the Christian Home.* Concordia Publishing House.

Our Family. Concordia — Tract on Christian Family Standard.

Various Authors, *Making Home Life Christian.* Parent Guidance Booklet No. 2. Concordia.

Chapter 4

Christian Family Life Education

Oscar E. Feucht

THERE IS A WIDESPREAD INTEREST in families. The many syndicated columns in the metropolitan newspapers and the feature articles in Sunday magazine sections of these papers, as well as the appearance of articles on the family month by month in practically all periodicals, is evidence enough that this interest is very real.

Family-life-education courses are being given in thousands of high schools, and there are few colleges that do not offer courses dealing with marriage. Family problems came to the fore especially in the depression of the 1930s and in the period of World War II. The sharp rise of divorces and the several waves of juvenile delinquency aroused the whole citizenry. Sociologists have supplied much new factual information. But they have called on church men and educators to give the moral and spiritual assistance without which family problems cannot be solved.

Churches have not been slow to take up the new task of family life education in a concrete manner. A few years ago the Roman Catholic Church in the United States had full-time family life directors in seventy dioceses. It is conducting well-planned and fruitful Cana Conferences all over America. Protestant churches are developing family life clinics and seminars for the training of pastors and workers with children, youth, and adults.

There are commissions on family life education in the native churches of Asia. Organized family life work is found in Burma,

Japan, India, Malaya, the Philippines, and Korea. A family week is observed by the churches of Hong Kong and Formosa. Western ideas of marriage and the family are challenging the joint family system of the East in which the father and, after him, the eldest son is the head of a total household, controlling housing, food supply, and all material things.

In England and on the continent of Europe the churches have likewise awakened to the needs of refugee families and to the problems of young mothers in particular. The war orphans, the postwar imbalance between the number of men and women, together with an alarming moral laxity, have given the churches real concern.[1]

A glance at the bibliography at the end of this book is a further indication that writing in the field of the family, both by the social scientist and by the church leader, has been, and still is, nothing short of prolific, new books appearing practically every week.[2]

It is impossible for the church to be silent on questions pertaining to marriage and family living — because God is not silent on these subjects.

1. Why Families Need Help

In the previous chapter we talked about the standard for the Christian family. It is the church's task not only to hold up goals but to give guidance toward their achievement and to supply some of the materials needed to help families approach a greater Christian consciousness.

This is all the more necessary since the hindrances are many and each family, in making progress, has many obstacles to overcome. The lack of strict worship patterns, the indifference to Sunday as the Lord's Day, the weakening influence of the church in the community, and downright human selfishness are formidable roadblocks. New freedoms in regard to modern living are breaking down old guards. Other factors are crowded housing, greater leisure, increase in the use of alcoholic beverages, the large place given to social entertainment. Sex appeal is played up in motion pictures, radio programs, television broadcasts, magazines, news-

---

[1] As witness such books as Gunnar Buhre's *Du und Ich von der Ehe.*

[2] Note also such periodicals as *Marriage and Family Living,* the journal of the National Council of Family Relations.

papers, advertising — with a terrific impact on our thinking. An Oregon doctor in an address to his medical society said: "We are experiencing a sex hysteria which is doing deep damage to our children. Never before in history have children been subjected — so young and so steadily — to an atmosphere drenched with so many sex stimuli." All these aspects of our culture have contributed to the secularization of our society. It is in this environment that our Christian people make their living.

Louise Bracher, in her book *Love Is No Luxury,* lists the following as present-day threats to the family: (1) Removal of external props (economic, religious, legal); (2) prevalence and acceptance of divorce; (3) increased association of the sexes; (4) the cult of success (keeping up with the Joneses); (5) romance and happiness goals (as interpreted by Hollywood); (6) prevalence of premarital sex experience and changing standards of sex behavior; (7) studies in the sciences relating to man (knowledge of mankind greatly increased); (8) separation of members of the family from each other (in war and peace; woman out of the home); (9) mobility of population (eight million American children moved in a single year, 1948 to 1949); (10) poor housing and inadequate income; (11) transfer of religious training outside the home; (12) lessening of parental controls; (13) forces outside the home interfering with the rearing of children (radio, TV, schools, etc.); (14) the fact of change, which brings new emotional strains and tensions on all families and calls for continuous evaluation and adjustment.

We are living in a rapidly changing civilization, and family problems are not confined to America. Families are in distress in every part of the world.

In the face of these obstacles, can the church do otherwise than help its families understand the situation in which they find themselves, and give them concrete help in achieving the goals for which Christian families must strive? There are Christian practices, such as family worship, that need not be sacrificed to the pressure of our age if the church will step in with a constructive educational program. The fruits of Christian family living are too valuable to be easily forfeited to the Juggernaut of "modernity."

2. Objectives of Christian Family Life Education

The findings of the social scientist (which some have called "secular") as related to the problems of the family have been very valuable. Research in this field has helped the church to recognize and more sharply to identify the needs of families and individuals. Both sociology and psychology have given the American people new insights for getting at family problems and have improved their skills in dealing with such problems.

It is, however, more than a smoothly functioning group of individuals related to each other by blood that the church is after. It wants more than the good family or even the religious family. The Christian congregation exists to help build — with all means God and human science have given — a truly Christian family. For this reason we should be clear in our objectives. In the Concordia Seminary workshop on the family in the summer of 1955, the following general aim was developed:

GENERAL AIM OF CHRISTIAN FAMILY LIFE EDUCATION

"Helping every family in becoming by the grace of God a spiritually growing, responsible Christian family unit."

"Helping — through the total program and fellowship of the Christian congregation and through community influences;

"Every family — the founding, expanding, shrinking, and aging families of the church and the individuals attached to these families;

"Becoming — the task is never quite finished; we are working at it continually; 'Der Christ ist immer im Werden' (Martin Luther); [3]

"Grace of God — by the divine influence of the Word of God and the sacraments (primary means), and by the other experiences and human knowledge which God allows us to discover and thus provides (secondary means);

"Spiritually growing — husband and wife, parents and children increasing in the grace and knowledge of Jesus Christ and in the Christian life, through the years;

"Responsible — assuming and discharging well the function of the family, the roles of its members, in marital and familial

---

[3] "The Christian is constantly in the process of development."

relationships, in church and community relationships; passing
on the Christian heritage — being a blessing to others in fulfilling their Christian vocation and mission in all areas of living;
"Christian — not merely morally decent and good, not merely
religious, but specifically Christian — trusting in Jesus Christ,
the Savior from sin, and living a life dedicated to Him in thankful response for God's mercies;

"Family unit — having cohesiveness and togetherness; being
united with the bonds of a common faith and by Christian love;
and acting as a unit of fellowship and service — to each other,
to the neighbor, to the church, and to the world."

Specific Aims in Christian Family Life Education

More specifically, the Christian home today needs a Christian view of marriage, help in developing well-adjusted Christian personalities, and specific training for Christian parenthood.
People in general need a new understanding of the importance
of the family. We must help the present generation to look
upon parenthood as the highest vocation, a career to be pur-
sued with honor and fulfilled with success. All the shiny products of modern industry have little value compared with a man
and woman who have the fear of God in their hearts and who
give to the world children carefully reared in the Christian
faith and well equipped to give a good account of themselves
in the world.

We should like to present for consideration five aims in
particular:

1) Enriching the spiritual life of the whole family and lifting
   the entire spirit and purpose of the home

2) Helping parents understand and appreciate their children
   and equipping parents with the necessary skills for the
   Christian nurture and training of children

3) Preparing children and youth for Christian family living
   and good homemaking

4) Providing guidance toward happy and successful Christian marriage to persons married or approaching marriage

5) Serving the founding family, the expanding family, the

shrinking and aging family, with a Christ-centered and church-centered program [4]

Every church will need to phrase its own objectives in family life education. Each year it may single out for chief emphasis one of the above aims. Its aims should grow out of its own "Parish Family Profile" (see Part VI of this book) and the needs of its families. The program in a young congregation with many young couples will be different from the program of a church where a large percentage of the members is in the upper age brackets. All who teach in the church should help in setting up the aims for a particular course, in terms of knowledge to be gained, attitudes to be developed, and skills that should be acquired by the individuals — children, youth, adults. Learning activities or projects are frequently as important as knowledge. The "how" is as important as the "what."

3. An Adequate Program

What kind of a program is needed to meet the needs and aims of Christian family life education? To deal effectively with the need, a ten-point blueprint of action is herewith submitted. It is "spelled out" in detail in a later chapter.

1) Thorough Christian indoctrination for young and old
2) Helping people establish and enrich family worship
3) Home visitation that helps to raise the standard of families
4) A practical program of service, especially to new families when they move into the parish and to parents after the birth of a child
5) Using your child, youth, and adult classes and groups to train for Christian family living
6) Premarital and postmarital counseling
7) A practical program of parent guidance and greater home-church co-operation
8) Helping young married couples and helping the aging family
9) Making literature available and accessible
10) Using Christian Family Week to evaluate and strengthen the program

---

[4] *A Family Life Program for the Parish,* p. 5.

Much more can be done in our work with children, with young people, with existing men's, women's, and mixed groups already functioning in the parish. What is your program for men doing to help equip the Christian husband and father for his responsibilities as head of the family and priest of the household? How much good would come out of a woman's program (planned for all the women of the parish) that centers on the Christian home! God has endowed woman to be the teacher of her children, has given her intuitive interest in spiritual things, and has conditioned her to be the natural homemaker by interest, skill, and temperament. Not to plan the woman's program of the congregation along the lines of the Creator's own design is to ignore something very fundamental in the church's life and work.

You will have noticed that this program is rather broad in scope. This is to be expected, since the family embraces all age groups and is involved in all relationships. T. D. Talmage wrote: "A church within a church, a republic within a republic, a world within a world is spelled with four letters H-O-M-E. If things go wrong there, they go wrong everywhere; and if things go right there, they go right everywhere."

The program suggested is also definite and concrete since generalizations are not enough. Mere verbalization will not be adequate today — if it was adequate at any time. Merely telling parents what to do (without supplying the "how") only increases their guilt consciousness. A sermon once a year can't say enough, nor can it supply the necessary skills. It is wishful thinking to hope that things will work out all right, when the whole community environment is mustered against the Christian principles set forth in the sermon. Putting all your confidence in the next generation being trained in the schools of today is forgetting that life patterns are formed by present-day adults, and that children revert to the adult example they find at home.

Young people have specific questions (mostly unasked) about dating. Couples are hard-pressed for a Christian answer to the problem of spacing their children. Married people have personality adjustments which they are not making and, as a result, live from week to week in tension, if not in open conflict. Only a specific program will give adequate help to these people.

Some suppose that the "traditional" church service simply preaching the "Gospel" is all that is ever needed. These people forget, however, that the epistles of the New Testament are specific and that Paul wrote a whole chapter to the Corinthians dealing specifically with their specific marriage and family problems (1 Cor. 7).

4. Part of the Regular Program

Preaching, worship services, and an educational program that are oriented in people's needs, bringing the full revelation of God to bear on life situations, are indispensable! Family life education at first glance may be misunderstood. It seems large and challenging. Some erroneously think that such a program as is outlined here will add new burdens to their church work. We hasten to correct this view.

It is admittedly a new approach for many, but it is not an additional program. It is not altogether new. Our fathers did some very fine work in building Christian families. Our task today is somewhat different and more difficult. What was adequate when the whole community was Christian and the whole environment was "controlled" by a Christian citizenry is no longer adequate now, when the whole world "rushes into your living room" via radio and television. What was passed on by parents to children in the more leisurely living of another, less tense and preoccupied generation is not adequately being passed on in our urbanized living of today.

Obviously more needs to be done, but this doesn't mean that a church is now to forget its other assignments and concentrate only on the family. Family life education is most effective when it becomes a normal part of the congregation's regular program of preaching and teaching. The more it is integrated with the whole church program — instructions in Christian doctrine, the regular preaching program, the work of elders with the families in their districts, the work with young people, the work of women's organizations and men's clubs, the work of the board of education and the stewardship committee — the better will be the results.

This program simply asks for new "values" in old forms. It should be part of the weekly, daily work of the local congregation, that is, the work of all its leaders, from the pastor to the

superintendent of the nursery department. A particularly great
opportunity awaits the teacher in a parish school to enrich his
teaching of all subjects and make his work count for the homes
of today and tomorrow.

"To have an effective church program of family life, a local
church will not necessarily have to do much more or even much
better than it is already doing. It will often merely have to do
different things. The program of family life may properly be
included in preaching, church school classes, organizations and
groups, such as women's societies, and in pastoral calling and
counseling."[5]

Where the pastor and the teachers and leaders of a congregation have done some reading in the field of the family and live
with eyes open to what is happening in their own congregation
and community, they can make their sermons, lessons, and topics
life-related by making them more family-related.

5. The Church Must Lead

The church is especially fitted to work with the family. It is
closer to the home than school or welfare agency. Eighty-nine
per cent of America's marriages are performed by clergymen.
The church enters the home at the time of marriage. It enters
at birth and Baptism, when the child starts to go to Sunday
school or parish school or confirmation class. The church comes
in to help celebrate anniversaries and successes. It enters in
sickness and health, in sorrow and death. The church has interest in the whole man. But, what is more, it has the Gospel
of Christ, which supplies that peace (and with it genuine happiness) which only Jesus can give. It is at the foot of the cross
that the family receives both the motive and the pattern for
Christian living.

The real scene of action is the local congregation. It is here
that the pastor must supply insights and understandings, propose programs and subjects, select study materials and train
leaders, make the family applications in the teacher-training
sessions of the Sunday school, and spearhead the entire family
emphasis. If the pastor is lukewarm or cold, if he does not
understand, his lay workers will not only be handicapped but
discouraged. The people look to their shepherd for leadership.

---

[5] Sylvanus Duvall in *The Christian Family in Changing East Asia,* p. 110.

One other group has a major role to play, namely, the committee on Christian education (in most instances, also, the board of elders). Its agenda should be revised to make room for this work, not merely once a year but at least once a quarter. A subcommittee should bring in special plans each year for integrating family life education into all courses and for the fruitful observance of Christian family week (see separate chapter on this subject).

Accepting this assignment will make it necessary to rewrite many a regulation for a board of Christian education in the local church. Working with homes and helping parents do their work (and not taking their work from them) is the master-stroke in education today — as it has been in every past day, since Moses wrote God's directive in Deuteronomy (Deut. 6:1-9).

Yes, the church must take the lead. But to do so it must have (1) a definite program; (2) this program must be spiritual; (3) the educative process must remain centered in the home; and (4) the church must equip both professional and lay leaders for family-life education.

DISCUSSION QUESTIONS

1. How many factors in modern life can you list which show the need for helping the modern family achieve a Christian standard of living?
2. If you were to propose a set of aims for family life education in your congregation, what would you suggest? What aim would you put first because needed most?
3. Going back to the blueprint for Christian family life education suggested, which of these activities do you now have in your congregation?
4. Why is the "routine, traditional" program of yesteryear no longer adequate today in meeting concrete family needs?
5. How can family life education take the lead in guiding the family? What help may it get from other sources and agencies?

SELECTED REFERENCES

Board for Parish Education. *A Family Life Program for the Parish.*

Bracher, Marjory Louise. *Love is No Luxury.* Muhlenberg, 1951.

Sheatsley, J. *The Bible in Religious Education.* (Now out of print.)

Handbook of Adult Education in the United States. (Section on churches.)

Buhre, Gunnar. *Du und Ich von der Ehe.*

PART II

The American Family
in Need

Chapter 5

What's Right and Wrong with the American Family

Theodore J. C. Kuehnert

No ONE WILL DENY that something has happened to the family, our basic social institution. We need but look about us in our communities and in our congregations, and we see that all is not well in the average modern home. In other words, the family of today is not in a healthy condition; it needs attention — understanding and help. Let us follow the tactics of a competent physician and diagnose our patient. Our discovery that the patient has a temperature is but the initial step. The fever thermometer has told but the beginning of the story. The cause of the high temperature must next be sought before any remedy may be attempted.

The American family has changed in structure and functions during the past several generations. These changes have not been initiated by the family itself. They have been the result of the impact of social trends. We have changed not only our foods, dress, and mode of transportation but our attitudes and points of view in many respects. We have acquired different habits and have discarded approaches to the solution of problems which our forefathers considered practically inviolate. These changes are reflected in our personal life, in our family relationships, and in our parish activities. Is it surprising to note that family life has changed? The changing trends have had their impact on all social institutions, and it was impossible for the family to remain unaffected by them.

1. The Family of Yesterday

In order to understand why the modern family is what it is, let us briefly look at the family of yesterday and note how it differed from the family of today. We shall see the family of yesterday in the type of home in which our grandparents spent their childhood. Then we shall note a few of the far-reaching changes which have exerted their influence on America's way of life since that time. Thus from our vantage point in the middle of the twentieth century we look at the typical family of a hundred years ago. In 1850 ours was an agricultural nation. The population was less than twenty-four million, of which eighteen million, or 75 per cent, lived in rural communities. As a result, "cultural islands" developed in various regions of the country — groups of people isolated by walls of religion or language or both.

Size and Occupation. — If we look in on this family of yesterday, we find on the average four or more children seated with their parents around the table at mealtime. Children were considered an asset in the home, for they would help to provide for the needs of the household. A father shared the sentiments expressed by the psalmist who compared children with arrows in a man's possession and exclaimed: "Blessed is he who hath his quiver full of them" (Ps. 127:5). This family was a producing unit insofar as its needs were practically all supplied by its members on and from the domestic domain — field, barn, smokehouse, cellar, kitchen, and spinningwheel.

Functions. — The chief responsibility of providing for and protecting the family rested on the shoulders of the father. While he was ably assisted by the mother, he enjoyed the respect and esteem of his wife and children. In cases of sickness, home remedies were applied, since doctors were scarce and, if available, had to be called from far away. The care of the aged was self-evidently an obligation of the family. Losses of property through fire and storm were repaired with the assistance of neighbors. Recreational activities were centered in and about the home. Near the fireplace or stove the group engaged in family games or enjoyed listening to one of the members reading from a book. Above all, family devotions had their place on the daily program. The family altar was an establishment in the average Christian home, and the Bible did not gather dust on the table in the best room of the house.

Attitude Toward Marriage. — When our grandparents had grown up into young men and women, it was self-evident that they looked forward to marriage. Marriage after all provided a source of security: a husband was a provider, a wife, a needed helper. The marriage partner was selected from among the acquaintances. The prospective son-in-law or daughter-in-law was not a stranger and self-evidently was a member of the same church denomination.

2. Cultural Trends

Industrialization. — With the building of factories, America changed rapidly from an agricultural community to an industrialized nation. The factories drew their needed workers, men and women and even children, from the farms. This meant changes in many respects: regular money income, types of tools no longer owned by the worker, occupation and work away from home.

Urbanization. — Sites of factories developed into cities, some of which soon grew into great metropolitan centers. The city drew people away from the farm. Its bright lights and various places and types of amusement, the enjoyment of which was made possible by the regular hours of work, were magnetic forces which drew the population cityward. But the change of residence from the open country to the city meant living in congested quarters. Soon evils of the city made their appearance in the form of commercialized vice, racketeering, and delinquency. The degenerating influence of city life, which Thomas Jefferson feared, became reality. Today our population is chiefly urban. In 1850, about 25 per cent of our population was urban. By 1950 urbanites constituted more than 60 per cent of our population (Census Bureau).

Technological Advancement. — Endowed by the Creator with the ability to reason, man has used his mind to discover the laws and harness the forces of nature. Invention has followed upon invention so that our age is designated as the age of science. As a result of this technological advancement, much drudgery has been removed from our shoulders in home, workshop, and on the farm. What our forebears had to accomplish through hard labor is done for us by power-driven machinery. The conveniences which we enjoy and take for granted were unknown to them.

Transportation and Communication. — Steam-propelled conveyances on land and water, which had substituted horseback, stagecoach, and river barge transportation, have given way to the speedy automobile, the diesel engine, and the jet airplane. Distances have been practically eliminated, and regional isolation has broken down. Telegraph and printing press, followed by telephone, radio, and television, have carried urban culture into every nook and cranny of rural America. More than that, these inventions have made all of us members of a world community.

Emancipation of Women. — In the days of our grandparents woman's place was in the home, where she was fully occupied with housework and the care of her family. Today women and girls find much of their activity outside the home in the business world side by side with men in factory and office. In 1890 only one in twenty-two married women worked outside the home; in 1950 it was one in four (Bureau of Census). Colleges now provide facilities for women to prepare themselves for wage-earning positions, professions, and business careers. Like men, women cast their ballots at the voting booths. One of the greatest social changes which would dumbfound our forebears if they could step into our midst today would be the present economic, social, and political emancipation of women. But we cannot turn the clock back; we must meet family life as it is today — not merely reminisce on the "good old days."

3. The Family of Today

The impact of the cultural trends has greatly changed our basic social institution. Our modern family presents a vastly different picture from the family of yesterday, both as to organization and as to function.

Earlier Marriages. — With the higher standard of living, more young people tend to marry at an earlier age than formerly. While in 1890 half of the women twenty to twenty-four years of age were single, in 1950 less than one third were single.

In 1890 the median marriage age for men was twenty-six years, and for women twenty-two years. In 1951 the average age for men was 22.6, and for women 20.4 years.[1]

Smaller Families. — While the number of persons in a family is on the increase at the present time [2] the average in 1950 was 3.4 persons, compared with 5.6 persons in 1850. There had been a steady decline of the birthrate prior to 1940. Since then the number of families with children (and the number of children in a family) has been increasing. While in 1940 there were 281 children in the United States per 1,000 women of childbearing age, by 1947 this number had risen to 367. From 1940 to 1950 the number of families having a third baby rose 57 per cent, and those having a fourth child was up 37 per cent.[3] Nonetheless there are a great number of childless or one-child marriages.

The reasons for smaller families are given: City life is not conducive to large families; children are no longer regarded as an economic asset; families have higher standards of living; more married women work outside the home; families are less stable.

Patriarchal Control on the Wane. — The impact of urban culture has contributed much toward the disintegration of family life. The family no longer lives and thinks as a group. Each member develops and follows his own interests. The patriarchal pattern is disappearing. Where the husband and father is still the nominal head of the group, his authority and influence are on the decline. In many families maternal domination is evident; and the filiocentric, or child-controlled family is not an isolated phenomenon on the American scene. These phenomena, too, are often the result of conditions practically beyond our control.

Functions of the Modern Family. — As indicated by the declining birthrate, materialism and pleasure philosophy have weakened the reproductive functions of the family. Under the pre-

---

[1] Kirkendall, Lester A. *Too Young To Marry?* Public Affairs Pamphlet, 1956.

[2] In Canada there were 224 children for every hundred families in 1948. By 1955 there were 237 children per hundred families. Eric Hutton in *Maclean's Magazine,* May 26, 1956.

[3] Duvall & Hill. *When You Marry,* p. 436.

tense of retaining a decent standard of living, the operation of
God's law of propagation, which He has vested solely in the
estate of marriage, is negated or obviated in many a marriage
today.

The care and rearing of children, formerly a self-evident
concern of the family, is largely delegated to other agencies.
This is a recognized weakness of present-day life. Parents rely
on the school and perhaps on the church to an increasing extent for guiding the physical, intellectual, moral, and religious
development of their children. Through the downward extension of our formal agencies of child training — the kindergarten, nursery school, beginners' department in Sunday schools
— the brief preschool period of home training has been short-
ened still more. As a result, the home influence during the
most impressionable years has been weakened.

The protective and recreational functions are no longer the
prerogative of the home. The sick, the aged, and the orphans,
formerly the wards of the family, find their care in community-
provided institutions. Diversified commercialized recreation sat-
isfies the individualized interests of the members and practically
nullifies the very attempts of competition by the family in this
area. Suburban living and television are new phenomena that
are bringing families together again — to a degree.

Last, but not least, the modern family seems to have relin-
quished or lost consciousness of its religious function. The family
altar has become as outmoded as the heating stove in the average
American home and has disappeared in most church-related
homes. The Bible is an unread book in many homes, and even
table prayers have become a discarded practice. Statistics show
that millions of American children grow up like pagans because
their parents, by precept and example, are depriving them of
all religious guidance and spiritual nourishment.

4. What Is Right with the Family?

Despite the ravaging effects of the cultural trends, the family
is still recognized as the basic social institution not only by the
church but by the state and society at large as well. The state
does not approve illegitimacy but makes the family the legalized
agency for the propagation of the race; the church recognizes
it as a means for the Spirit of God to create in children a con-

sciousness of their relationship to their Heavenly Father; and society regards the family as the chief agency through which the child becomes a socialized individual. Basically, the family has retained its functions even though these functions have been more or less delegated, but not entirely surrendered, to other institutions.

An aspect of family life which sociologists believe has been considerably strengthened is the affectional tie between husband and wife and parent and child. One of the purposes of marriage, companionship, stands in sharper focus today than was evident generations ago. While the giving and receiving of affection has always been considered a basic function of the family, the demonstration of it is much greater today than it has been in previous times. We hear husbands and wives publicly use terms of endearment which formerly were regarded out of place in our puritanic culture. Demonstrations of affection are also more obvious today in the observance of wedding anniversaries and birthdays through personal gifts to the extent that such practice has become highly commercialized (family birthday and Mother's and Father's Day greeting cards, flowers, specially boxed sweets, etc.). Family vacations in the automobile are common. In short, companionship, one of God's purposes of marriage, seems to be recognized and attained to a greater extent today than formerly.

Affectional, Cultural Aspects. — Writers in our popular magazines frequently have stressed the affectional aspect of marriage and family life in modern society. One such writer admits that the family has changed, that in an economic sense it is no longer what it used to be; but he states that "family solidarity is not based solely on economic necessity but on the deepseated eternal needs of men, women, and children." [4] Other writers make similar observations.

In spite of the loss of the historical functions of the family — economic, protective, educational, recreational, and religious — it is necessary to realize that the family still retains two intrinsic functions. While various forces are shearing from the family its institutional significance, it still maintains its affectional and cultural activities. More and more the American family is becoming a union of

---

[4] "The Family Is Still America's Backbone," *Coronet,* July, 1949.

husband and wife, parents and children, based upon the
sentiment of love, common interests, and companionship.[5]

5. What Is Wrong with the Family?

The change in organization and function has altered the pattern which the family assumed generations ago. If we merely
see the changed pattern and make it our criterion of evaluation,
our analysis is bound to be superficial. Then the spotlight is
turned on symptoms, and the causes are ignored.

Evidence of Family Disintegration. — While some aspects of
family life appear to have improved, nevertheless it is evident
that the family has lost much of its former stability because so
many new threats and dangers have arisen. The family is no
longer that coherent, integrated group, unified by bonds of loyalty, common interests, mutual understanding, and deep concern on the part of each member for the welfare of the others.
Husband-wife and parent-child relationships frequently show
that all is not well. The prevalence of the broken home, notably
the mounting divorce rate which has risen to one divorce to
four marriages in 1946, is an alarming omen. The sensuality
which characterizes our modern way of life, reflected in the
appeal to sex in modern entertainment and advertising, and
revealed by the prevalence of extra-marital sex relations and
various types of sex perversion, according to the Kinsey [6] report,
is, to put it mildly, alarming. Another example of deterioration
is the waning of responsible parenthood and of filial respect.

Causes of Deterioration. — The family consists of individuals.
In the personalities of the individual members one must look
for the causes which have weakened the family and will continue
to sap its strength. The chain is as strong as its links make it
strong. This is highly significant for the church in its program.

Why do many marriages prove unsuccessful? The records
of courts and social workers supply the answer. Maladjusted
personalities create problems which are found almost insoluble.
The family is the area for human interaction. Here personalities
find their truest expression. Here reality must be faced.

---

[5] Ernest W. Burgess and Harvey J. Locke, *The Family — From Institution to Companionship.* New York, American Book Co., 1945, pp. 510, 511.

[6] Alfred C. Kinsey, et al., *Sexual Behavior in the Human Male.* Philadelphia, W. P. Saunders Co., 1948.

When maladjusted personalities enter marriage, they are soon faced by disillusions which manifest themselves in disappointments. The marriage partner is found to be one who does not measure up to expectations. The result is personality clashes caused by differences in attitudes, habits, or interests. Marital discord follows not only many hasty marriages but frequently mars the relationship of couples who have taken the traditional and orthodox road into the estate of matrimony.

The chief basis of such personality maladjustments is found to be emotional immaturity.* Students of marriage and the family regard it the main source of domestic discord. Paul Popenoe, a prominent student and writer in the field, gives the following striking description of emotionally immature persons: "These people may be fully grown physically. A man may be 6 feet tall, 30 years old, weigh 180 pounds; but in his emotional and social development he may be no more than six years old or even six months old. He is not ready for marriage." [7]

6. The American Family Needs the Church

The Modern Family Is in Distress. — This is being recognized in an increasing measure not only by students of society, but the church is focusing its attention on the family. It observes that the wholesome influence of the family is waning. This is especially reflected by the problems which confront the church in its educational program. Work in school, Sunday school, and Bible class is hampered by lack of home co-operation. Many of our young people find their companions among those not of the household of faith and incline toward the moral standard of the world with tacit approval of their elders. Marital discord among the parishioners is no longer an isolated problem which challenges the ministry today. [8]

The Church Preparing. — Aware of this grave, challenging situation, the church is girding itself for action. Leaders have met,

---

* This includes spiritual immaturity.

[7] Paul Popenoe, *Modern Marriage*, A Handbook for Men. New York, Macmillan Co., 1944, p. 1.

[8] Number of divorces reported to Synod's statistical office for 1954 was 1198. At midcentury Roman Catholics had 1 divorce for every 25 newly constituted marriages; all Protestants 1 divorce for every 10 new marriages; Missouri Synod Lutherans 1 divorce for every 20 new marriages. Also see Landis & Landis, *Building a Successful Marriage.*

have analyzed the situation, and have drafted plans for instruction and guidance of parish workers. Forums in family living and marriage institutes are being arranged for the purpose of making the laity conscious of the situation and enlisting their help in the rehabilitation of the home.

The church cannot stem the tide of cultural trends. We Christians can and must, however, condition individuals, especially our youth, the prospective founders of families and homes, to fulfill their God-intended mission in life. Holy Writ supplies the basic principles for Christian conduct in all its phases. In Scripture we find the compass for the family now adrift on stormy waters. Many families having trouble feel that life is that way and that not much can be done about it. The church is in the world to show them what Christian family life can be like.

DISCUSSION QUESTIONS

1. Is blaming the family for the prevailing ills in society justified? Discuss.
2. How do the functions of the family today differ from those of the nineteenth century in America?
3. How does the growth or decline of the following play into the problem: personal piety; church attendance; home devotions; the small, closely knit community?
4. What has led to smaller families? to the decline of patriarchal control? to the equalitarian pattern in husband-wife relationships?
5. How do maladjusted personalities create almost insoluble family problems?
6. What evidence have we that affection and comradeship are stronger family ties today than they were formerly? But is this the full answer to our perplexing family problems?

SELECTED REFERENCES

Burgess, Ernest W., and Locke, Harvey J. *The Family.* New York. American Book Co., 1945. Ch. 16: "The American Family in Transition."

Geiseman, O. A., *Make Yours a Happy Marriage.* St. Louis. Concordia Publishing House, 1946.

Kirkendall, Lester A. *Too Young to Marry?* 1955. Public Affairs Pamphlet.

Nimkoff, Meyer F., *Marriage and the Family.* Boston. Houghton Mifflin Co., 1947. Ch. 4: "Modern American Family."

Duvall and Hill, *When You Marry.* Association Press, 1953. Ch. 8, 14, 20.

Chapter 6

Family Crises

Theodore J. C. Kuehnert

CRISES MUST BE FACED in all phases and walks of life. They are inevitable in marriage and family living. A crisis is a turning point, "a decisive change which creates a situation for which the habitual behavior patterns of a person or a group are inadequate." A crisis creates a shock which tests the temper, the stability, of one's personality. Adequate training for life should include preparation to meet crises courageously and effectively.

1. Types of Crises

Natural and Imposed. — Since the family represents an arena in which people meet people, it is but natural that critical situations arise which test the stability of the group and the emotional maturity of the individual in varying degrees. Some critical situations arise beyond the control of those who must face them; these are natural and unavoidable. Others grow out of situations created by those whom they confront; they are avoidable and may be termed imposed. Prolonged illness and bereavement are of the former type; disgrace through one's conduct illustrates the latter.

Causes. — A crisis may suddenly and unexpectedly strike into a family. The sudden death of a parent or a child, the unexpected loss of the husband's job, the destruction of property by fire or storm, are experiences which create emotional strains and frequently have disastrous effects on personalities. Likewise, infidelity of a mate or delinquency of a child may cause personal disorganizations often beyond repair. In whatever form it may appear, a crisis in life is the result of sin. All people alike are victims of sin's consequences: sickness, death, sorrow. Man's

sinful and perverted heart causes him to stray from the path
which God has bidden him to walk. By such departure he brings
shame and unbearable grief on those nearest to him in life. It is
of vital significance that this be recognized by all concerned —
by those who personally experience crises as well as by those
whose counsel and guidance are to help others weather storms
and recover from shocks which crises have caused.

Effects. — Not all crises have disorganizing effects on individuals or groups. The death of a husband and father may knit
the survivors into a closer and more fully integrated group. The
widowed mother and her children now form a united front to
cope with the exigencies of life. The critical experience through
which the members of a family have passed frequently strengthens the bonds of understanding, loyalty, and regard for one another's welfare. If death was the result of prolonged illness, the
care and sacrifice of wife and children may have contributed
toward the development of kindness and patience and forbearance, which resulted in the emerging of a fuller and richer
personality.

Unfortunately, not all critical situations have wholesome effects. In many instances the results are devastating. Individuals
are observed to go to pieces physically or mentally, and some
Christians lose their spiritual balance as a result of a crisis which
they experienced. The life of a whole family can be changed
considerably when a member must be placed in an orphanage,
a children's home, or a hospital for the mentally ill.

2. Aspects of Family Crises

Crises Related to Husband and Wife. — Disruption of the husband-wife companionship creates critical situations which strike
deeply into the hearts and souls of men and women. Some of
these separations are the result of natural causes, while others
are self-imposed critical experiences in life. Death is responsible
for three fourths of our "broken" homes.

The death of a mate calls for drastic readjustments by the
surviving partner. These adjustments involve family support,
keeping the household going, seeking employment, guiding children. A feeling of loneliness is experienced; the sex life, natural
in normal marriages, has been disrupted. Where "widowhood"

is the result of divorce, haunting pangs of conscience frequently bring strains which prove to be extremely severe. Divorce is an admission of failure; it represents the shattering of a dream. It makes the divorced person conscious of having exercised poor judgment in the selection of the mate or of having been unable to make satisfactory marital adjustments. In a succeeding marriage comparisons are frequently made between the new and the former mate. All this creates tensions which are apt to become real crises.

Childless marriages frequently cause critical developments in husband-wife relationships. When the desire for children is not shared by both mates or when the absence of children is due to natural sterility, frustration or disappointment may have serious effects on personalities. Childless marriages have a high divorce rate.

Crises Related to Children. — Turning points in life are likewise the lot of children. Perhaps the first major change which children face comes at crossing the threshold of adolescence. While both sexes are affected, girls experience the greater tension. The appearance of menstruation in the life of a girl brings with it a deviation from her previous behavior and mental state. This changes her mode of life. Lack of proper parental guidance at this turn of the road can have serious aftereffects.

Children are vitally affected by the behavior of their parents. They are constant observers of the relationship between their fathers and mothers. Strains and tensions leading to marital discord do not escape the notice of the child, regardless of its age. Teachers and school nurses have discovered that the unsatisfactory conduct of a pupil in school had its roots in the scenes which the child witnessed daily at home. Children of divorced parents are subjected to experiences which may mar the happiness of their childhood, the normal development of their youth, and, later, the success of their own marriage.

In the lives of children there are other experiences which cause tensions. When a boy or a girl leaves home to attend college, the separation from the family presents a turning point in his or her life. New surroundings, new friends and associates, new responsibilities, as well as new temptations, call for mature judgment and often for a complete readjustment of life.

Crises in Various Stages of Married Life. — It has been found that the first years of married life are the most critical. They reveal whether, and to what extent, personality adjustments can and will be made. Nevertheless, the forces and conditions which bring about disruptions of marital relationship, or family discord of one type or another, are not respecters of time and age.

Tensions are created by difference in religion, by disagreement on child training, or by problem children. Delinquency of one member in the family, perhaps intemperance of the husband and father, or a disgraceful step in the conduct of a grown son or daughter, strikes a blow in the later stages of married life. The husband-wife relationships may be seriously affected by sexual frigidity which at times accompanies the menopause in a woman's life. Old age may bring to married couples economic insecurity, invalidism, unemployment. Loneliness caused by the children's leaving the family circle to establish their own homes, adjustments to a daughter- or son-in-law, and finally the bereavement through the death of a spouse, are severe strains.

3. Crises Created by Social and Economic Conditions

The impact of cultural trends is reflected by the overall picture which the modern family presents. We observe our sophisticated youth in rebellion against the authority of their elders. Women revolt against the status of husbands. The restlessness of men eager to explore new areas fills the air with discontent. The prevalence of estrangements, separations, desertions, and divorce is evidence of a growing disregard for the sanctity of marriage. These general signs of our time set the stage for family crises to arise.

Effect of War. — Marriage and the family are profoundly affected by war, and resulting dislocations strike deeply into the family group. Sons and husbands are drawn into military service, and thus bonds are severed. Women, including mothers of young children, are attracted by high wages and by the need for workers in industry. They often exchange their household occupation for gainful employment away from home. Hasty marriages are contracted. The moral standard, especially with regard to sexual behavior, is lowered.

Influence of Depression. — The well-being of the family depends on regular and adequate income to supply its various needs. When unemployment of the breadwinner closes the channel through which the family gets its sustenance, great dislocations may result. The wife will have to seek employment, and children must look for work even if their educational career is thereby interrupted, while the husband and father takes over the housework. Thus the status and the role of family members are completely reversed. If the family is compelled to go on relief, the stigma which attaches to that change may give rise to a crisis. Economic depressions cause families to double up in homes. In order to decrease expenditures, parents take into their homes the family of a son or a daughter, or the parents make their home with the children. In such cases the in-law problem may create critical situations.

Studies and records of family life made during the thirties show that the depression did not affect families in the same manner. While in some instances the imposed changes produced a greater family unity trained in thrift and charity, and caused the adoption of a wiser philosophy of life, the greater trend was in the opposite direction. Family demoralization and emotional strain became evident by the increase of desertions, drinking, vice, crime, delinquency, and mental abnormalities.

4. Crises for the Unmarried

Our modern culture must make us conscious of strains and tensions which develop into critical situations for the unmarried adult members of society. The prolonged period of education postpones marriage for many young men and women. The philosophy of our age releases the sexual impulse, and the availability of contraceptive devices makes premarital sex relations the experience of many of the youth today, with resultant repercussions on the family.

Illegitimacy, or unmarried motherhood, strikes into many families. The Children's Bureau reported (on the basis provided by twenty-five state health departments) more than 9,000 illegitimate births during a period of three months in 1942.[1] The welfare agencies of the church find that membership in a Christian church is in itself no protection against personal disorganization and family disruption caused by this irregularity of conduct.

---

[1] Ernest R. Groves and Gladys Hoagland Groves. *The Contemporary American Family.* Chicago, J. B. Lippincott Co., 1947, p. 559.

The best of families are not immune to such experiences. Aside from its basic cause, the sin-weakened heart unable to control a natural urge and to resist temptation, the unwed mother problem has its roots in our culture. "A considerable part of the extra-marital sexual relationships of young American women are motivated, not by the desire to escape organic tension, but to gain and hold favor with the male who is sought as a means of fulfilling urges that go far beyond physical intimacy. Sexual freedom thus becomes an expediency in the case of many." [2]

It is needless to emphasize that not only the unmarried mother but her child and parents, as well as the child's father, if his identity is revealed, experience crises which completely change their patterns of life.

5. How the Christian Faces Crises

The Christian is not a fatalist who accepts every turn in life as inevitable. True, there are natural, unavoidable situations in life, such as prolonged illness and widowhood, which he meets in submission to God's will and with full confidence that these experiences must "work together for good to them that love God" (Rom. 8:28). On the other hand, for conduct which is within the control of the individual or group, the Christian finds guidance in Holy Writ. God's principles and directives are definite and clear. The Holy Spirit gives the Christian the assurance of strength to control his urges and power to withstand temptation.

God has especially enshrined, as it were, the institution of marriage and has safeguarded the family and home with the commandment "Thou shalt not commit adultery." Numerous passages in Holy Writ offer guidance for husbands and wives, for children and youth. Examples and consequences of infidelity, unchastity, lust, and other offenses which disorganize the family are recorded in Scripture to make us aware of our natural inclination toward evil and to put us on our guard lest we become victims of the carnal mind, which is enmity against God.

Crises are tests for the Christian, and the family is an arena in which he must expect, and be prepared to face, various critical situations.

---

[2] Ibid., p. 298.

6. Need for Understanding and Sympathetic Helpfulness

Individuals confronted by crises need help. Society realizes this more and more. Our mental institutions are overcrowded with victims of personal disorganization. Guidance and counseling are regarded as the need of the hour.

The church cannot stand by complacently. Its own membership is affected. Every pastor will testify that problems which arise in family living increasingly challenge him in his ministry. Teachers of children must wrestle with situations which have their roots in family disorganization.

In our expanded program of Christian education in the local parish the preparation for family living is an evident need. In supplying this need, emphasis should be given on the proper levels to the permanence of marriage, the privilege of parenthood, the responsibilities of child training, the respect for personalities, acceptance of the will of God, willing obedience to Christ — in short, the various aspects of Christian living which fall into the area of family life.

Effective guidance, especially of adolescents, requires, first of all, understanding. Symptoms must not be confused with causes. Analysis and diagnosis make knowledge and orientation an essential prerequisite. Where understanding was lacking, attempted guidance has not only proved ineffective but in many instances has been harmful. Sympathetic helpfulness is motivated by the law of love. Legalistic procedure is contrary to the practice of the Master, who substituted stone throwing with the kind and forgiveness-assuring verdict and counsel, "Neither do I condemn thee: go, and sin no more" (John 8:11).

DISCUSSION QUESTIONS

1. How should effective counsel and guidance distinguish between natural and imposed family crises?
2. How are the effects of widowhood similar and different for the surviving husband and wife?
3. How do children become the victims of family crises?
4. Show how our modern social and economic conditions tend to create critical situations in family life.
5. How does modern culture create strains and tensions for the unmarried adult members of society?
6. Discuss a possible program of training and guidance in family living for your parish.

SELECTED REFERENCES

Brink, Frederick W. *This Man and This Woman.* New York. Association Press, 1948. This 79-page booklet is an excellent guide for
young people contemplating marriage.

Elmer, M. C. *The Sociology of the Family.* Boston. Ginn and Company, 1945. Ch. 18: "Adjustment of Family Life in Times of Crisis."

Geiseman, O. A. *Make Yours a Happy Marriage.* St. Louis: Concordia Publishing House, 1946.

Goldstein, Sidney E. *Marriage and Family Counseling.* A Manual
for Ministers, Doctors, Lawyers, Teachers, Social Workers, and
Others Engaged in Counseling Service. New York: McGraw-Hill
Book Co., 1945. Ch. 1 and 15.

Groves, Ernest R. and Groves, Gladys Hoagland. *The Contemporary
American Family.* Chicago. J. P. Lippincott Co., 1947. Ch. 11:
"Sociological Aspects of Family Life."

Duvall and Hill. *When You Marry.* Association Press. 1953, Ch. 13.

Chapter 7

The Importance of
Working with Families

Oscar E. Feucht

To a larger or smaller degree churches have always ministered to families: in sickness and health, in sorrow and death, at Baptism, confirmation, marriage. Many a pastor of yesteryear has been closer to the home needs than the family physician.

Close family contact is still maintained in most town and country parishes. But in larger churches, especially in the cities, such contact has become more impersonal and infrequent. Fortunately, the tide seems to be turning, and churches are focusing new attention on the home, in many instances through organized home visitation.

In our concern for the individual we may forget the family as such. Indeed, many churches think chiefly of "the duty the families have toward the church," without proper regard for "the duty the church has toward families."

The time has come when we should re-examine our basic philosophy of parish work. It is particularly for this reason that a chapter on the importance of working with families is justified.

1. Primary Institution of God

In our highly organized society we are apt to forget the primacy of the home and to set up strategies and programs that are secondary. God made the family first. It existed long before church or state. God made the home the center. Out of it developed the tribes that later became nations. The first families built altars to God and worshiped Him with sacrifices. Down through the ages the family has been the basic unit of society. History has seen a number of experiments which tried to ignore this arrangement of the Creator. All of them resulted in dismal failure. The latest of these was made in the Soviet Union.

When we turn to the Bible, we find that the story of the church and of civilization is told in terms of families. Family trees (genealogies) are faithfully preserved. The great Messianic promises were given to families and were passed on from father to son. The Bible employs the vocabulary of the family to help us understand who God is and what He does for us. God's people in the Old Testament were organized according to the twelve families of the sons of Jacob. Religion was connected with the daily living in the home. The celebration of the Passover, antecedent of the Lord's Supper, took place in families. Much of the ministry of our Lord is connected with homes and families, and the Apostle Paul begins the practical applications in his letters with his "table of duties" for the home. Martin Luther considered the family primary and introduced each portion of his Small Catechism with the rubric "As the head of the house should teach it to his children."

2. Cradle of Personality

Parents have children "not to have and to hold, but to have and to mould." And this moulding process begins very early in life. "The importance of the whole educational system is trivial compared to the influence of the home in the most formative years when mental action patterns are being developed," is the way one college president put it. There has been much emphasis on the importance of the early years, because the way a child's fears are met and his daily needs are dealt with makes a great difference in the kind of person he becomes. When the Bible says "train up a child in the way he should go" (Prov. 22:6), it underscores these words of a modern educator: "The paths which the adults' feet are to travel find their origin in childhood."

Educators have demonstrated the value of a good environment. The potential for most children is very high. But something in their training must set off the spark that will make them outstanding men and women. Father and mother must give a child dependability, scrupulous honesty, and the joy of working with others. They must show what a radiant faith is like. Parents must see beyond toilsome training and endless correcting to the years when the spiritual harvest of their work becomes visible. They must have a vision of excellence. "Go through the traits that make up a beautiful personality, and you will find in the family life all the occasions and opportunities for their acquisition." [1]

3. Greatest Teacher

The home is potentially the greatest teacher. Not that we could for a moment do without schools. They are more necessary than ever. But education is wider than the schoolroom. It begins before we are six and continues for a lifetime — a lifetime largely lived under the influence of a home. The school has the child thirty hours a week, the church (where there is only a Sunday school) less than two hours, and the home seventy-three hours (exclusive of sleep). The schoolteacher sees the prim pupil, and the church sees the Sunday child all dressed up (and on its best behavior); but the parents see the child as it is.

Why is the home superior for Christian training? It exerts a continuous, unbroken influence. Over the child parents have an authority possessed by no other persons. This is coupled with the confidence which children have in mother and father, a trust children give to no one else. The home supplies many natural teaching and learning situations. Parents apply the Ten Commandments as they are needed — when an untruth is spoken, when there is quarreling among the children. But they also apply the Gospel and overcome a sense of guilt with the words of Jesus, "Be of good cheer, your sins are forgiven."

According to the Biblical pattern given us in Deuteronomy 6, it was through the parents that the child was to learn God's love and care and so get a sense of security, to learn God's Word and Truth and so get a sense of authority, to learn right from wrong and so get a sense of morality, to learn to communicate with God in prayer and so get the highest privilege accorded to man — worship.

And all this is best learned from parents. A mother asked an educator, "When does the education of a child begin?" He replied, "Twenty years before the child is born." You see, everything that goes into the training of mother and father helps to

---

[1] Dr. Samuel L. Hamilton at Conference on Family Life, Cincinnati, Ohio, 1948.

make them what they are. They can pass on to their children only as much as they have and are. "The young are not apt to learn religion or to be Christian unless their immediate environment, the home, is Christian in attitude and act, more than in mere verbal expression." [2]

"Sad to say, it is also in the family that growth can be arrested, and in some homes personalities are marred and scarred by some of the most devastating, humiliating, frustrating, and degrading interpersonal relationships. There, also, is life-changing, but the change may be for the worse." [3]

"Dad, why don't you wear a Wilkie button?" said a six-year-old one day during the time Wendell Wilkie was running for the Presidency. His mother and father looked up in great surprise. Evidently the child had been hearing more than the parents expected. The little lad, on the basis of a chance remark, had already put his dad into the Republican party! Much is learned from merely incidental remarks. If children pick up their political leanings that way, you can be sure that they also pick up their religion — from what we say or don't say, what things we value and don't value, and from the way we react to situations. Parents are teachers. All parents teach religion or irreligion.

4. Agency of Evangelism

Who brought you to Jesus? Very likely, it was a father and mother who brought you to the Lord in holy Baptism. As soon as you could talk, they taught you "Abba Father, Amen," and, a little later, simple table and bedtime prayers. They first introduced you to Jesus and opened the Bible to you. The Christian family, committed to transmit the faith to its children, has always been the most effective evangelism agency.

Conversely, let us think of the more than twenty million children and young people not under regular religious instruction. Why are they among America's spiritually illiterate? Is it because no father and mother get a Sunday morning breakfast for them, and dress them for Sunday school? It is the way many adults spend Saturday night that keeps them and their children away from church on Sunday morning. Wesner Fallaw is quite

---

[2] Wesner Fallaw, *Modern Parent and the Teaching Church*, p. 25.

[3] Samuel L. Hamilton, at Conference on Family Life. Cincinnati, Ohio, 1948.

right when he says: "It is unrealistic and unwise to think that a child or adolescent can change himself from futile or anti-social and irreligious living into purposeful Christian living, if he has to overcome both his own drives toward perdition and also the prevailing values and conduct of perdition-bound parents." [4]

In the poem "The Lost Sheep," based on the Biblical story, the unknown author emphasizes that the Savior spoke of a *sheep*, not of a *lamb*.

> For the lambs will follow the sheep, you know,
> Wherever the sheep may stray; When the sheep go wrong,
> It will not be long Till the lambs are as wrong as they.
>
> And so for the sheep we earnestly plead,
> For the sake of the lambs today; If the lambs are lost,
> What terrible cost Some sheep will have to pay.

5. Transmitter of Culture

Some of the finer things of life have been perpetuated through family customs and practices, for instance, family worship and the Christian celebration of Christmas in the home. The Christmas tree, the carols, and the family "hymnsings" came over from the country that gave us "Stille Nacht." These good things came to us by way of families who have preserved many other fine folkways and noble traditions. For generations some Christian families have closed their Sunday social visits by singing a hymn together and with an evening prayer.

Good manners and courtesy are learned in family relationships. And so are good English and love for books and fine music and good art. Habits of Bible reading, church-going, and daily prayers are come by in much the same way. A family transmits a positive or a negative attitude toward the church, Christian missions, other races and nations. In fact, the whole outlook on life is, in most instances, the by-product of the culture, or the lack of culture, in the home. The good and the bad are passed down through families.

6. Barrier to Evil

In the spring of 1952, when the Missouri River was at flood-stage, the city of Omaha was threatened seriously. The water was backing up into the city through a sewer. A barge was

---

[4] Wesner Fallaw, *The Modern Parent and the Teaching Church*, p. 53.

loaded with steel, and this mass of metal was dumped at the point where the sewer emptied into the river. It plugged the opening, and disaster was averted. Similarly, the flood waters of secularism, the philosophies of godless communism, the poisonous streams of moral filth, can sweep over our youth unless someone is alert and can raise a dike or close a trap door to keep the onrushing evil from our children and young people.

The best barrier to worldliness is the Christian home that maintains its standards. There are times to be firm and not waver. A father's no, spoken in time, can save a child from a whole series of mistakes and from a life of unhappiness.

We are living in a time when the sex magazine, lurid comic books, and mass media of communication make it very easy for retaining walls to fall down. Old safeguards no longer hold. On what may the church rely as a true "league of decency" to hold off the enemies of our youth and of our nation? It can rely on Christian parents if their own consciences have not been dulled by lax thinking and living. Aroused parents in many cities have taken remedial action. America needs more such stalwart citizens who are not ashamed to stand for moral honor and decency. Such citizens in the future will come — whence they have come in the past — from good Christian homes.

7. Bulwark of the Church

Concerning the training of the people in the Old Testament the *New Standard Bible Dictionary* says: "Training of the young appears to have been entirely in the hands of their parents, especially the fathers. No trace of any institution resembling the modern school is found." The synagogue did not come into its own until 500 B. C. This means that the faith of Israel was passed on chiefly through home teaching and religious ceremonies.[5] Some of these have continued to this day. Modern Judaism has preserved a high regard for the family and has kept the father as a teacher of religion in the home. The Jews have propagated their religion throughout the Christian era, being in the minority in practically every country in which they lived. Historians have called this "one of the strongest civilizations of which we have any record." And what was the secret?

---

[5] There were also teaching priests and leaders. See 2 Chron. 34.

Centering religion in the home and making the father the priest of the household!

No mere Sunday religion is good enough. True faith is a living thing. It is constantly asserting itself. Unless religion is lived in the home, how much faith do its occupants have? At every point the sacred must penetrate the secular until all is sanctified by the Word of God, by prayer, and by faith in Christ.

Healthy families make a healthy community. Spiritually strong families make a strong church. Only as every family is made a spiritually growing and responsible family unit can the church rely on it to fulfill its mission; only then will it yield its time and talents, its sons and its daughters, for the extension of the Kingdom of our Lord. No congregation is stronger than the families that make up its membership. A parish is more accurately evaluated by the caliber of its families than by the number of its communicants.

The church is people. And people are largely what families make them!

8. Cornerstone of the Nation

A chief of police told a parent-teacher association in a fashionable school district of one of our flourishing cities, "I could tear your hearts open with true stories of your sons and daughters." The Children's Bureau estimates that the number of children and young people brought to juvenile courts in 1954 because of delinquent behavior was nearly half a million. This is one out of every forty-one American children in the ten-to-seventeen-year bracket.[6] J. Edgar Hoover, director of the Federal Bureau of Investigation, seldom makes a speech, writes an article, or allows himself to be quoted without some reference to his conviction that only more religious education and Christian training will change the heart and give us dependable citizens of which the nation can be proud. President Calvin Coolidge said, "What America needs is more religion." Then he added, "the kind of religion that is lived in the home."

During the war a church leader in Kansas City told the writer: "I have been called into conferences with the police department, with the board of education, and with the social

---

[6] U. S. Department of Health, Education, and Welfare.

welfare agencies to consider the problem of neglected children. And every conference has ended at one place, the doorstep of the home. Why aren't more churches setting up a concrete program to help the home? I know of only two local churches with an effective program." If the real problem is parental delinquency, should not the church be the first to offer assistance?

Dr. Erdmann Frenk sums up the Family Life Committee's appeal for the primacy of the family when he writes: "Religion is the undergirding of the family, the moral timbers on which the home rests. Without religion the home soon begins to crumble and decay because of the absence of certain moral disciplines which only religion can supply. Where the wish and will of God are ignored, there sooner or later selfishness, lust, and greed become the motivating factors in life, and with them come relationships which are usually debasing and degenerating." [7]

DISCUSSION QUESTIONS

1. How does God rate the family as an institution in His scale of values? In what way does God show the priority He gives to families?
2. Discuss the following statement by an eminent educator: "Early in childhood are grown the emotional roots of the great religious experiences of subsequent life."
3. How is religion being taught indirectly in your home? How is it taught directly?
4. Discuss the question: "Does the church ever really have the child if the parents do not give moral support to the church?"
5. What family practices and customs that contribute to good culture is your home continuing?
6. What examples from reading or experience can you cite to show that a good home can be a mighty barrier against evil?
7. Why do you regard as good stewardship the plan of assigning families of a parish to the elders for more frequent contact?
8. How many outstanding citizens can you name who were the products of Christian homes in the nation? In the state? In your town or community?

SELECTED REFERENCES

Fallaw, Wesner. *The Modern Parent and the Teaching Church.* Macmillan, 1947.
Wolbrecht, W. F. (Ed.). *The Christian Family in the Modern World.* Concordia Publishing House, 1948.
Kildahl, Harold B. *Family Affairs.* Augsburg, 1948.
Groves, Ernest R. *Christianity and the Family.* Macmillan, 1942.

---

[7] Erdmann W. Frenk, *Staying Married,* p. 38.

Chapter 8

The Church, the Family and Community Resources

Paul W. Jacobs

---

1. Families Have Varied Needs

As CHRISTIANS WE CANNOT FORGET that the family is an institution of God and that we must make every effort to help it to secure and maintain a normal, healthy existence.

Children reared in familes in which there is constant strife and where they are unloved will find it very difficult to gain the awareness that God is love. Parents who are confused about spiritual values will not be able to pass on any clear concept to their children.

The church can pride itself on the low rate of divorce among its parishioners. Divorce, however, is only one symptom of an unhappy family circle. Tradition, moral censure, and other factors keep families together even in the most unfortunate conditions. But in such conditions the marriage partners are not adequately fulfilling their obligations to meet the spiritual, social, and emotional needs of themselves or their children.

While other organizations wish to preserve the family because it is the socio-biological unit best fitted for the rearing of the young, for the Christian Church the purpose of all family rehabilitation is not only to bring about physical well-being but to place and keep Christ in the family.

While the church has diligently attempted to meet the spiritual needs of the family, it has frequently failed to recognize that families have other needs. In other words, the total needs of the family, the needs of the body and the mind, are not always kept in view. The church wonders why Johnny Smith, whose parents are in church every Sunday and who completed eight grades in the parish school, was sent to the state reformatory for stealing a car. The church also wonders why Helen Jones, who answered most of the questions in her confirmation class, was discovered to be pregnant and had to be sent to a home for unmarried mothers in a nearby city, where her child was delivered. Evidently there are needs which home and church failed to meet in the cases of Johnny Smith and Helen Jones.

That church ministers best to its families which remembers that health of body, mind, and soul are interrelated.

2. The Church and Related Services

From ancient times the church has been a refuge for those who are in distress. Even today people who would not go to any other source for help with family problems will frequently turn to the church. The church has met these requests for assistance with varying responses. In many instances it has been of real help. Pastors who have a good intuitive sense, as well as a strong feeling for people, have made wonderful contributions in stabilizing family situations. Some pastors, however, have felt rather helpless and have been unable to give much assistance. Some have looked with disdain upon persons who have not been able to manage their personal lives and have been unwilling to do anything except sit in judgment.

The church has frequently stood apart from the general community. While bemoaning the fact that family life is deteriorating, it has been fearful of using community resources which have been established to help preserve families either by service to the entire family or by service to one of its members.

During the past fifty years great progress has been made in the study of human relations. Psychology, psychiatry, social work, sociology, economics, medicine, anthropology, etc., have supplied us with a body of knowledge which, though still not complete, is valuable in helping individuals to adjust themselves to the stresses of everyday living. The social sciences have given us new insights into family needs and problems. They have also given us new skills for meeting such needs. The church should be aware of the nature and the scope of this new knowledge.

Some congregations are beginning to utilize the skills and techniques of these disciplines. They have found ways of resolving the conflict between secular philosophies and the Christian ideal by means of a co-operative approach. The pastor recognizes that he does not have the training or the experience to provide certain types of help for his parishioners. He also realizes that poor counseling can often lead to irreparable harm.

3. The Pastor Augments Himself

The pastor has been prepared for the teaching and preaching of the Word of God. He is also called upon to minister to the sick, the dying, and the bereaved. Many a pastor feels that he is not adequately prepared to provide counseling in marital problems, parent-child problems, or personal problems that are social, emotional, or economic. The pastor can supplement his service to parishioners, however, by the utilization of specialized techniques that are available in the community. In other words, he should be encouraged to add another ministry — the ministry of referral.

Are we still inclined to believe that social agencies are organized only to care for the economically disabled and improvident? In a study made a few years ago by a large family welfare agency which annually serves over six thousand families, it was learned that 14 per cent of its clients were engaged in engineering, law, teaching, research, and other professions; 33 per cent were electricians, painters, pattern workers, watchmakers, and other skilled persons; 10 per cent owned their own business, such as retailing shops, contracting, printing, and jobbing enterprises; 20 per cent were sales people, civil service employees, and office workers; and 23 per cent were students, housewives, semiskilled, and unskilled persons. Four out of every five of these persons were self-supporting, and 14 per cent were willing to pay a fee for the service which they desired.

4. Using the Church's Own Welfare Agencies

The church will, of course, first turn to its own social and health organization in preserving and strengthening the family life of its members. Within one church body of less than two million members (1955) there are seventeen hospitals, two sanatoria, nine orphan homes, sixteen homes for the aged, one home and school for the feeble-minded and the epileptic, nineteen home-finding societies, and two schools for the deaf.[1] These

---

[1] The Lutheran Church — Missouri Synod.

agencies, in general, offer only specific services. However, in a few instances they are flexible enough to offer limited services to families in local parishes.

As an example, the principal of a parish school felt that the home conditions of a fifth-grade boy were contributing to the child's behavior problem. He called on the local denominational child welfare agency and asked if this agency could help him. The organization assigned the case to one of its workers and began a treatment plan, not only with the boy but also with his parents. The teacher, the pastor, and the social worker combined their efforts in this plan of treatment, and eventually the child and his family responded favorably.

5. Using Community Welfare Services

Some local churches use trained personnel from their own congregation as a family advisory council to serve individuals and families with special problems. Such a council is usually made up of the pastor, an elder, a physician, a social worker or psychiatrist, and a lawyer.

Pushing back the curtains, the local church will discover community resources close at hand and willing to serve.

To use these agencies effectively it is necessary to have an understanding of their functions, their limitations, and their place in the community. The public agency is supported by tax funds. Its functions and the extent of its services are usually limited by law. Private agencies are supported by voluntary contributions. In general they are more flexible in the type of service they can give. Some organizations meet specific needs, while others offer a wide variety of services.

Agencies also differ in the quality of service they offer. Some are able to employ persons who have graduate training in social work. Others are not so fortunate and employ untrained or partially trained workers.

Family Service Society. — One of the most valuable resources for the church's use is the local private family service society. There are some two hundred and forty of these agencies in the United States which are affiliated with the Family Service Association of America. These societies must meet certain professional and ethical standards before they can obtain membership in the national body. They are staffed with professionally trained persons, most of whom have had two years of graduate training in social work. Each worker is under close supervision so that the individual receives the service best suited to his needs. Some of these agencies provide psychiatric and psychological consultation for their workers so that the clients may receive the benefits of these specialized disciplines.

The family welfare agencies often help parents who are experiencing difficulties, for instance, in dealing with problems of their children, or in helping low-income couples who are setting up housekeeping. They have in many instances been able to help the husband who, because of his wife's attitude toward him and his children cannot concentrate on his job; the mother who is upset over her husband's apparent insistence that she make all the decisions in relation to the home and the children and who begins to feel that he no longer cares for her; and the student who is so anxious to please his parents that his worry produces school failures rather than success. These are some of the situations which, if nurtured on misunderstanding, fear, or fumbling advice, result in domestic crises and disturbed relationships.

Since poor health brings severe pressure on the stability of the family, it is important that the church know the health resources in the community. The public health doctor and the school nurse usually can provide health examinations and preventive measures also for the children of a parish school.

Medical Social Service. — Hospitals can be called upon to assist patients and their families with those social and emotional problems which interfere with treatment and hamper recovery. For instance, medical social workers of the Wheat Ridge Foundation are now located in a number of communities to assist patients who have tuberculosis, as well as their families, in working out those perplexing social problems that arise during the various stages of this serious disease.

Statewide rehabilitation programs, designed to provide vocational guidance and retraining for persons disabled by accident or disease, are available to the citizens of most communities.

Mental Health Guidance. — Poor mental health on the part of a member of the family can do much to disrupt the family life. At one time it was considered a disgrace to admit that a member of the family was "mentally slow" or "a little queer."

Persons were sent to the mental hospital and often left without any hope of recovery.

Authorities tell us that one out of ten persons will eventually have to spend some time in a mental institution. The church should recognize that emotional disorders occur regardless of class or creed. It should acquaint itself with the facilities available to its parishioners who need help when these conditions arise. Because of more extensive knowledge of dynamic psychology, many more persons, who suffer from emotional disorders, can now be helped. As in other illnesses, the sooner these disorders are detected and treated, the better are the chances for recovery.

In most urban communities it is possible to obtain psychiatric services. Child-guidance clinics and clinics for adult patients are available in many cities. Some states maintain traveling psychiatric clinics so that persons in rural areas may avail themselves of this service.

The United States Veterans Administration not only maintains hospitals but provides vocational and educational guidance centers in many communities. In many cities the American Red Cross maintains chapters which provide casework services for veterans.

County Welfare. — The church in the small or rural community will not find a wide variety of health and welfare agencies available. There is, however, in every county seat a public welfare organization which is charged with the responsibility for administering various types of public assistance. The personnel of these public assistance offices are acquainted with the social services within the locality as well as within the state. The pastor frequently can also obtain a list of resources available in his state by writing to the State Welfare Department at the state capital.

By using social workers, judges, doctors, marriage counselors, and other resource persons available in your community, as speakers, panel-discussion leaders, participants in parents' meetings, couple groups, youth seminars, and the like, your church can enrich its family-life education. This is only another way of using community leaders in the church.

6. Making Referrals

The pastor should make it a point to obtain a broad picture of the total community organization of social services. When a particular problem comes to his attention and he feels that this problem can be referred to a given social agency, he should consult the agency's supervisor before making a referral. In this way he can be sure that the organization to which he is referring is equipped to handle the problem.

One should face the fact that not every person will accept a referral to a social agency. However, some of this resistance can be overcome by a description of the agency's services, the skill of its workers, and its reputation in the community. The agency's supervisor can be of great help in assisting the pastor to make the appropriate explanation to the individual. It is also well to remember that the agency may find it difficult to live up to any extravagant claims for its services.

After making a referral, try *not* to direct the agency's plan of treatment. If there is a feeling that the planning is unrealistic, it is well to visit the agency to obtain further information.

The agency may not be able to share all its findings with the pastor. When the social worker discusses the case with the pastor, he must determine what is confidential and what is not. The same relationship with respect to confidence exists between the social worker and his client as that which exists between the pastor and the parishioner. It goes without saying that details of case histories should be kept in strict confidence.

Delays can and do occur in the best of organizations. Pressures of work, as well as the lack of a staff — or the lack of a staff large enough — can result in poor service to the individual. Public agencies are frequently hampered by red tape. In some instances the incompetence of a worker may be the cause for delay. If one feels that the service is poor, it is best to arrange for a conference with the supervisor.

Public or private health and welfare agencies will not solve all the church's family problems, or all those which affect its members. There are many gaps in every community which, because of a lack of resources and trained personnel, cannot be filled. Agencies which do exist are often restricted as to the amount and type of service they can offer. Although knowledge regarding human behavior has developed considerably in the past years, there is still much that needs to be learned. Not every situation can be corrected even by the most highly skilled staff.

Both the church and welfare agencies should be aware of their own limitations. Welfare workers should learn to recognize spiritual problems and to refer them to the church. Church workers should learn to recognize social and health problems and refer them to the proper agency.

7. Strengthen Community Services

The church should be interested in strengthening and improving its community welfare resources. When the community suffers, the members of the congregation suffer. Social agencies are anxious to have the co-operation of the church in the administration of their programs. The church can be a leavening agent in the development of health and welfare activities in the community, and it can encourage its members to contribute to the enrichment of these services. Some can serve as board members. Some can serve as volunteer workers. All can and should make financial contributions for the support of these agencies. The citizens of your locality should be able to say, "*There* is a church which is concerned about families."

8. The Church's Unique Ministry

The church makes its own unique contribution to the stability of family life by preaching and teaching that Jesus is our Savior and by stressing the gracious love of God. All aid should be looked upon as a means to that end. No program of family-life education is complete unless it has as its ultimate objective the spiritual welfare of its participants. This involves not only the preaching and teaching of spiritual truths but an integration of these truths into the personality of each individual.

In all dealings with families it must be remembered that the church remains a church. It has a unique service to give — a service no social agency is able to render. The minister, on the one hand, may be swept away by psychology and may fail to give the spiritual help which his parishioners need. On the other hand, he may completely ignore the material, emotional, and physical sides of situations which come to his attention and give only "preachy admonitions" instead of the dynamic Gospel and service to the whole man, physical, mental, spiritual, and social.

The basic cause of all problems in human relationships is sin. The church, however, does not complete its ministry merely by pointing out this fact. It must also call sinners to repentance and teach the Gospel, the channel of grace through which the Holy Spirit may work faith in the heart of the sinner. This is the unique mission of the church.

This mission, however, is carried out in a social order in which individuals and families are frequently exposed to poverty and want, sickness and sorrow, creating mental and emotional pressures which often tend to distract them and to cause them to close their hearts to the work of the Spirit. As an expression of its concern and love the church will help to remove these hindrances. This implies that the church will guide people in the solution of their social and emotional problems.

As in the past, so in the present the church feeds the hungry that they may be led to an increased awareness of the love of God as reflected in Christian charity. It guides persons with twisted emotions to skillful scientific help, when necessary, to express its interest in the whole man. It aids wives and husbands who find their relationship one of bitterness to resolve their differences that they may live as "joint heirs of the grace of life." It applies Christian truths in the lives of church members to prevent marital problems from arising. This means, then, that the church will bring the transforming power of God to cleanse and heal every area of life.

There are, of course, additional reasons why the church should serve the social and emotional needs of people. Among these are the powerful impact which the ministry of mercy will make upon the world, and the general obligation imposed by Scripture upon all Christians to practice mercy and "to do good unto all men." The church wins a better hearing for the Gospel by its acts of kindness, service, and helpfulness.

Too frequently the church has identified itself with those who were seemingly successful in managing their lives and has neglected those who, for one reason or another, suffered misfortune. The souls of these persons are just as precious in the sight of God as those who have received more in the way of temporal blessings. The church cannot in good conscience reject these people.

The church and the health and welfare agencies can work co-operatively. Each has a distinct contribution to make to the treatment of the total personality of the individual. Misunderstandings which have arisen in the past between these agencies can, humanly speaking, be overcome. Each needs to study more fully what the other has to offer. As they combine their forces, they will help persons not only to more adequate ways of living but also to an increased spirituality which has, as its ultimate end, the salvation of souls.

Jesus in His ministry "went about . . . teaching . . . preaching . . . healing" (Matt. 9:35). The ministry of the church today should include the whole man — body, mind, and soul. Christian love has concern for all the needs of the family — physical, mental, spiritual, and social.

DISCUSSION QUESTIONS

1. Should the church use the verified findings of science in its ministry to families? If so, how?
2. How can your parish give leadership in family service to your community?
3. How can your church better serve the families "on the other side of the railroad track"?
4. What new understanding did this chapter give you?

SELECTED REFERENCES

Nixon, John L., and Hiltner, Seward. *Community Helps on Pastoral Problems.* Federal Council of Churches of Christ in America. 297 Fourth Ave., New York 10, N. Y.

Stroup, Herbert H. *Social Work, an Introduction to the Field.* American Book Company, New York.

Elledge, Caroline H. *The Rehabilitation of the Patient.* J. B. Lippincott Co., Philadelphia.

Social Casework. Published by the Family Welfare Association of America, 122 East 22nd St., New York.

Survey Mid-Monthly. Survey Associates, 112 E. 19th St., New York.

Public Affairs Pamphlets. Public Affairs Committee, 22 E. 38th St., New York 16, N. Y.

Hiltner, Seward. *Religion and Health.* Macmillan, 1943.

PART III
The Church and Family Guidance

Chapter 9

Winning the Family for Christ

Oscar E. Feucht

DOES THE CHURCH REALLY HAVE THE CHILD unless it also has the parents?

There are many fine examples of children being won to the Savior without any co-operation from the parents. There are other examples of little children leading their parents into God's kingdom with their simple acts of devotion or with a tender word of testimony and invitation. God has mightily used the words of a child.

But we must not forget that much more often it is the parent who brings or leads the child to Jesus. When parents are spiritually persuaded, they naturally bring their children to the Lord. Witness the Baptism of entire families in Bible times, in our times.

A child needs the spiritual and moral support of both mother and father. When one of the parents is indifferent or even antagonistic toward religion, this is felt at once by the child. When both parents are also going to church and Sunday school, the child gets a new sense of certainty and security.

Evangelism today seeks not only the conversion of the individual but is making determined efforts to enlist the whole family for worship and study in God's house. It is this dual approach that is needed: one to the child, the other to the parents. Neither dare be neglected. This is good stewardship in evangelism!

But how shall we win the family as a group for Christ?

1. Use Appeals that are Understood

Many human factors play a part in winning of people to church membership. One of these is confidence in a church and its members. The "This Is the Life" television program and such Gospel broadcasts as "The Lutheran Hour" are excellent means for establishing such confidence. Religious broadcasts and telecasts give the family an opportunity to evaluate a church before they attend its services. Often months (and even years) of casual acquaintance precede the day when an unchurched neighbor or friend accepts the invitation to get a better understanding of Christian teaching.

Effective evangelism appeals first to values which the prospect already appreciates or understands. Ask your prospect if he ever attended church or Sunday school. Many *know* that they should be going to church, since it has been a tradition in their families for generations. An appeal to conscience is effective. Sharpen the conscience by saying, "We are asking you to do what you know you should be doing"; or "The Bible is God's Book for the guidance of our lives. Learn to know and follow it. It is the Book of Life." Frequently people are disturbed over moral laxity among youth and recognize the need of giving children the fundamentals of good citizenship. Often it is not possible at first to go beyond merely moral values, which are only a by-product of the Gospel. But frequently these will be enough to awaken a sense of need for those things which only the church supplies. Testify to the spiritual lift you get from the church service and explain, for instance, how one verse of the Scripture changed a very dark day in your life into a bright day. The opportunity to speak of "sin and grace" may not come on the first visit, or it may not come until a clear understanding of human guilt and eternal salvation is gained through the evangelistic sermon and the Christian doctrine course.

2. Testify to What Jesus Means to You

Effective evangelism is positive and Christ-centered. It is simply telling others what Jesus means to us who have accepted Him. This sharing should be natural and as spontaneous as possible. Every believer should learn to put his testimony into his own words rather than simply borrow the statements of another. However, it is well to help every Christian to become articulate in this respect. This can be done in the regular courses of the Sunday school. Thus, for instance, a young people's Bible class studying Mark, chapter ten, came upon the words of Peter: "Lo, we have left everything and followed you." Jesus answered, "Truly, I say to you, there is no one who has left house or brothers or sisters or mother or father or children or lands, for my sake and for the Gospel, who will not receive a hundredfold now in this time, houses and brothers and sisters and mothers and children and lands, with persecutions, and in the age to come eternal life" (Mark 10:28-30 RSV). In applying this passage the teacher asked the question: "Just what does Christ and Christianity mean to you?" In answer to that question this class developed six talking points: peace, hope, fellowship, wisdom, character, purpose.

WHAT JESUS MEANS TO ME

Peace. — Rom. 5:1 — that peace which passes all understanding, the result of having received the forgiveness of sins by faith in Christ. This is the beginning of happiness and, in fact, of a whole new life. We are never happy when we live in sin and are running away from our own consciences. Peace with God is the beginning of all other Christian blessings.

Hope. — 1 Peter 1:3-5 — that hope which buoys us up in every hour of trouble, which supplies courage and comfort in every need, which brings new strength through prayer because it connects us with the resources of heaven. This hope comes to its climax when the lights of the world go out and the lights of heaven go on in our resurrection to eternal life through Jesus Christ, who overcame death for us with His own resurrection from the grave.

Fellowship. — 1 John 1:3, Acts 2:42 — that fellowship which results from being united by a common faith with fellow Christians all over the world in the one holy Christian Church. The Christian faith unites us with the great men and women of God in every age, unites us with the prophets and apostles, and, above all, with Jesus Christ our Savior, our Lord, but also our Brother.

Wisdom. — 2 Tim. 3:15-17 — that wisdom which comes from Christ, of whom it is said that in Him are hidden all the treasures of wisdom and knowledge (Col. 2:3). The whole marvelous content of Holy Scriptures, the greatest book in the world, be-

comes yours as you read and study the Bible and apply it to
life. There is no higher or greater wisdom than the wisdom God
gives us.

Character. — 2 Cor. 5:17 — that character which is the fruit
of faith in Jesus Christ and is produced by the Holy Spirit, who
makes us new creatures and gives us such gifts as love, joy,
peace, patience, kindness, goodness, faithfulness, gentleness, self-
control (Gal. 5:22). We receive Christian character as we grow
up into Christ more and more, and as the image of God is re-
stored in us (2 Cor. 3:18).

Purpose. — Acts 1:8 — that purpose which Christ gives every
believer, namely, the evangelization of the world, the building
of the kingdom of God by means of the teaching and preaching
of the Gospel in every nation. This is the greatest purpose with
which man can identify himself. It is the biggest enterprise on
earth. It is building the one kingdom that will endure when all
others sink in dust and ashes.

To be able to speak on any of these points with conviction —
and in your own words — helps you in winning families for
Christ. For these are positive values which families actually need.

3. Appeal to a Better Understanding of the Bible

Most Americans have a Bible. Many of them seldom or ever
read it, while those who often do so have difficulty in reading it
with understanding. Someone needs to help them discover the
doctrines it teaches, to demonstrate to them the devotional use
of the Bible, and to show how to apply the Bible to everyday
living. Many people do not know the fundamental rules for Bible
interpretation. Others are quite confused with regard to the
Bible's message because they cannot distinguish the Law in the
Bible from the Gospel in the Bible. They don't know how these
are related to each other. Even those who have gone to Sunday school frequently have only a vague idea of what is meant
by "sin" and what is meant by "grace." All need some Philip
who will guide them (Acts 8). The church which gives them
an orderly concept of Christian truth does these people a great
service.

More churches are awakening to this need. Adults who have
been led to faith in Christ and have a real desire to know the
Bible are forever thankful for such guidance. During his parish

ministry the writer developed the following fifteen-lesson course under the title "God and Man":

The Voice of God in the Bible
God and His Chief Creation, Man
Man's Relation to God
Man's Relation to Man
Man's Failure — Sin

+ + +

Christ Meets the Consequences of Human Failure — The Atonement
Christ Earned for Us a Blessed Hereafter — Heaven and Hell
Fellowship with God Through Faith
Fellowship with God Through Baptism
Fellowship Confirmed in the Lord's Supper

+ + +

Talking with God in Prayer
Walking with God in the Christian Life
Working with God in the Church and in the World
Keeping with God by Avoiding Unchristian Associations
Union with God's Church on Earth Makes for Union with God in Heaven

There are many other arrangements of Christian doctrine. This one has proved to be very helpful because it is so easily remembered and is so closely related to life.

4. Use Family Appeals

The kingdom worker who would gain families for Christ should also be equipped to use appeals that are directed to families as families. These appeals are not complete in themselves, but they strike deep into the heart. They are to be adapted to the particular family with which you are dealing.

Where there are *small children,* emphasize the fact that the first four or five years are very important, as important perhaps as the four college years, and that the teaching of religion begins practically at birth. Tell these young parents that life ways and attitudes are largely determined during the preschool days. Parents are teachers of religion by their attitudes, habits, interests, home life. Explain the help which the nursery department letters

give to parents of young children. Then *drive home your point.*
But parents cannot give what they do not have!

Where there are *school age children,* impress the fact that
our children are children only for a short time. Each year is
precious. To lose a single year of schooling is considered a great
handicap. The same is true of the child's spiritual growth. Using
every precious year to help the child get spiritual knowledge is
vital for the development of right attitudes toward God and such
skills as prayer and Bible use. During these school years parents themselves must give spiritual guidance. A father may send
his boy to Sunday school; but if he himself does not go to God's
house, the boy at age fourteen will say, "Dad, I'm grown up now;
Sunday school is for kids." Many persons drop out of church at
this age simply because their parents did not take them to Sunday school and church and did not give them the example of
a life *with* God. It is not enough to have a religion *about* God!
Parents themselves need to come into the church — *and this is
the point* — because their example is far more effectual than
the Sunday school!

Where there are *young people* in the family, the appeal may
be directed to their future. You want your sons and your daughters to do well in school, to establish themselves in good jobs,
to become reputable and successful citizens, to make the right
choice in a life's mate, and to set up a home that will not be
broken by divorce. It is the church that will contribute most
to the achievement of every one of these goals you have in mind
for your growing children. The church offers your youth the
most important ideals for life, and with the Gospel it supplies
the power to achieve these ideals. But — *and this is the point* —
your young people will *listen* to the church but are very likely
to *follow* the living pattern they have in their homes! Where
father and mother do not lead with their own testimony to Jesus
and with examples of Christian discipleship, young people have
a formidable obstacle to their spiritual development.

Where there are *young married people* who are to be won,
the appeals will take a different turn. Experience has shown
a very close relation between religion and a happy and successful marriage. The divorce courts indicate that most of the break-
ups occur where husband and wife do not have a common faith
to hold their marriage together. In Dane County, Wisconsin, for

instance, in the year 1954, only two out of every ten couples divorced were members of any church. It stands to reason that where husband and wife believe alike, go to church on Sunday, become interested in Christian work, and have fellowship with other couples who also believe in Jesus Christ, their own life will be enriched, and their marriage will be safeguarded. We appeal to you to come to the class and learn what the Bible tells us about the Christian faith, because — *and this is the point* — the Christian faith is like cement; it helps to hold marriages together and makes them happier and more successful!

Where there are *older adults* to be won for Christ, the Christian family appeal may begin with the saying, "There are no happy old people except Christian old people." Is there a reason for this statement? Is it based on experience? How does the Christian faith help older folks? It helps to take away their fears of tomorrow and gives them confident trust in their heavenly Father. It assures them that whatever mistakes have been made in the past, they are forgiven through the cleansing blood of Jesus Christ (1 John 1:7). As for the future, the Christian looks forward to the fellowship and happiness of heaven. To carry us through our old age we have wonderful promises of the presence of Jesus and words of comfort and hope which only the Bible gives. In the church we maintain friendships with other older adults and find activities that make our lives useful to the very end. The church, you see — *and this is the point* — has something to give older folks which cannot be found anywhere else; the peace and security that Jesus gives!

These appeals to the family are realistic. They can be understood. They touch the heartstrings. They deal with children and their parents, young couples and their future. The church must talk a language its prospective members can readily understand.

5. Enlisting the Whole Family

The local congregation should be equipped to receive whole families not only as fellow-worshipers in the church service but also as fellow-students of God's Word by setting up Sunday school classes for all ages. Many congregations are content to have only the children enrolled in Sunday school, and make little effort to enroll also their parents, in fact, all the family. Enlisting parents, of course, means having an alert Sunday school secretary and superintendent who ask, "Where is your father today, Johnny?" or "Where are your children, Mr. and Mrs. Jones?" Getting a good record of every Sunday school pupil's family is important. The enrollment of a child should start a chain-reaction type of service to the home: a teacher visits in the home to explain church-home co-operation; the pastor appeals to parents to "bring," not "send," the child; the adult department leader invites to parents' class or Bible class and leaves a descriptive folder on the subjects being studied. Eventually the parents are enrolled in the pastor's class in Christian doctrine.

Each family should be asked to read a portion of the Bible every day and to have prayers. One Oklahoma church almost got 100 per cent co-operation from parents when it proposed a definite plan with specific directions, assignments, and helps. As parents are enrolled in parents' classes or Bible classes (weekday or Sunday), and, along with their children, grow up in the faith, they prepare themselves to be the priests of God in their own household. A mission-minded church will reach out for the whole family!

6. Using Families to Win Families

Has it ever occurred to you that the early church for many years assembled chiefly in homes? That Christ carried out much of His ministry in the homes of people? That the Christian home is one of the best "display pieces" the Christian Church has?

Sharing Christ is normal and natural; first of all in our own homes! There are millions of homes where only one or two members of the family go to church. Many have become indifferent and need an evangelistic approach with appeals they can understand, given in terms closely related to their own needs. Most of us have relatives who are still uncommitted to Jesus Christ. Sometimes they are not won because the efforts made are argumentative instead of positive and helpful expressions of "What Jesus means to me." The home is the first place where our faith is to show itself and flow over into the lives of others.

The home is also a sort of informational center for others. Does the neighbor lady who has a problem come over to your home to seek advice or comfort? Does she bring questions about religion? Does she ask "Won't you explain what this verse in the Bible means?" Do your neighbors have deep disappointments, critical illnesses, great sorrows, wounded hearts that need to be soothed? These questions reveal the missionary opportunities every Christian family has. It need only make use of them! Our wives and mothers especially have wonderful opportunities almost every day to let the Gospel light shine into somebody's heart.

The Christian home itself is an exhibit for Jesus. The family that not only works and plays together but also worships and prays together witnesses to its faith. Religion is life, and life is religion — living with God. Christ and the church are not "subjects on which the family is silent." Hymns are sung, the Bible is read, prayers are said, and God is in the daily conversation. Each day is lived in faith that the heavenly Father will provide for all our needs, that Jesus forgives all our sins, that heaven will be our eternal home. The children of such a home will rise up to bless their God-fearing parents (Prov. 31), and the whole community will feel its beneficent influence.

A truly Christian home will send forth a stream of blessings into the world. It will prepare sons and daughters of whom the church may be proud, who make good in the sight of God and find favor with men (Luke 2:52) because they have sought first the kingdom of God and His righteousness and because God has fulfilled His promise and has added unto them "all these things" (Matt. 6:33). The greatest glory of the Christian home is its living products, the jewels it sends out into the world.

A Texas church has won national recognition in evangelism. Its chief missionary agencies are the homes of its members. Its families have set up in their homes 150 Bible study groups. These classes meet Sundays and weekdays, mornings, afternoons, evenings. Needless to say this is a growing church. In a very special sense its families have been, and are being, used to win families for Christ.

DISCUSSION QUESTIONS

1. What kind of appeals will the average prospect understand best? How can the appeal to conscience be used?
2. What are your own talking points in telling others what Jesus means to you?

3. How do you "sell" the orientation course in Christian doctrine which your congregation gives to adults who are inquiring into the faith?
4. Reread the special appeals to families. Tell how you plan to use one of them in the next few days when talking to an unchurched acquaintance.
5. Does your church have a procedure by which systematic approaches are made to enlist the whole family in Sunday school and church? If not, what should you do to set up such a plan?
6. How can the following activities help to make our families soul-winning units? Family reunions, cottage Bible classes, deaths in the neighborhood, a wedding in the family, a neighborly visit.

SELECTED REFERENCES

Gockel, H. W. *What Jesus Means to Me.* Concordia Publishing House.

Green, Bryan. *The Practice of Evangelism.*

Kettner, Elmer A. *A Message from Your Church.*

The Christian Family in Changing East Asia (a seminar report).

An Invitation (Tract). Augsburg Publishing House.

Enlisting People in the Bible Class. Board for Parish Education.

Chapter 10

Family-Centered
Education

Oscar E. Feucht

JACOB SHEATSLEY, IN HIS BOOK *The Bible in Religious Education*,[1] devotes one of the chapters to Christian education in the home. He bases it very properly on Deut. 6, where God instructs the Children of Israel to carry forward a family-centered program of religious education. It must be remembered that those words were spoken about a thousand years before the synagog (church school) came into general use. The chapter ends with this statement: "We can look only to Christian homes for religious *training;* and since many homes are only nominally Christian, where likewise no Christian nurture can be expected . . . it becomes apparent how tremendously great the problem of Christian education is — *at its roots.*"

From New Testament times to the present the church has been conscious of its duty toward children and youth. The catechumen classes of the early church bear witness to that consciousness. Christian schools and Sunday schools are a comparatively recent development, dating back chiefly to the Protestant Reformation. However, as schools were established, teachers trained, pedagogy developed, and industrialization revolutionized society, the church relied more and more on schools, frequently losing sight of the role which the home, under any circumstance, must play if religious education is to be effective. This chapter is an exploration into this problem.

1. Some Disturbing Facts

The words of a minister who has shifted the emphasis of his ministry toward greater service to families should give us all

---

[1] Wartburg Press, about 1929.

food for thought. "While it is evident to all that the effectiveness of the church is determined largely by what happens in the family, the amazing fact is that the typical church gives little attention to marriage and family life education."[2]

That many churches have not in practice realized the importance of the home is evident from a study reported in the International Journal of Religious Education.[3]

A study was made of the withdrawal from Sunday school of 700 persons under twenty years of age over a period of years, for other-than-good reasons. There were but three instances in which either father or mother was enrolled in the school or known to be actively supporting it.

Sixty-nine members of a church school were traced throughout their Sunday school life, from the Beginners' Department to their time of withdrawal. The reasons for their withdrawal were listed. It was found that more than 80 per cent of the other-than-good reasons for their leaving stemmed directly from parental influence or example or act, intentionally or unintentionally.

Studies of members of senior and young people's groups tracing membership through the Sunday school showed that more than 90 per cent of those who remained in school, progressing through the various departments, came from homes where parents were church members and actively supported the program.

Studies of church accessions of church school members indicated that some 90 per cent of these had a Christian home background on which the church could build.

The study concluded that many children from non-Christian homes go to Sunday school, but schools seem unable to bring them to a commitment to church membership without home support.

Conditions will vary from church to church. But the pastor who analyzes the work of his church school in the course of years will find much in the records which corroborates the findings above. Have we concentrated so exclusively on the child

---

[2] Dr. Roy Burkhart at Intercouncil Conference on Christian Family Life, Cincinnati, Ohio, 1948.

[3] *International Journal of Religious Education,* April 1943.

in the church school that we have practically by-passed the child's most important teachers — the parents? A glance at adult Bible class enrollments will answer this question. Even where a good system of parish schools exists the temptation has been to let professionally trained persons take over almost entirely. This focus on the school is illustrated also by the fact that parent-teacher organizations have given much of their time to help the school rather than to engage in parent education.

"Protestantism professes to advocate the priesthood of believers. Yet, so far as education is concerned, we have left the training of the child to a priesthood of teacher specialists. Let the church first understand that the problem of adequate Christian education is really the problem of educating parents and, in fact, the entire adult body of the church."[4]

Repeatedly, Christian educators have sounded the warning that we "give more attention to helping parents do their job and less attention to acting as substitutes for parents."[5] They have called on the church to act on the assumption that the family is the basic unit in religious education.[6]

Dr. Martin P. Simon, editor of *The Christian Parent,* puts it this way: "The common fallacy runs like this: 'God made the home responsible for the training of the children. BUT since the home is not doing its duty, we must have schools and Sunday schools.' We must indeed have schools and Sunday schools. But the conclusions as drawn are still wrong. Since the home is not doing its duty, therefore we must show the home how to do its duty and co-operate with the home so it will learn to do its duty."[7]

2. Some Basic Considerations

To say that education is telling on the part of the teacher and listening on the part of the pupil is an oversimplification. To think of education as restricted to a schoolroom and some textbooks is likewise greatly limiting a process as old as man

---

[4] Wesner Fallaw, in *Christian Century* as quoted by *Concordia Theological Monthly,* March 1946, pp. 217, 218.

[5] Harry Munro in *International Journal of Religious Education,* May — June, 1944.

[6] Prof. Paul Vieth, Yale University.

[7] From a conference paper.

and one that existed before schoolroom or text existed. No teaching actually takes place unless learning results.

Teaching may be defined as person-to-person sharing. We (Christian persons) are to be intermediaries of the Holy Spirit (a Person) to children, youth, adults (persons) so that Christ (a Person) may by the miracle of conversion be formed in their lives. This accounts for the fact that so much of Scripture is in biographical form. In each generation God wants it to be "translated" back into biography.

"Christian religious education," says Dr. Samuel L. Hamilton of New York University, "is therefore much more than instruction in Christian doctrine. It is personal reconstruction, change, growth, toward life more abundant. It involves the removing of human obstacles so that the Holy Spirit may change us by divine power into new creatures in Jesus Christ.

"All individual personal growth is interpersonal. At every stage of life, from birth to death, the family in the home can provide the setting, the occasions, the atmosphere, the inspiration, the behavior patterns, the controls, and the dynamic of the most profoundly forming and transforming interpersonal relationships of human existence."[8]

Parents have more time with the child than school or church. Parents are closer to their children than anyone else. Parents have access to all sides of a child's personality. Parents have natural learning situations for the training of the child. Parents alone can see to it that learning is translated into doing, living, being; that faith is not divorced from life.

Christian teaching should not be restricted to the home. The church has a definite charter to teach this truth of God (Matt. 28:19, 20). It is always the church AND the home doing it together in harmonious teamwork. The church cannot do it alone. The home cannot do it alone. By its very nature both teaching and training are co-operative tasks. Christian education cannot be institutionalized.

3. Some New Thinking for Teachers

There is a tremendous new challenge for all Christian educators in this new emphasis on family-centered education.

---

[8] Intercouncil Conference on Christian Family Life, Cincinnati, Ohio, 1948.

It makes new demands on adult education. It asks all teachers to develop good rapport with parents. It signals some new approaches that must be carefully conceived and well tested.

How can one really enlist parents? How give them the attitudes and skills needed to help their children? In our civilization with the mother, too, out of the home more than ever before, how can parents find the time? Must not the family acquire new disciplines in the use of leisure time for constructive purposes?

An even larger corps of still better trained teachers is a new and pressing demand of our day — the world over. But must we capitulate to modern "secularization"? Isn't the trend to the suburbs and more time in and around the home something to be seized by the church?

But how seize it?

It appears that serious consideration must be given by every church to the following:

1) A parent-guidance program for all parents, not only the interested and active but also the peripheral members
2) New devices for involving the home in the teaching program of the church, assignments to parents, family Bible-reading program, parent-teacher conferences
3) Keeping parents spiritually growing persons by life-related, Christ-centered classes for all adults on a weekly basis; and using Sunday for study as well as worship.

The question is often asked, "What about the homes where the parents are either indifferent or unchurched?" It is hard enough to get co-operation from more interested church members. There is very little advance lesson preparation on the part of many pupils. Most parents just "don't take time." This is acknowledged. But it must not deter us. It only accentuates the need for family-centered education. The more parents are excused, the less they will do. The more the church "gives in" to such a situation, the farther it recedes from the heart of the educative task. The church is here to change things rather than to be changed by things.

Various church bodies have been reckoning with this issue. Our own "Life in Christ" Sunday school materials [9] have direc-

---

[9] Concordia Publishing House.

tives for parents (Parents' Guide). The nursery department
materials are directed chiefly to parents. The Presbyterian
Church (U. S. A.) in October 1948 issued its new Sunday school
materials strongly geared to parents and to teaching in the home,
with a lesson quarterly intended both for parent and teacher, and
supplementary readers for the children in book form. It was
seven years in the planning and writing stage. Parents are told,
"We are doing this together with you, but not for you." About
two thousand persons were used in introducing the new teaching
method and materials. Called the first serious attempt to implement home and church through a common curriculum, it is
based on the premise "that the family is the center of religious
education, which is to take place and actually does take place
not only on Sunday morning, but every morning and every
evening in the home."[10]

Up to a few years ago the Amish in Pennsylvania had no
Sunday schools, yet they did a very effective job of transmitting
their faith to children and children's children. The secret of
their success was the strong element of religious teaching, conversation, and worship in every Amish home.

4. Some New Thinking for Pastors

It has been encouraging to find pastors responding eagerly
to the call for family-life education. Yet they labor under some
severe temptations. One of these is the constant reminder (what
with imposing new modern edifices) that they are building congregations. So much of their activity revolves about a physical
edifice of brick and mortar — and about its upkeep and attractiveness. But really, are not pastors first building the holy Christian Church by building up persons who are in Christ, who are
born in families and get their chief nurture of body and soul
in families?

The Christian ministry is a service of winning and keeping
souls for Christ. In an earlier chapter we have related evangelism
to families. All through this book a program of service through
many varied and most interesting ministrations is indicated. The
church is people. Through the church's ministry God is helping
people become what God wants them to become.

---

10 Dr. R. V. Kearns, Jr., at Intercouncil Conference on Christian Family
Life, 1948.

Hundreds of pastors have been disturbed by the fact that the church in organizing its work often has contributed to the "dismemberment" of the family. The strict age division in education, the separate meeting nights of various groups, and the segregation of sexes, have played a part. Is there no way in which the church can bring together members of the family who during the day are separated by going to their separate schools or places of work?

Pastors are asking: Can we not do more things in the church as families? Must we not consolidate meetings on one or two nights a week so that parents can be with their children? How can we weave family-life education into the regular teaching agencies and processes? Should not the parish be divided into smaller groups of families in the same neighborhood? Should the elders and deacons focus more on enlarging home visitation and helping families function effectively for Christ? Is a new family-conscious program needed?

Teaching and preaching helpfully and practically means more life-related sermons and Bible lessons. Working with families is reflected in the quality and in the content of the sermon. Working with families is not "more work," but a shortcut to "effectiveness." What the home is, the church will become. So why not give more attention to the things that make the difference?

One of the pastors at the River Forest workshop in 1949 saw the new opportunity to rethink his ministry when he said, "Everything in our past practice suggested using the family for the church. We must reverse that!"

We have enlisted the family for the church. We must now enlist the church for the family!

5. The Theory in Practice

But will it work?

In a series of regional workshops the emphasis has been on the practical side. Pastors in every part of America have made suggestions. Sectional conferences dealt with every phase of family-centered education. The responses of these conferences are assembled in the composite "picture" which follows.

A child comes to the door of the church and is enrolled in the Sunday school. During the week the Sunday school teacher makes contact with the parents. After they have visited the church and have attended one of the Bible classes, they are invited into the pastor's class on Christian doctrine. They gain new convictions directly from the Word of God and display their new interest in the Christian faith in many ways. They are especially receptive to new learning.

One church family becomes very much interested in them, and the two families exchange visits. The new family is given guidance (by demonstration) on how to make family worship meaningful also to the children and on how to vary the procedures and make good use of devotional materials. The Christian Family Standard is given them; the work and some of the history of the local congregation is shared; the larger work of the church body is described. For this the sponsoring family has a neat "new members' kit" of printed materials and guidelines.

The church elder or deacon in whose territory the new family lives makes frequent calls. These calls deal with the happiness and the usefulness that come with the stewardship of life. The horizons of the new family are widening — and they like it. The women have set up neighborhood circles which meet in homes. Here the new family gets acquainted with other families of the congregation which live in close proximity to them. The assimilation of the new family is accelerated by the parent-home and missionary topics discussed by the women in their circle meetings. The men's program is equally helpful. It includes such projects as world-wide missionary broadcasts and telecasts, and a special ministry to the aging. More and more the members of the new family feel "we belong."

The teachers of the parish school and the Sunday school confer personally with all parents, and the new family is given every help in understanding the objectives, the methods, and the part parents are to play in Christian teaching and training. There are quarterly parent-teacher meetings (for all parents, by the way). And the educational features are for the purpose of helping parents to be better parents. The nursery department of the Sunday school begins these home contacts at the birth of a child. And the contacts do not stop when the child is enrolled in a Sunday school class.

The age-level needs of children as they grow from grade to

grade (and out of one problem stage right into another) and the specific needs of young people, young adults, and parents (in fact, all adults, also the aged) are provided for by the various classes of the Sunday school, where fifty-two Sundays a year life-related, family-related, and always Christ-related teaching is done. The objectives for each class, the courses, and the methods are chosen with care. Living the lesson is emphasized in teachers' meetings and in parents' meetings. Courses in Bible, doctrine, missions, evangelism, church leadership, marriage and the family, homemaking, world work of the church are given. The board of education's subcommittee on family life sees to it that there is good integration with the total teaching program in all agencies and groups.

The parish plans for families as such. Four times a year it has well-planned family nights and fellowship programs. Instead of drawing various members of the home away on different nights, it has arranged a weekly church night. Committees, youth and adult groups, arrange to have a joint opening with Bible study and then go to class, society, committee. All meet again for a social half hour and close the evening with prayer. "We are not so many isolated individuals," say the elders, "we are one fellowship in Christ, we are one family." To serve the varied needs of the family, a library is well stocked and staffed, and a family guidance tract rack in the church vestibule contains thirty different items related to the family and its needs.

The role of the pastor is very strategic. He has freed himself for more visiting in homes, especially the homes of new families and families that need spiritual assistance. He is more than ever in demand for counseling. Members are asking him to have a home-dedication service when they move into a new house. He works closely with the young married peoples' club and teaches the group on Sunday morning. He always has some part of the sermon that is especially addressed to the children — and more and more *are* attending. He takes children into consideration when he chooses some of the hymns, and frequently the sermon is applied especially to families. The pastor encourages families to sit together in church. The doctrinal teaching has not changed. If anything, it has become more practical and realistic. There is simply a new emphasis.

6. Also Church-Centered

Can the home do it alone? Certainly not. The organization of our society does not permit parents to have the time or the know-how (in most instances) to give a balanced education to their children. The school and the church are more necessary than ever. But there is a still more important consideration. Home fires must get coals from the fires that burn at the church. Without a Christian church there would be no Christian home! Who has preserved the Bible, established and nourished Christian training schools, provided pastors and teachers? Is it not the church?

Christian education cannot be properly home-centered until it is properly church-centered, and neither type of education can be Christian unless it is Christ-centered. Homes must get the *church spirit*, and churches must get the *home spirit*. The church is the only institution which can give parents the sort of training they must have if they in turn are to be Christian home builders.

What the church is, the home will become. And what the home is, the church will become. The smaller family of the home and the larger family of the church are one and the same family if both are "in Christ."

"The Christian church and the Christian home as institutions are closely bound together. They are like Siamese twins: if you cut them apart you may sever an artery of life and cause one or both to die. The church cannot function as she should in a disordered world unless she employs the home as her main reliance in Christian nurture. And I feel certain that the family cannot be a Christian family or a happy family unless it stays in the circulation of those spiritual influences of which the church is the great custodian." [11]

Such is the vital role of the church!

DISCUSSION QUESTIONS

1. What are some of the disturbing facts which have troubled Christian pastors and teachers?
2. How would you define the processes which we call Christian education? Is your concept too small? Is it adequate?

---

[11] Dr. Samuel L. Hamilton, Intercouncil Conference on the Family, 1948.

3. What are some of the thoughts teachers and pastors will want to take from this chapter in rethinking their ministry?
4. Did you find the ideas outlined in the section "The Theory in Practice" practicable in your congregation? Which of them can you introduce this year? Which are you already doing?
5. Why must Christian education always remain properly church-centered?

SELECTED REFERENCES

Fallaw, Wesner. *The Modern Parent and the Teaching Church.* Macmillan, 1947.

Munro, Harry. "The Family-Centered Curriculum." (Article: *International Journal of Religious Education,* May and June 1944.)

Ligon, Ernest M. *Their Future is Now.* Macmillan, 1940.

Smart, James D. *The Teaching Ministry of the Church.* Westminster, 1954.

Grewenow, George. *The Application of Lutheran Teaching to the Home.* Board for Parish Education, American Lutheran Church, mimeographed.

Sheatsley, Jacob. *The Bible in Religious Education,* Wartburg Press, about 1929. Out of print.

Chapter 11

Helping Families Worship

Oscar E. Feucht

"WHERE TWO OR THREE ARE GATHERED TOGETHER in My name, there am I in the midst of them" (Matt. 18:20). The Lord Jesus speaks these words to all who gather in His name. What He says applies not only to congregational worship but to family worship in the home, which is, essentially, reading the Word of God and praying together as a family. God speaks to us through His Word to give us courage, comfort, and peace; to supply directions for each day, and to help us keep our purpose clear — glorifying God and serving men. Members of the family, in turn, express to God their thanks and present to Him their daily needs.

Looking back over twenty centuries of Christian experience, it is no overstatement to say that family worship has been, and still is, one of the most fruitful practices within the Christian Church. No other single custom in the Christian home contributes so much to keeping it functionally Christian. Family worship has nourished and developed some of the world's greatest churchmen, statesmen, teachers, and leaders. It is as ancient as Noah building an altar for his family, and Abraham gathering his whole household about him for prayers. It is as modern as millions of contemporary Christian families all over the world who regularly hold their family devotions. For Christian people it is a practical necessity. How otherwise can they live *with* God?

There are various estimates as to the extent of this practice today. It is admitted that we are not living in an age conducive to home worship. Some estimate that only 10 per cent of the church families still maintain family devotions. A recent survey in one church body discovered that approximately 35 per cent of the families have such devotions at least two or three times a week.[1]

The "spirit is willing, but the flesh is weak." The Old Adam puts many roadblocks in the way of family worship.

While the chief responsibility rests with the family itself, the church also has obligations to light the fires on the family altar. Many churches have naively taken for granted that their people have such worship, use the materials supplied, and know how to adapt these materials to family needs. Church leaders are mistaken when they think their people have the "know-how" of family worship. Actually many adults do not know the simplest rules for reading the Bible devotionally or composing their own prayers. Many seem to be practically helpless without a prayer book. The interferences from the side of modern living are considerable. After the second or third failure many families stop trying. Unfortunately, many families have never even tried. Family worship cannot be "taken for granted."

Families need and want help. What is needed most perhaps is more and better motivation.

1. Why Build Family Altars?

Wherever God's Word is in use, God Himself is at work. God uses many agencies to instruct His people and build them up in the Christian faith: the sermon, the church service with its hymns and prayers, Christian schools, Sunday school classes, the pastor's confirmation class, and the like. One of the means God has used mightily is family worship.

Families that worship together in the home —

1) *Learn to Know the Bible.* Daily Bible reading gives a firsthand familiarity with the Bible attainable in no other way. Rich indeed is the family that lives in the Word of God (Col. 3:16), while the family that denies itself this heritage is poor however rich it may be in worldly goods.

2) *Face Life with God.* Family worship supplies a message from God for each day. It fortifies spiritually each member of the household against error and sin. Every family faces forces

---

[1] *Bible Reading Practices in The Lutheran Church — Missouri Synod,* E. J. Fritze.

that can be overcome only by spiritual power. The Bible gives courage, comfort, hope — for a life with God (Rom. 8).

3) *Grow in Reverence and Prayer.* In family worship we learn to listen to God and be still. We also learn how to meditate on God's Word and how to pray. In family worship God daily speaks to us, and we daily speak to God. What a tragedy for children when they seldom or never hear and see their parents in prayer.

4) *Spiritually Train Their Children.* While instruction may well take various forms, a daily period for Bible reading, comment, discussion, and questions and answers is provided when the family worship period is wisely used. Family worship prevents soul starvation.

5) *Talk More About Religion.* Where family worship is established, religion ceases to be merely a Sunday affair or "a subject seldom discussed." Instead, the Christian faith will be a natural part of family conversation and daily living. Daily family worship invites Christ into the home as the daily Guest.

6) *Strengthen the Church.* Experience shows that the families that read God's Word are the backbone of the parish. Family worship reinforces the lesson of the school and the Sunday sermon; it strengthens the influence of the church and develops Christian workers.

7) *Develop Christian Citizens for the Nation.* God-fearing parents that lead their children to Christ through instruction and prayer are the greatest barriers against evil. Whatever makes good Christians also makes the best citizens.

8) *Unify and Enrich the Home.* Family life has its moments of strain and friction. Where families worship together, disharmony, tension, and distrust are dissolved; fear and anxiety disappear, and a sense of true values is constantly renewed. Marriages about to be broken up have been saved through family worship. Nothing does more to unify and enrich a family spiritually than regular family worship.

2. Patterns of Family Worship

Since the values and benefits of family worship are so great, the practice dare not be discarded but must be fostered for the good of the individual, the family, the church, and the world.

Therefore we proceed to discuss ways in which family worship may be conducted to be more fruitful and satisfying.

Where home devotions are cold, conducted in a mechanical way, and made an exercise tolerated rather than enjoyed, the younger generation will tire of the practice and will not care to establish it in their own families. On the other hand, family worship can be conducted in such a manner that it is an experience children will not want to forego and which young people will cherish as one of the greatest contributions to their lives. How can we help the families of today achieve the latter and prevent the former?

There has been real strength in the family worship patterns of the past: regularity, an air of reverence, solid Bible interpretation, deeply spiritual prayers. But there have been some weaknesses too: mechanical reading, lack of comment or discussion, language over the heads of children, lack of personalized prayers. If family worship is to be improved, we must help remove the weaknesses and cultivate those things that make family worship strong.

One of the most helpful things families can do is to choose patterns and procedures that meet the needs of the respective family and still keep the worship period deeply spiritual. Materials used should be changed from time to time to give variety and develop interest. With such a vast store of selections from Scripture, hymns, prayers, suffrages, orders of home worship, and ways of conducting family devotions available, there is no excuse for sameness. Much variety is possible.

There are centuries of good usage back of our *devotional manuals*, prayer books, and books of meditations. In these books the spiritual insights of great men of God are preserved for our generation. The modern devotional booklet, produced by most denominations, has perhaps done more than anything else to cultivate again the devotional life. A paragraph or verse from Scripture is read. Then follows the commentary and prayer, the Lord's Prayer and the benediction. We can make these aids more useful and personal if we add our own words of comment, questions, observations, experiences. Many of the prayer books contain a longer prayer for each day of the week.

Reading a Scripture selection without a printed commentary is another pattern. The leader may or may not comment or discuss. Prayers are read from a book or composed on the basis of the reading. A definite reading program should be selected, such as the lectionaries (reading lists) in Bibles, hymnals, and such daily Bible reading guides as *Light for Your Way*.[2] Some choose a chapter a day and a short psalm; others prefer a shorter selection, with more time for meditation and absorbing its meaning. The Bible should be read by units of thought, usually the paragraph. There should be purpose back of all Bible reading. It should not be merely a "holy exercise that blesses all in the doing thereof." Actually we should be looking for something. The leader should suggest things to look for and so help to make it a mutual undertaking. There are many stimulating questions that may be used: (1) What does this Scripture say? What does it mean? What does it mean to me? As first one member and then another tells what the paragraph means for daily faith and life, the Scripture portion becomes personal, meaningful, helpful. Another set of questions is: (2) What did you not understand? Where do you find a directive for faith and life? Where did you get new understanding? As these questions are answered in the family circle and are reflected in the prayers, the true receiving and giving of worship takes place. A third set of questions that can be used as a change is: (3) What are we to believe? What are we to be? What are we to do? The answers, of course, must come from the Scripture portions read.[3]

This pattern requires more resourcefulness on the part of the leader, but it is richly rewarding. With a little more guidance and practice, many Christian people can get much greater benefits from their family devotions. These benefits are: reading the Bible according to a plan, learning the art of personal meditation, cultivating the skills of individual, free prayer. One of the weaknesses of the use of devotional materials is that people become wholly dependent on them and never develop devotional skills of their own.

Family participation is desirable in practically every type of family worship. Several patterns cultivate this more than others.

---

[2] Formerly *Feeding On His Word*.

[3] For similar approaches see Chapter Two of *Building Better Bible Classes*, by Feucht.

The father may take the lead with a call to worship saying, "Let us have our evening prayers" or "Lord, open our eyes that we may see wondrous things in Thy Law." Another member of the family may suggest a hymn. It may be sung without accompaniment and from memory. Instead of the hymn, parts of a psalm may be used to help prepare the heart for worship. The Scripture reading follows, with brief comments, explanations, and several applications of the text to the family. The prayer grows out of the group by the use of sentence prayers. The leader begins with an invocation and a sentence of adoration and praise. Then each member of the family adds one sentence until the circle is completed and the leader closes with "And this we ask for Jesus' sake. Amen." Where there already is some training, each person may add a different element to the prayer: praise, thanks, confession, petition, intercession, dedication.

Such a practice will supply a valuable element of training. All will learn to pray spontaneously or extemporaneously, but with purpose and forethought. Do we underestimate the ability of the common man to pray? In southwest Missouri the writer heard a Christian farmer conduct morning devotions with a free prayer that astonished because of its spirituality, depth, and scope. In Minnesota he heard six children in a pastor's family use sentence prayers on a Sunday morning, each asking the Lord to bless the teaching of His Word that day in another part of the world.

Where there are children the pattern should be kept simple. Yet even here great variety is possible. If the children already know the Bible story, one of them should be given the privilege of telling it (in a devotional manner). The mother or father then reads the story from the Bible. Questions are asked and answered. They should deal not only with the facts of the story but with its meaning for the child. What does God tell us? What does He want us to believe? What does He wish us to do to please Him? Children, too, as we have seen, can contribute sentence prayers. Another procedure is to ask members of the family to mention one or more things they wish to have included in the prayer. These will grow out of their experiences, concerns, and desires; they will include "gifts for which to be thankful," "sins to confess," and "petitions for those in need." The devotional leader then weaves these into a closing prayer followed by the Lord's Prayer and the benediction.

The daily family devotions may also be closely *related to the Sunday school lesson.* Most lesson quarterlies suggest daily readings in the Bible. This is true of study materials on the child, youth, and adult levels. We live in a day when there seems to be little time for homework. However, those who have a devotional period each day can use it for such Bible reading. As each reading throws additional light on Sunday's lesson, it is not only comprehended more fully but applied more thoroughly. From Monday to Saturday the subject of the lesson is kept in mind and applied at school, at work, and at play. The decline of Scripture memorization can be arrested with this method if daily the whole family repeats the memory verse. Suppose the subject of the pastor's catechism class for the week is "faith" and there are four or five longer Bible stories given as examples. Frequently these cannot be discussed in class. In the family worship period they will present dramatic illustrations of great faith and can be dwelt on until their lessons are absorbed.

Those who like to have their devotions more formal may follow the Morning or Evening Suffrages in *The Lutheran Hymnal* or read psalms in unison or responsively, sing hymns, recite portions of the catechism, and use some of the great prayers that have come down to us, such as, Luther's morning and evening prayers, old and new collections of prayers.[4] Litanies may be chosen, suited to the season or day. Silent prayer may be used frequently. The hymn book is a rich store of devotional literature. The writer observed youth groups in a worship session build their worship around a single hymn, singing the first stanza, reading in unison the second stanza, meditating quietly on the third.

Actually the patterns are limited only by the limits of our imagination and resourcefulness.[5] Families should employ variety within the basic pattern: Word of God, comment and discussion, personalized prayer, benediction.

---

[4] *A Chain of Prayers Across the Centuries,* Fox; *Collects and Prayers,* Muhlenberg Press; *A Diary of Private Prayer,* Baillie; and similar books.

[5] *Our Family Worship,* Poellot; *Guideposts to Creative Family Worship,* Gebhard.

3. Meeting Age Level Needs

Parents are asking, How can we have family devotions with *very young children?* Even before a child can talk, he can observe the devotional practices of the parents and get one of the most important lessons: a right attitude toward God. At first the devotion will be connected with simple Bible story pictures. They will be extended as the child's ability to grasp grows. They will be informal rather than formal. They may be part of getting dressed in the morning or going to bed at night or part of the afternoon story hour. At first they may be no more than a spiritual song like "Jesus loves me." Song, Scripture verse, story, prayer, picture will be used. The worship period may grow out of a question asked, or a walk into the garden, or a visit to a park, or conversation or play.[6]

School-age children are most eager to hear the great stories of the Bible. So great is the number of these stories that no Sunday school curriculum can include them all. For the primary child the stories need to be simplified as we find them in Sunday school lessons and Christian children's magazines.[7] Most of the devotional manuals are written for adults in language and in concepts too difficult for a child. Fortunately, new devotional books designed especially for children are appearing on the market.[8] Publishers are also cataloging devotional materials by age levels. Yet the parent must assume the role of teacher in retelling, explaining, and applying Bible stories and drawing prayer thoughts from them. As indicated above, every church supplies lessons with daily Bible reading that can be used in the home. Parents need demonstrations, helps, and guidance for conducting devotions meaningful to the child according to his needs and advancement.

As children grow into their teens, they are more and more influenced by their peers and by the fads, patterns, and activities of high school. This is a danger period for family worship. *At this time youth's interest is likely to lapse unless worship patterns are adapted to its needs.* Young people must be given

---

[6] See *Guiding the Young Child,* by Ellen K. Jagow.

[7] For instance, *The Christian Parent Magazine,* published at Highland, Ill.

[8] *Bible Readings for the Family Hour,* by Martin P. Simon, and *Little Visits with God,* children's devotions by Simon and Jahsmann.

opportunity to participate; for instance, reading devotions in their turn, each member reading and explaining a verse of the Scripture portion; each taking his turn in leading in prayer; using sentence prayers; comment and discussion geared to youth's questions. At youth camps our young people often plan their own group devotions and surprise their leaders with their spiritual interest and ability. Then why do we adults not permit them to do this at home? Devotional materials that have illustrations from life, challenging stories from mission fields, or incidents from the lives of great Christian men and women appeal to youth.[9] Using a modern Bible version, some modern prayers in the language of today will help to recapture the interest of teen-agers.

Old folks need especially the comfort and counsel of the psalms and the promises of old age and heaven to cheer their days and keep them useful members of the body of Christ. Some special materials are available for them.[10]

4. Family Worship Problems

The hindrances to family worship are many. But none of them is insurmountable, just as there is no problem in regard to church attendance that cannot be solved where there is a will to do so. In fact, any group of Christians confronted with one of the problems dealt with below would in half an hour come up with some effective solutions. Where the spirit of Christ is, there also family worship can be held and will triumph over any unfavorable circumstance.

"We Don't Have Time"

Finding time is the most mentioned hindrance. When is the family together? This is becoming a big question in America. Shift work, meetings held early and late, community activities, school and church programs are cited as barriers. But we do read the newspapers (at least the comics), listen to the ball game on the radio, spend hours before television sets, and take time for business, work, sports. We have time for the things we want to do. Increased motivation to strengthen the will is in-

---

[9] Such as *Day By Day with Jesus,* Calendar, Bertermann; Reuben Youngdahl, *Going God's Way.*

[10] *Treasures of Hope, Burden Made Light,* Doerffler.

dicated here. The family that *wants* to do something about it *can* do something about it. Time *can* be found!

Self-discipline

Even when a convenient time is found, strong resolves are needed to prevent exceptions until the habit is formed. Here prayer will help. So will good planning to keep the devotions limited to the time available. But what about the interruptions — the favorite program on radio or television, the telephone, the unexpected caller? Family worship belongs to Christian living — to living with God. Do we need to build up some self-discipline, love for Christ, a sense of responsibility for a family's spiritual welfare? Christian families need a Christian sense of values! Let the Christian family realize that it cannot live like unbelieving families; it must be a light in its street, an oasis in the neighborhood; it must set its own rules as to what comes first, with the love of Christ the moving force.

Atmosphere

The greatest hindrance is an unfavorable climate in the home. Think of the seventy-nine split families in a church of 450 communicant members, where either husband or wife is not a member of any church, or a member of another church. What shall one do in such cases? Often the tensions and conflicts involve religion. We dare not forget the words of a great missionary leader who said, "Upon the women of America rests the responsibility for the prayerless homes of our country." It is upon the Christian spouse, husband or wife, that the burden falls — the duty of spiritual leadership. Someone must take courage for Christ and not act in fear and faithlessness. Someone must take the initiative and start, be it in ever so modest a way — first with an extended table prayer or a short devotion,[11] at a convenient time — and with charity in the heart, and with much prayer.

Inexperience

Sheer timidity has kept many from beginning. They have never experienced home devotions. They feel they would be embarrassed. They fear that they could not read devotions well

---

or pronounce some of the difficult words in the Bible, or know

[11] Devotional book, *Two Minutes With God*, Hoh.

how to ask questions or to answer questions put by their own children. Or it may be that an earlier experience with home devotions was negative. God does not ask for good grammar or flowery speech. He asks for our hearts and true faith. The church can do much to remove these obstacles by giving all members simple materials, guidance to the ABC's of family worship, and opportunity to observe sample home devotions. This condition, more widespread than we think, calls on the individual, on the one hand, to strengthen his ability in the use of the Bible, and on the church, on the other hand, to give every one of its members specific training in the skills of family worship. How can one really be a priest of God without exercising priesthood in one's own home?

"Church Is Enough"

Unfortunately, another condition also prevails. It is best described in the lame excuse, "We go to church regularly and there get enough religion for the week." This is tragic, of course, because it reveals a sickly Christianity, an externalism foreign to the spirit of true discipleship and genuine Protestantism. The Christian faith is a dynamic, life-giving, life-changing thing. We may well ask such people whether they have the spirit of Christ and live *with* God. We should appeal to them to develop a Christian philosophy of living! Unfortunately, they operate in a vicious circle — little Word, little strength.

It is clear that help is needed. The church should not merely bewail the situation. People need assistance — simple but *essential rules* are needed to help these people: (1) Daily Word and prayer are a part of living as a Christian. (2) Find and use the best time available. (3) Begin in God's name, using a suitable pattern and simple materials. (4) Be regular. (5) Start with part of the family if all are not yet persuaded. (6) Make it a happy experience; don't force family devotions in a legalistic manner. Let the love of Christ be the motive. (7) Plan and pray for success.

5. How the Local Church Can Help

Practically every family needs help with regard to family worship. All new families and 75 to 85 per cent of the church's old families need help in establishing or re-establishing the family altar. Those that have it need help to improve it and make it more fruitful. We shall only briefly describe some of the means.

1) Training children. One pastor increased Bible reading 90 per cent in his Sunday school through a special Bible reading program. Ask parents to follow the Bible readings of the Sunday school lesson in daily home devotions.

2) Train young people in youth groups and encourage them to carry on at home.

3) Give basic guidance, sample devotions, helpful materials to all couples in the premarriage counseling program.

4) Work especially with new families to get them started. Prepare a new member kit which includes tracts on family worship, and a list of devotional materials for all age levels.[12]

5) Display devotional materials — on bulletin boards, in the church office, the church library, the church narthex at all times — and set up a larger, special display once a year.

6) Dramatize and demonstrate family worship from time to time — in a church service, in meetings of parents, men, women, youth. Skits and plays and guidelines for these are available.[13]

7) Use audio-visual aids, recordings, filmstrips, films — to show "how to get started," "patterns of family worship" (see references at end of chapter). Follow with good discussion.

8) Conduct a home visitation, using your own flip-chart, packets of materials, tracts. Discuss in a practical way the benefits and nature of family worship with every family in the parish.

9) Use the Covenant Home Plan developed by Faith Lutheran Church, Los Angeles, to enlist a larger number of homes as "Family Altar Homes."[14]

---

[12] Concordia Publishing House Leaflet. *45 Book Selections for Your Daily Devotions.*

[13] For instance, *How to Conduct Family Worship*, Louise A. Manka. *Parish Education*, May, 1949; *Living Closer to God Through Family Worship*, Ruth E. Schwartzkopf. *Parish Education*, January, 1954; *Secret of Security*, L. J. Dierker; *Don't Be An Ostrich*, G. L. Wind, available from The Board for Parish Education.

[14] *Spiritual Power for Your Congregation*, by C. W. Berner, pp. 23 to 31.

A complete manual, *Building Family Altars in Your Parish*, is available to local churches (board of elders, board of education, stewardship committee). It outlines procedures for increasing and improving the practice of worship in the home.[15]

It develops these chief parts:

I. Why Build Family Altars
II. Ways of Conducting Family Worship
III. Materials that Help Families Worship
IV. How to Build Family Altars (eight plans)
V. Family Worship Project
VI. Keeping Altar Fires Burning
VII. Who Shall Be the Builders?

A pastor, a layman, and a board of elders in a Texas church [16] produced their own practical manual on family worship. In a home visitation it was taken to each family in the congregation. It contains —

An Introductory Letter
Motivation
Ways of Conducting Family Worship
Ten Methods "Described"
Suggestions for Praying
Developing the Spirit of Reverence
Ten Methods "Demonstrated"
Bible Reading Guide for Family Worship
a) "Four Months with Jesus"
b) Golden Chapters
c) Selection of a Choice Passage from Each Book of the Bible
d) Bible Stories for Children

As the local church sets up, as one of its major tasks, the establishment and improvement of family devotions in every home, it will help make its homes true workshops of the Holy Spirit.

---

15 Board for Parish Education.
16 Trinity Lutheran Church, Corpus Christi, Tex.

DISCUSSION QUESTIONS

1. What percentage of the families in your parish hold family devotions at least two or three times a week? (Try a survey in all Sunday school classes.)
2. What reasons would you advance to induce a new family to conduct family devotions?
3. John and Mary have four children, ages 3, 5, 7, and 9. What family worship method would you suggest to them?
4. The Millers have three teen-age children, ages 13, 17, 19. What methods and materials can they use to keep these young people interested and participating?
5. Select one of the problems in Section 4 of this chapter. What reasons would you develop in dealing with a family having that problem? Or divide class into buzz groups and assign a different problem to each group for further study and solution.
6. Considering your own congregation, which of the activities listed in Section 5 would you use over a five-year period to increase and improve the practice of home devotions?

SELECTED REFERENCES

Baillie, John. *A Diary of Private Prayer.*
Board for Parish Education. *Building Family Altars in Your Parish.*
Berner, C. W. *Spiritual Power for Your Congregation.*
Hoh, Paul J. *Two Minutes With God.*
Doerffler, Alfred. *Treasures of Hope.*
Doerffler, Alfred. *The Burden Made Light.*
Herzberger, F. W. *The Family Altar.*
Bertermann, E. R. *Day by Day with Jesus.*
Simon, M. P. and Jahsmann, A. H. *Little Visits with God.*
Simon, Martin P. *Bible Readings for the Family Hour.*
Jagow, Ellen K. *Guiding the Young Child.*
Gebhard. *Guideposts to Creative Family Worship.*
Hegland, Martin. *For His Name's Sake.*
Schramm, Edward W. *At Jesus' Feet.*
Fritze, Edwin J. *Bible Reading Practices in The Lutheran Church — Missouri Synod.*
Film: *Faith of Our Families,* 40 min. Black & white.
Filmstrip: *At Home With God,* with recording, 15 min.

Chapter 12

How a Nursery Department Helps

Arnold C. Mueller

A PASTOR WHOSE SUNDAY SCHOOL has had as many as 800 little ones on its nursery (cradle) roll said: "The cradle roll has meant as much as any other thing in the growth of our church." Another pastor asserted that the greatest field for evangelism lies in the nursery department.

These are far-reaching statements. If it is true that the nursery department is a powerful force for building the congregation from within (Christian education), and that it is a powerful force for building the congregation from without (evangelism), every church should, without fail, inaugurate a nursery department and develop it to the utmost. Moreover, a well-ordered nursery department, as we shall see, is the means through which the congregation strengthens the home, and this will be the chief emphasis in this study.

1. Belongs to a Full Educational Program

The nursery department that is fully organized and functions well, will help the church in many ways. This department

provides an additional contact with the home at a strategic time (the birth of a child),

guides parents in the first steps of Christian child-training with counsel and materials,

follows up at once on the implications of Baptism (Christian training),

enrolls the child soon after birth in the Sunday school and the church program, frequently leads to the evangelization and instruction of the parents if they are unchurched,

helps the parish develop an important type of home visitation through lay workers.

EXTENDING THE EDUCATIONAL LADDER

The educational ladder of the Sunday school has been extended upward to include all youth and adult members of the church. It has been extended downward into the preschool or kindergarten and nursery age. The nursery department concerns itself with babies and children under four years of age — *and their parents.*

The downward extension of the ladder has been dictated by the realization that the child's education begins at birth. If the child's education begins at birth, the teaching responsibility of the parents and the church cannot be deferred to some later age. The Lutheran Church has always advocated child-training at the earliest possible age. When Christian parents present their children at the baptismal font that the children may be born again and become children of God, both the parents and the sponsors assume the responsibility of bringing up the children in the nurture and admonition of the Lord. Today it is the nursery department of the Sunday school that gives the first assistance to parents for their task.

CHURCH AND HOME NEED EACH OTHER

God has given identical educational assignments to the home and to the church. In declaring parents responsible for the Christian training of their little ones, the Scriptures assume that fathers and mothers, being members of the church, will be duly instructed with respect to their duties and will fulfill those duties conscientiously (Deut. 6: 6-9; Eph. 6: 4). It has, however, become apparent that many parents today are incapable of bringing up their children in a God-pleasing manner without special help. Even well-meaning parents who want their children to grow up to be sincere Christians and upright citizens need all the assistance the church can give them.

Christian leaders, aware that the future well-being of the church and the nation depends on building strong Christian homes, are designing a blueprint of Christian education which they hope will achieve what the traditional pattern can no longer attain. This is apparent from the transformation which the Sunday school, the most widely used instructional agency of Protestantism, has undergone over the years. Originally ungraded and poorly organized, the Sunday school now has a completely articulated program for people of all ages, and is trying to bring its program into the home.

The average Sunday school has been most successful on the elementary level; it has been least successful on the nursery (preschool) and Bible class (youth — adult) levels. These are the two divisions of the Sunday school that must be strengthened if the educational work of the church is to help toward the restoration of the truly Christian home, and if the home, in turn, is to be a source of strength to the church. Yes, the need is urgent! The church must help parents fulfill the greatest task God has laid upon them. The nursery department will prove an excellent means to that end.

2. Objectives of the Nursery Department

We may state the objectives of the nursery department as follows:

1) To awaken in parents a sense of responsibility for the religious instruction and training of their little ones and to give them initial guidance

2) To establish and maintain a bond of unity between the parents and the Sunday school and church

3) To give the church additional access to the homes of the unchurched where there are preschool children

Through its nursery department the church reaches into the home and tries to establish a friendly relationship, the prerequisite for gaining the co-operation of parents. It has been said that the road to the hearts of parents is through the children. Parents can be reached more effectively through their children than in any other way. But unless the parents are actually gained for the church, it is not likely that the church will hold the children very long. As a rule, parents are especially receptive to religion when a new baby comes into the home.

The Sunday school, through its nursery department, seeks

first of all to reach fathers and mothers. A large number of parents belonging to church, and still more parents who only send their children to Sunday school, are careless about Christian nurture. Some of them are ignorant of the most elementary rules of child training. Nursery workers bring into the home stimulation and guidance for Christian education in the important early years. They acquaint the parents with the church's service to child, youth, adult. They help parents to understand their children better. They give them help for the Christian rearing of their children. In many cases the parents do not realize that the chief responsibility for the teaching of religion rests with the home and that every home is doing a teaching job. This teaching job may be good, bad, or indifferent; but it is potent. On the other hand, most parents who have genuine concern for the moral and spiritual growth of their children really welcome the help which comes through the church's nursery department.

One of the objectives of the nursery department is "to gain access to the homes of the unchurched." A department of the church that can enter such homes has the prospect of gaining both the parents and the children for church membership. That is why the nursery department has been heralded as a primary force in evangelism. Today evangelism begins at the bedside of the young mother. The church that makes the first contact with the mother frequently has the best chance of bringing the parents and the child into its fellowship. In 1955, 4,500,000 babies were born in the United States. The church has unlimited possibilities for winning souls and building home and church through an active nursery department.

If we involve the parents in the educational program of the church when the child is young, we are almost sure to gain the children for regular attendance at Sunday school. The enrollment of the Sunday school can be gauged by the number of babies on the nursery roll. A large nursery roll means a large Sunday school, and the more children we enroll in the Sunday school, the more opportunity the Holy Spirit has to impress the saving message of the cross on human hearts and thus to extend the church. It is, therefore, little short of tragic that so many Sunday schools have not yet projected a full-scale nursery program.

Recent years have shown more interest. New Sunday school plants are providing more space for three- and four-year-olds. Enterprising young and old churches are discovering the many benefits and new joys of working with young parents. One church in New York State with 590 communicant members has 150 children on its nursery roll. With fine insight and justifiable pride one Sunday school superintendent said, "Here is the secret of a large Sunday school and the church's future," as he pointed to a larger nursery roll and spacious quarters for the care of children from birth to age four.

3. Focus on the Home

The nursery department records the names of children who at the age of three will be eligible for the nursery class of the Sunday school, and at the age of four will enter the beginners' department. We must be careful, however, not to give parents the impression that their early home-training program is of minor importance and that the real job of Christian nurture will be done later when Bobbie and Jane attend Sunday school. Parents are to know that their home-training program is more important than any program the church may devise.

The nursery program, while originating in the Sunday school, must *center in the home.* It does not substitute for the parents or relieve them of their responsibility. Its chief purpose is to help parents surround the young child with Christian attitudes, teaching, and training. This great task needs direction and stimulation. It begins even before the baby is born. If the training program of the home is strong, the parents will, without much persuasion, avail themselves of the educational agencies the church provides for young and old. On the other hand, the church that presumes to "take over" what only parents can do will be weakening Christian education both in church and home. No congregation will enjoy a healthy spiritual growth if it "substitutes for parents." We must by all means help parents do the job they are to do.

Now let us look at the nursery department. It subdivides into (1) the nursery roll, (2) the church nursery, (3) the nursery class.

4. The Nursery Roll

The organization of the nursery roll is simple. It should be an integral part of the Sunday school structure. The pastor and the Sunday school superintendent select as nursery superintendent or leader a competent Christian woman who understands and loves children. When the work grows, the superintendent chooses one or more helpers to assist her especially with home visits. Home visitation is the chief task of the nursery workers. One of them visits the mother soon after the birth of the child. She speaks to the mother about God's saving purpose for the baby and asks permission to enroll it.

Even during the first visit the worker may give the mother the prayer cards of the personalized cradle roll, and the tract *So You Are Parents*. The worker might also leave a suitable tract on Baptism with the parents, for the mere reading of such a tract usually prompts the parents to have their child baptized.

With enrollment of the child begins a regular and systematic contact with that home. During the first three months several calls will be important, to establish closer friendship and to indicate genuine interest. It is only natural that the pastor himself should also call. Arrangements for the baptism will supply a good opportunity to discuss the privileges of Christian parenthood.

Thereafter the nursery worker calls at least once every three months, personally taking one of the letters of the *nursery program packet* listed at the end of this chapter. When a personal call is impossible, the letter should be sent. Each of these letters brings a different message on Christian child-training suited to the development of the child. The first letter speaks of the standards and goals of a Christian home. The second tells father and mother how important the first four years of life are for the child's personality. Suggestions are made for the first prayers to teach, pictures to explain, Bible stories to tell.

The child soon begins to ask questions about God, the Bible, Jesus, the church, and the world it is beginning to discover. The nursery worker will suggest ways to answer these questions. She will direct to simple Bible story books with pictures for the very young child; explain the helps the church has prepared for parents, such as the *Parent Guidance Series* booklets and the best books in the field. *Growing Up with Jesus,* a manual which presents the basic rules of child training, and *Guiding the Young Child* are especially helpful.

Because the first two years are vital for the proper Christian training of a child, it may be well to present the parents with a copy of one of these books before the baby is a year old.

When the child has reached the age of two, the superintendent will begin delivering or mailing the *Story Picture Lessons for the Nursery Roll* (26 leaflets). Besides the stories and prayers for the child, each leaflet has a message for parents, and together these messages constitute a short course in child-training. Personal delivery of the leaflets gives the visitor an excellent opportunity to maintain contact with the home, to give encouragement and offer a word of counsel to parents.

Funds should be made available for the free distribution of leaflets, the manual, or another book and other nursery materials. Even if the congregation must pay the entire cost, the returns in the way of better Christian homes will make this a fruitful investment.

5. The Nursery Class

When the child has reached the age of three, it is ready to be enrolled in the nursery class. Special lesson materials are available for three-year-olds: leaflets, pictures, activity materials, and teachers' guides. There is much evidence that children of this age absorb attitudes, knowledge, and skills from the nursery course. If no class for three-year-olds exists, the Sunday school should provide the parents with *My Nursery Bible Lessons* — to be taught at home. (The manual *Growing Up With Jesus* will be especially helpful because it shows the parents how they can combine instruction and training in the daily program of Christian education.)

Three reasons may be given for adding a nursery class. First, parents began sending their three-year-olds to the beginners' department, which was too advanced for them. Secondly, it was found that three-year-olds are capable of learning little prayers and songs and profiting by Bible stories and simple instruction and activities. Thirdly, educators have discovered that the preschool years are very significant for religious training.

Whatever our feeling may be about sending three-year-olds

to Sunday school, the church faces a practical situation. A great educational advantage is lost if the child from one to four is neglected. Unless we receive these little ones, many may be lost to the church and to the Savior, and a valuable spiritual contact with the home may be forfeited.

The nursery class program is somewhat more informal than that of the beginners' department. Since the interest span of tiny tots is short, the program will have a variety of activities. The superintendent of the nursery roll or another qualified person may be the leader of the nursery class. Teachers of three-year-olds should have both *training* and *experience* with preschool children, or arrange to get these by reading books and observing other nursery class teachers.

Directions for organizing and managing the nursery roll and the nursery class will be found in books listed at the end of this chapter.

6. The Church Nursery

Babies and small children are often a disturbance in the church service — also to the parents. Rather than have their children become a source of annoyance to others, parents stay home or take turns in going to church. Such irregular attendance, however, deprives parents of spiritual growth and guidance just at a time when they need it most. This practice also keeps young adults (who are in their best years of learning) from the Sunday school's Bible classes.

Many churches find that the church nursery is a happy solution, and it is a very simple matter to arrange for it. A room is set aside for babies and small children. The only equipment needed are baby beds and a few tables, toys, and books. The congregation will put a competent woman in charge of the nursery, and this woman will enlist other women, or girls of high school age, to help her. If there is an early and a late service, none of them need ever miss church. Otherwise they may take turns in serving so as not to miss church often. Many churches overcome this problem by using a public address system to bring the worship service into the nursery room.

The secret for getting young parents with small children back into the Bible class (parents' class, couples' class) is to extend the church-time nursery so that it is open also during the time of the Sunday school session. This gives the young parents not only a chance to study God's Word in a class but it also supplies the fellowship with others which they desire. Without such nursery service a Sunday school unwittingly cuts off one of its most promising sources of growth.

Parents may safely entrust the care of their babies and little children to the nursery personnel while they attend Bible class and the morning service. A properly trained nursery leader will have something constructive and spiritual planned for the two-year-olds and three-year-olds, such as simple Bible stories, nursery songs, finger play, prayer sentences, and Bible pictures. When the children are three or four years old, the parents should take them along to the worship service. Thus the church nursery does not interfere with early training in church attendance. Properly conducted, it prepares the small child for public worship.

7. Training Nursery Workers and Parents

Observation, reading, and *conference* are the means through which nursery workers will equip themselves for their task. Visiting Sunday schools that have a nursery department will give them a chance to see a nursery class in operation. They may also go to a day nursery and there observe trained workers in action. The nursery department superintendent and her teachers, helpers, and workers should have regular meetings for the purpose of study and planning.

In the early stages of the work the group will study books which deal with objectives, with the use of pictures, and with the telling of Bible stories. The program should be carefully outlined on the basis of sound principles. Nursery workers need to be resourceful, but they also should be acquainted with the many plans and materials for nursery children developed in recent years.

PARENT GROUPS

It is difficult to devise and keep in operation a scheme of parent visitation through which all parents, churched and un- churched, are approached regularly in the interest of sound home training and co-operation with the church and its program. Even if a good system of nursery visitation has been made to function, two or three parent meetings a year will still be desirable and helpful. At such meetings parents receive guidance that cannot be given them under any other arrangement.

You may begin by inviting parents to be observers in the nursery class. From this may develop parent classes, mothers' meetings, mothers' clubs, or parent-teacher meetings. Mothers' meetings may be held on Sunday afternoon or at some other convenient time. Parent classes are best attended when scheduled on Sunday morning as a part of the Sunday school Bible class program. Direct Bible study should alternate with training courses for young parents. As a rule, parent-teacher meetings in the evening are to be preferred to mothers' meetings because then both fathers and mothers are able to be present.

A well managed nursery department is more than "a sentimental baby-admiration club" and far more than keeping a record with "colorful booties tied with pink or blue ribbon" to a scroll in the church vestibule. It is setting up (1) a nursery roll with a program of home visitation, (2) a nursery class for three-year-olds, (3) a church-Sunday school nursery to make possible church and Sunday school attendance of parents with very young children, and (4) the training of both nursery workers and parents. It is focused on the home, and yet it is a key to both the inward and outward growth of the church.

DISCUSSION QUESTIONS

1. What obligation do parents and sponsors assume at the baptism of a child?
2. To what extent has your church used the nursery department to gain unchurched children and their parents?
3. Why is the educational program of the church likely to be most successful when the congregation centers the training program of the preschool child in the home?
4. Give the chief reasons why every congregation should inaugurate a nursery department.
5. Outline a program of work for the superintendent and visitors of the nursery roll.

SELECTED REFERENCES

Annual Packet: *Parent Teacher Materials.* National Lutheran Parent-Teacher League.

Erb, Alta. *Christian Nurture of Children.* Herald Press, 1955.

Jahsmann, A. H. *Concordia Nursery Program Packet.*

Jahsmann, A. H. *Teaching Little Amalee Jane.* CPH.

Mueller, A. C. *Growing Up with Jesus,* a manual. CPH.

Various authors. *Parent Guidance Series:*
   "Your Child and You"
   "Making Homelife Christian"
   "Happiness is Homemade"
   "Guiding the Young Child." CPH.

Jones, Elizabeth. *Nursery Children and Our Church.* Judson Press, 1955.

Brennemann, Helen Good. *Meditations for the New Mother.* Herald Press, 1953.

Athy, Marion Poppen. *In the Nursery* (a manual). Castle Press, 1953.

Strang, Ruth May. *A Study of Young Children.* Abingdon-Cokesbury, 1944.

Stelzner. *Methods for Workers with Nursery Children.*

Chapter 13

Getting the Church into the Home

Erdmann W. Frenk

WHEN THE "CHRISTIAN CENTURY" PUBLISHED a series of articles on "Great Churches of America" (1950), it reported that it had found certain common elements in all of these great churches. Most of them enjoyed strong pastoral leadership, and some had developed very efficient lay leadership; but all carried on unusually extensive programs of home visitation and education. The religion of these churches was marked by its ability to leave the pulpit and its Sunday setting, to invade the home of the parish, there to become a vital factor in everyday living. What is more, all of these churches had made very careful arrangements for the proper channeling or piping of their religion into the homes. It is this channeling, alias "Home Visitation," that is presented briefly and suggestively in this chapter.

THE EARLY CHURCH AND THE HOME

The early church was the *familia Christi* in the fullest sense of the term, and it functioned as such. Home and church, for all practical purposes, were closely related. The priesthood of all believers was a reality. One lived for the other, and all lived for Christ. Church services frequently were conducted in the home. Moral ideals were pictured in the language of the home. Educational directions were addressed to the parents. Even its charities had a distinct home ring. The church was in the home and the home was rooted in the church. This does not mean, however, that there were no family problems and that all Christian homes were perfect (1 Cor. 7).

Conditions changed rapidly with the beginning of the fourth

century, when the church became institutionalized. The drift
now was away from the home. The church began to function
independently of the home, at times in deliberate opposition to it.
And with years the gap and the rift between the two became
greater. To be sure, the church still had a message for the home,
and pulpit utterances relative to marriage morals and family
ideals are not wanting in the Middle Ages. Yet the church,
down through the years, became an institution wholly separate
and apart from the home. Its interests were in itself and not in
another institution.

Luther and the Christian Home

Martin Luther as a man "of the people, by the people, and
for the people" could not help but be interested in the religious
health of the home. One cannot read his sermons without feeling his grip on the conscience of the common people. A faith
which did not claim the entire man in all of his social relationships was no faith at all, he emphasized time and again. His zeal
for religious schools in the interest of better home life needs no
restatement. His Table of Christian Duties were no afterthought
in a catechism which he wrote specifically for home use. Time
and again he stressed the truth that church and home stand or
fall together. As a result, he did not hesitate to use every legitimate means to channel his religion into the homes of his day.
He was as much interested in the reformation of the home as
of the church. He had a stake in both and left no stone unmoved
to bring the two to bear upon each other.

We face a like need today. The church of our day must find
ways and means of moving more effectively into the homes for
the mutual benefit of church and home. And this influence upon
the home must be something more than casual or oblique. Occasional sermons just won't do. Neither is the solution found in
formal Christian education, especially if it is restricted to the
elementary level. It must be something more definite, distinct,
detailed, frontal — with carefully defined goals and the necessary
techniques and implementations to reach these goals.

Fourfold Program of Visitation

To us a program of home visitation would offer the highest
hopes of making our religion more effective and influential in

our family life and home relations. And by home visitation, we hasten to add, we mean something more than an occasional canvass of the homes of our parish in the interest of funds, pledges, or some other stewardship commitment.

In our own parish,[1] numbering approximately 2,500 souls, we have consistently carried out a fourfold program of home visitation, the character of which we shall describe briefly. And lest anyone suspect that what we are about to describe is applicable to a large parish only, we immediately add that we have used this selfsame program with like effect in smaller parishes. With minor adaptations it can be used in any parish. Our directions are addressed chiefly, though not exclusively, to pastors and church councils. We point briefly to pastoral visitation, elder visitation, every-member home visitation, and teacher visitation.

1. Pastoral Visitation

Every pastor visits homes. It lies in the very nature of his calling to do so. When he, like Moses, feels sensitive to the burdens of his people, he will share these burdens with them in their homes. There will be a natural priority and sequence in his visitations. First the sick and the dying, then the aged and the shut-ins, then problem homes, mission homes, or the homes of the catechumens — these will and must be visited by the pastor and most probably in the order indicated. Congregations expect this. They have a right to expect it. Pastors and congregations profit immeasurably by it. Yet when we speak of pastoral visitation, we mean something more than these occasional crises ministries which are common to every normal pastorate. We mean a consistent program of visiting every home in the parish over a given period of time, irrespective of whether those homes present particular problems and emergencies or not. We refer to a persistent, perennial program of pastoral calling at all the homes in the parish for the express purpose of stimulating and directing the spiritual life within the home. In connection with such a program of pastoral visitation we make the following specific suggestions:

Good Routing. — Block out all the homes of the parish, barring none, irrespective of the size of the parish. Group those

---

[1] St. Peter's Lutheran Church, Joliet, Ill.

most conveniently visited. A route ticket listing the name, address, the communion frequency, and the contributions of the individuals in the past fiscal year will prove very serviceable in making the proper approach. The reverse side of this route or call ticket may be used for the missionary memoranda which pastoral visitation invariably awakens.

Fixed Time. — Have fixed hours for pastoral visitation. We formerly thought that the hours from three to five were the most ideal. We now know that the period from four to seven offers greater possibilities. Three to four afternoons a week, with from three to four calls scheduled for an afternoon or early evening, will be a sufficiently heavy program. This tempo may have to be reduced during the Advent and Lenten seasons.

Give Notice. — Announce your intended visit to the homes in question. Phone them a day or two in advance, or send a post card. We include our list in the announcements which we still make from the lectern in the course of the service. One church prints the list in its weekly bulletin. Announcing the homes to be visited beforehand not only enables the home to prepare for the visit but makes the pastor sure that he will find the family at home.

Clear Aim. — Have a clear picture of the aim and purpose of the visit. Essentially it is to set up the counseling and confessional "booth" in every home. Never enter the home unless armed with definite data relative to church and communion attendance and such other items as you may want to discuss with the family. It is at home visitations that golden opportunities for pastoral counseling will present themselves in the field of marriage, Christian education, youth, missions, the family altar, etc. It is not strange that pastors given to home visitation invariably have large adult membership classes.

Encourage Expressions. — Encourage the parishioners to speak freely on the occasion of such visitations. Give them a chance to present their problems. Mothers especially will welcome the opportunity for pastoral counsel and guidance. We have known of families that literally held a caucus in anticipation of the visit of the pastor and presented a full slate of problems to him. Pastors must be on their guard against monopolizing the conversation on such occasions lest they defeat the very purpose of their visit.

Leave Tracts. — Leave behind some tangible evidence and reminder of your visit. Tracts, booklets, a reading list, a congregational statement on premarital counseling or mixed marriages, a family check list, in fact, anything that fits into the general scope of the visit will do. This is a simple way of reinforcing and prolonging the benefits of the visit. This implies careful selection, stocking of tracts and other literature. The general family packet (see end of chapter) has been assembled for this purpose.

Keep Records. — Good record-keeping belongs to good soul-accounting. Take time to evaluate the home. The problems as presented by the home as well as any other item which especially impressed the pastor should be carefully noted for future reference and study.

Keep Confidences. — Without violating confessional or pastoral confidences, discuss these problems later with the elder of the district insofar as they pertain to him. Take the more common problems and put them on the docket of the elders' meetings.

Pastors who consistently carry out a program of home visitation are unanimous in their praise of its value. The home, the church, and the pastor — all profit from it in a manner and measure too vast and varied to be described within the confines of this chapter. Experience definitely proves that home-visiting pastors make for church-going congregations. Ministries become people centered. The pastor becomes a spiritual "father" to his people. The church functions again as the *familia Christi*.

2. Elder Visitation

This, in some respects, is the most profitable type of visitation, superior, under some conditions, even to that of the pastor. Certainly, of all lay visitation this is the best. While the pastor visits each home on an average of once a year or once in two years (our church has 1,000 homes), the elders and their assistants do it four times a year. It is true that the pastor visits the homes in a more representative and official capacity than do the elders; yet it is likewise true that, being laymen, the elders at times invite a more ready confidence and rapport than does the pastor. We know of no type of visitation so productive of good for both church and home, if properly performed, as elder visitation. To make this possible in our own parish we have increased the number of elders to thirty, each having one or more assistants, and each responsible for about thirty homes or seventy-five communicants. We add here some practical directions relative to this type of visitation.

Good Example. — Encourage all elders and assistants to set their own households in order before they endeavor to counsel others in home matters. This is just plain common sense (1 Tim. 3:12).

Train for Visitation. — Educate, enlighten, train, and condition the elders for the tasks of home visitation. They above all others must be oriented in the dogma and practices of the church lest they do more harm than good. Whatever the particular aim and subject of the visitation may be — and this will vary from time to time — they must know it and be able and anxious to share it with others. Attendance at the elders' meetings under these conditions is imperative. Infinitely wise is the pastor who will make the most of the educational possibilities of the elders' meetings. Needless to state, while the elders may distribute the quarterly financial statements on the occasion of their visits, the real purpose and long-range aim of their visits will not be a financial one. It will be essentially the same as the pastor's aim, i. e., the spiritual stimulation of the home.

Spiritual Men. — Spiritualize the elders for their tasks. Let them feel the overflow of your own enthusiasm and personality. Remind them of the great need of humility and prayer. Tell them frankly to begin their visits on their knees and to seek the guidance of the Holy Spirit. Awaken in them the mind of Christ, and make them especially sensitive to mission opportunities.

Prepare Parish. — Prepare and condition the congregation for the visit. Announce it on one or two Sundays prior to the period of visitation. Parishioners need to be reminded that they must receive these elders in the name of Christ and consult with them as brethren in Christ (1 Peter 2:9; Col. 3:16; Luke 22:32).

Remain Evangelical. — Tell the elders never to argue or to scold but to present the truths and needs, as they see them, in an evangelical manner and to report all major problems to the pastor.

Problems. — If the problems are not too personal, urge the elders to present and discuss them in subsequent elders' meetings.

Elder's Wife. — Encourage the wife of the elder to accompany him on his rounds at least once a year as a goodwill gesture. The pre-Christmas season is most ideal for this joint visitation. Through the eyes of his wife the elder will see things which, but for her, might completely escape him.

Every congregation has its fringe families, namely, those households in which faith is seemingly at a low ebb and on the verge of being given up entirely. These especially need frequent attention on the part of the elders. (For additional suggestions on reaching fringe families see Part VI of this book.)

Our elders are best qualified for this work. Their office assumes added dignity and meaning when they do it. The thirty families entrusted to the elder and regularly visited by him become his personal parish. He visits them in time of sorrow. He shares with them their moments of joy. He becomes their spokesman when they need a congregational spokesman. His word of counsel dissolves many a misunderstanding, throws light on many a problem, softens many a temper, and serves as a tie to bring home and church into closer relationship. The value of this type of work to the elder is tremendous. While chosen for the position of elder because of his high caliber of manhood and spirituality, it is home visitation more than any other function that raises the elder to a high level of consecration and service. In this service dollars-and-cents matters for once are forgotten, and the culture and care of the soul become the great issues. We cannot recommend this type of visitation too highly.

3. Every-Member Home Visitation

Most churches have an every-member stewardship canvass once a year. Many churches also carry on some organized evangelism visitation in the homes of the unreached in their community. There is a third type of visitation which differs from both of these. It is the systematic and purposeful visitation of all members and families of the parish during a specified period of time by trained volunteer workers of the congregation with nonbudget, spiritual objectives in mind. It has been used very successfully in many Protestant communities and is usually referred to as a congregational home visitation.

Select Workers. — The best leadership of the congregation is solicited and trained. They go forth in teams of two, having a definite purpose and supplied with materials — during the weeks preceding Lent, during National Family Week, before the parish observes its annual Missions Sunday, or in early fall, when the congregation enters upon a new season of work. The workers are sometimes called "the Seventy," after the seventy whom the Lord sent forth (Luke 10:1, 2), although the actual number may vary.

General and Specific Aims. — The general objective is "to strengthen the families of the congregation spiritually," that is, to inspire one another to love and good works and to growth unto the stature of Christ (Heb. 3:12; 10:24, 25; Eph. 4:13; Col. 3:16).

Specific purposes are decided on the basis of parish needs by the board of elders or a planning council. Thus individual churches have chosen one or more of the following: weekly church attendance, frequent and meaningful participation in holy communion, enlisting others for Christ, the world mission of our church, building the Christian home, Bible reading and home devotions, daily prayer and a prayer calendar, reading church periodicals, enlistment in the Bible study program, finding a place in the work of our parish (talent enlistment).

Prepare Guidelines. — Usually a manual is prepared for the workers which outlines the entire visitation. Thus one visitation having as its purpose the improvement of church attendance, provided the workers in such a manual with vital facts to be used in their visits on church attendance in America, why a Christian goes to church, how worship fills a felt need, church-going as a privilege, how the liturgy helps us worship, understanding the sermon and taking it home, and the family pew.

In another such visitation a check list was left in every home for use in a family council. It asked each family to discuss a few simple questions on the church in the home, the church-going family, the whole family in God's school, the family and Christian living, the family as kingdom workers, and the Christian family in the world. (See part VI of this book for this check list.)

Instruct Workers. — The workers are instructed and given their materials in one or two training meetings. The training is similar to that given for a personal-evangelism visitation. The members of the congregation are prepared through sermon and church bulletin. The teams of workers get their assignment cards, are sent forth with prayer, and make a report on each call.

The advantages of such an organized home visitation are that the whole parish is reached in a comparatively short time and that a greater number of the members of the church, both men and women, participate in a task which otherwise might seem practically impossible. The benefits come not only to the families visited. Often the visitors get even greater joy and spiritual help from the project. Especially is the common fellowship in Christ greatly strengthened. Like other types of visitation, this trains lay volunteer workers, develops a family-centered church, and strengthens congregational solidarity. Personal contact manifests a deep, personal interest in the people, more so than sermon, parish paper, or circular letter. Such visiting is essential for good stewardship because people whose spiritual health is good are usually more liberal in Christian giving.

Through family visitation we not only discover the real needs of the homes and extend the ministry of the pulpit, but we help to recapture some of the lost concern for our fellow Christians and the good practice of sharing our faith — the practice so prominent and so effective in the early church.

4. Teacher Visitation

This type of visitation is limited to the homes in the parish having children in the parish school or having the children and youth in the Sunday school. Briefly, it is a program whereby the superintendent, department leaders, class mothers, or teachers enter the homes of children to make the acquaintance of the parents, to gain an insight into the home conditions, to seek the co-operation of the parents in the training of the children, to acquaint the parents with the educational aims and ideals of the school, and to throw whatever light they can on the problems of the home, especially as they pertain to children and youth.

This type of visitation has been done quite generally by our parish school teachers, especially during the summer months and in preparation for the opening of a new school year. A concerted effort on the part of our Sunday school teachers in this type of visitation has not been as general as it might be.

Good Planning. — There is tremendous value for home and school in teacher visitation, if properly done. Careful planning must go into such a visitation. It should be concentrated, if possible, on no more than two or three weeks, unless done by an individual like the superintendent or parish worker, when it becomes a perennial program. The home of every child should be visited. The teacher should appear at his or her best.

Definite Purposes. — The goodwill and the co-operation of the parents should frankly be sought. After all, the chief aim and ultimate purpose in making the visit is to win the willing co-operation of the parents in behalf of the training of the child, as the teacher sees it. Religion is the support of the family, but the family is also the support of religion. Accordingly, the problem of the child, as known to the teacher, should be shared frankly with the parents. The missionary possibilities of the home should not be overlooked. The groundwork for the later attendance of the parents at the parents' evenings and Bible classes should be laid. Teachers should keep a careful record of each visit, with the thought of discussing their discoveries later with the superintendent, the pastor, or the other teachers in the teachers' meetings.

Include Preschool Child and Parent. — In this connection we point to the value of the quarterly visitation of nursery- or cradle-roll mothers in the homes of the children assigned to them. Congregations that have an active program of home visitation on the part of the cradle-roll mothers lose a minimum of children, whereas the child loss in congregations having no checkup between the year of birth and the year of school enrollment is staggering.

The value of a home-visitation program on the part of any church cannot be overstated. It is the connecting link between church and home — second to none. It is the real secret of many a flourishing congregation. It raises tremendously the level of spirituality. In our own parish it has stimulated communion attendance, enlarged our adult classes, increased our offerings, deepened our mission consciousness and possibilities, articulated the "home" element in our preaching, and brought about a homogeneity between church and home which has definitely domesticated the religion of this parish. Its values to the home are equally great. It makes for the enrichment and ennoblement of all participating in it, be they lay or clergy. It gives tangible expression to the priesthood of all believers and the concern of one for the other. Church bells and doorbells must ring together. Where they do, the cause of Christ invariably prospers both in the home and in the church.

DISCUSSION QUESTIONS

1. What effect would regular, periodic visitation of elders in the homes of your parish have on the spiritual life of the individual members, the families, and the congregation at large?
2. Can the four types of home visitation referred to in this chapter be carried out in your congregation, and, if so, how will you start?
3. Why are the number, the character, and the spirituality of elders so important in the visitation of a congregation?
4. Just what is the difference between stewardship visitation, evangelism visitation, and an every-member home visitation? Can these three be combined in one?
5. Just how does your congregation show that it is the "family of Christ"?

SELECTED REFERENCES

Blackwood, Andrew. *Pastoral Work,* ch. 7—11, 19, 27. Westminster Press, 1945.

Lindhorst, Frank A. *The Minister Teaches Religion,* ch. 8—11. Abingdon-Cokesbury, 1945.

Dicks, Russell L. *Pastoral Care and Personal Counseling,* ch. 5—7. 225 pp. Macmillan, 1945.

Dolloff, E. D. *The Romance of Doorbells,* 197 pp.

Eakin, Mildred, and Eakin, Frank. *The Church School Teacher's Job.* 228 pp. Macmillan, 1949.

DeJong, Peter Y. *Taking Heed to the Flock.* Baker Book House. 1948. 85 pp.

Sweet, Louis, and Sweet, Malcolm. *The Pastoral Ministry in Our Time,* ch. 3—6. 192 pp. Fleming H. Revell Co., 1949.

Visitation Evangelism. Moody Press, 1955.

Sweazey, George E. *Effective Evangelism,* ch. 8, 9, 13. 280 pp. Harper and Bros., 1953.

Today, Vol. 4, No. 3, p. 20 ff.
    Vol. 4, No. 8, p. 5 ff.

General Family Packet — 19 tracts. CPH.

Filmstrip: *The Visiting Teacher.*

Chapter 14

Do Parents Need
and Want Help?

Arthur L. Miller

IF WE AGREE THAT THE FAMILY is the basic agency of Christian education, we must ask if our parents are prepared to meet their responsibilities for Christian guidance, training, and leadership in the family. We shall be better able to answer this question if we analyze, in the first place, the question as to what makes a good home.

WHAT A GOOD HOME SHOULD SUPPLY

Dr. Alice Keliher, of New York University, answers this question thus (at the National Conference for the Prevention and Control of Delinquency): A good home is one in which

1) the child knows he is loved and wanted;

2) he does not have either too much or too little;

3) he has a place to play in and keep his things;

4) he feels he belongs to the family, and they to him;

5) his parents accept his mistakes as a part of growing up;

6) the child shares in the family-planning at points where he is able;

7) he has freedom in proportion to his age and ability;

8) he feels he is loved as much as other members of the family;

9) he is given a growing faith in the existence of God and of a moral law;

10) there is discipline and correction as needed.

It is clear that Christianity can penetrate all ten items listed by Dr. Keliher in her analysis of what makes a good home, and that religion is not reserved merely to point nine. Nonetheless, it takes a careful analysis of the total home situation for parents to provide an environment in which these criteria are met.

1. The Function of Parents as Teachers of Religion

In emphasizing the influence of the home in Christian education, we emphasize the fact that parents are teachers of religion. What is included in the religious teaching that parents are to provide in the home? What is the function of parents as teachers of religion? In answering these questions there come to mind the telling of Bible stories, hearing of the child's bedtime prayers, saying grace at table, conducting family worship, and going over the child's lessons from the parish school, Sunday school, or other educational agencies. These are important matters, and certainly they must receive attention. They are not enough, however, and much of our failure in Christian education lies in the fact that these external matters are often considered sufficient. Let us examine several fundamental considerations of the function of parents as teachers of religion.

1) The child tends to develop successfully as the family situation makes it possible for him to do so. This is as true in spiritual matters as it is in matters of diet, health, and mental development. If the child is to gain an adequate concept of God, he must find God in the complete pattern of daily home life. Do father and mother live in the fear and love of God? Do they display a faith in God that helps them confront all problems courageously? Do they earnestly seek to do God's will? In short, does the family live in fellowship with God?

2) The family that seeks to provide effective religious education for its members will recognize that its daily practices and customs reflect the values that are important to it. While the Christian family is *in* the world, it is not *of* the world; and it refuses to conform to the things of the world. It sometimes denounces and sometimes ignores the secularism, materialism, and intellectualism so rampant in the world. It holds itself aloof from the envying and strife in the world, the lust for power and possessions, and sinful

pride. Instead, it seeks to practice the Christian virtues of love, service, sacrifice, gentleness, and meekness. In emphasizing Christian values the Christian family provides for a discussion of current incidents and problems. The family weighs and considers these matters from a Christian point of view and in this corporate consideration gives its members a profound educational experience. Each member of the family goes from such discussions strengthened and better equipped to stand against the false standards so often offered by society.

3) The family that seeks to provide effective religious education for its members will integrate faith and works. Teaching is primarily a matter of influence, and the superior value of the example over precept has long been acknowledged. Despite this recognition of the importance of the good example, it is a fact that lack of consistency between precept and example has made ineffective much of the Christian education offered in the home and in the church.

If, then, the role of Christian parents as teachers of religion requires so comprehensive an understanding of the way in which children learn, and if the fact that the commonplace, everyday occurrences in the home have high educative value, it is quite clear that parents need assistance in spelling out the implications of God's Word for Christian training in the home.

2. The Need for Parent Education

A well-known specialist in the field of human behavior has this to say about the requirements of an adequate parent: "It probably takes more endurance, more patience, more intelligence, more healthly emotion to raise a happy human being than to be an atomic physicist, a politician, or a psychiatrist." There is no doubt that the raising of children is a difficult task that makes great demands upon parents. If we recognize that the children are gifts of God that He has entrusted to us for guidance in their spiritual development, we become ready and willing to put into the task all that it requires. It is a fact that some human beings seem to be much more ready to devote time to the training of dogs, horses, or other animals than they are to give time to the much nobler task of training children. Thus it will be seen that it requires the application of a great deal of intelligence to rear a child, and the application of a great deal of *Christian* intelligence to rear a *Christian* child.

Dr. Goodwin Watson, of Columbia University, has provided a convenient test to emphasize this important point. Note the following multiple-choice statements:

1) Religious and moral development is dependent (wholly, almost entirely, to a large degree, partly, very little, not at all) on the experiences which come in infancy, childhood, and youth.

2) The influence of parents in the home training is (the only, the greatest, a very large, a slight) factor in determining the experiences which come in infancy, childhood, and youth.

3) (All, most, many, few, very few, no) parents are adequately trained to guide wisely the experiences of their children which will be influential in matters of moral and religious development.

4) The ordinary church devotes (all, most, much, some, little, none) of its time and effort to help the parents with their problems of child nurture.

A careful study of these four multiple-choice statements, and an objective attempt to mark the answer which appraises the actual situation correctly, will indicate the tremendous importance of infancy and childhood for Christian education, the importance of the influence of parents in home training, the fact that few parents are adequately trained to guide the moral and religious development of their children, and the fact that the church has been tardy in recognizing that parents need guidance in the early training of their children. Our secular institutions and the newspapers and magazines have given much attention to this need for parent education. Many of the articles and pamphlets that have been produced are helpful to parents; many of them bring psychologically sound advice. Few, if any, of them, however, bring a Bible-based and Christ-centered approach to the training of children. By omitting the "one thing needful" these articles and pamphlets neglect the basic consideration in the Christian training of children and contribute to the further secularization of the thinking of parents.

3. Do Parents Want Help?

It is quite clear from the previous section that all parents need help in the training of their children and that Christian parents also need help for the Christian training of their children. The question arises, however, as to whether parents actually want help, or if they are perhaps not conditioned to participate in the program of parent education.

Jean Carter reported in *Parents in Perplexity* [1] that the number of parents actively participating in some kind of parent education runs into the millions. There is no doubt that this estimate by an individual who had surveyed the whole field of parent education is substantially correct today. It was reported in the *Handbook of Adult Education of the United States, 1936* that some kind of parent education program was available in every city, in many towns, and in 60 per cent of the rural counties of the nation. While these programs varied from the occasional lecture on a special phase of child development to an intensive and extensive study program, this does indicate widespread participation in parent education.

Further evidence of the very keen interest of parents in the matter of child training and parent education is evidenced by the subscriptions to magazines devoted to parent education. We are perhaps most familiar with the *Christian Parent Magazine,* edited by Dr. Martin Simon. The secular field with such periodicals as *Parents' Magazine, The National Parent-Teacher,* and similar publications, many of which have a very wide circulation, indicates that there is widespread interest in periodicals which are definitely educational and which definitely deal with parent education.

A further evidence of the fact that parents want help lies in the widespread participation in parent-teacher groups. There is widespread participation in parent-teacher groups in the public schools, the National Parent-Teacher Association having member groups in all the states and publishing a special magazine, topic studies, and conducting national conventions dealing with topics of child training and parent education.[2] There is also ev-

---

[1] Jean Carter, *Parents in Perplexity,* pp. 33, 34. New York. American Association for Adult Education, 1938.

[2] Membership in the National Congress of Parents and Teachers as of fall 1955 was 9,409,282.

idence within our own church, namely, that according to the latest available statistics over 800 groups have organized as parent-teacher groups. Some of these have only informal programs, but many of them have a systematic program of parent education.

From all this it is quite clear that parents are concerned, that parents are interested, and that parents want help in matters of child training. Given the opportunity, they will participate in programs that seek to meet their needs in this important area.

4. Mistaken Notions to Overcome

If parents need help in child training and want help in child training, the responsibility of the church to provide for parent education is clear. It is a vital need that demands action. In working to organize parent training, however, there are a number of mistaken notions to overcome.

1) The happy-go-lucky carelessness which insists that if you let nature take its course, everything will come out all right. This is not true in farming, nor in business, nor in school — nor is it true of child training.

2) The idea that good child training is merely the application of good common sense. No matter how much native common sense you have, you need special training to become a mechanic, a carpenter, a doctor, a lawyer, or a minister — and you also need some special training to become an effective parent.

3) The idea that "once a year" child training is adequate. A good sermon on the importance of Christian education in the home is important — a good lecture on child training equally so — but it is too little attention to a tremendously important subject.

4) The "too many organizations already" attitude. The argument is given that the church is already overorganized — that there are already so many organizations that to add another is unwise; for nobody will come, nor will anyone have time to lead the organization. While the arguments seem plausible, when given in connection with the important matter of parent training, they will not stand. It may be necessary to drop less important or-

ganizations. Another possibility is to graft the parent-training program on an existing organization.

These mistaken notions must be attacked, and we must emphasize the worthwhileness of the parent-education program.

5. The Aims of a Program of Parent Education

In setting up a program of parent education to meet the needs of parents, it is well to begin by defining the aims of such a program. These might be tersely stated as follows:

1) To enrich the spiritual life of the parents
2) To help them better understand and appreciate their children
3) To provide the parents with skills for the Christian nurture and training of their children
4) To help make personal and family worship increasingly effective
5) To lift the entire spirit and purpose of the home

It will be helpful to analyze these aims somewhat more in detail.

The aim "to enrich the spiritual life of the parents" emphasizes that parents as Christian teachers must be growing in Christian understanding and knowledge. Dr. O. A. Geiseman says in this connection: "Show me a home in which husband and wife are devout children of God, in which sons and daughters are loyal disciples of Christ, in which the spirit of the Lord fills the atmosphere, as it were, and I will show you a paradise in miniature." Christian parent education will differ from any program of secular parent education in the great emphasis it gives to increasing the spiritual understanding of the parents.

The aim "to help them better understand and appreciate their children" is important because of our need as parents to recognize that in human development variability is normal and that each individual is a unique personality. There are problems in the rearing of even the best of children. These problems can be approached intelligently. These problems can be approached from a uniquely Christian viewpoint by providing guidance in helping parents understand their children, in helping parents solve whatever problems arise.

The aim "to provide parents with skills for the Christian nurture and training of their children" emphasizes that education begins in the home, where the child learns to speak, to walk, to handle things, to play, to demand, to give, and to experiment. No doubt there is no more far-reaching educational institution than the family; for within the family the individual experiences adventure and safety, contentment and rebellion, co-operation, sharing, self-reliance, and mutual aid. When the full impact of the statement that during the first six years of childhood the individual learns more and learns it more permanently than he will ever do in any other six-year period of his life is clear to us, we will recognize the tremendous importance of giving the child adequate guidance during this important period.

The aim "to help make personal and family worship increasingly effective" stresses the importance of family worship in fostering and preserving family unity. There is no doubt that the family altar strengthens family ties. From the diverse interests that young and old may have, it gathers the members before the throne of God in the bond of common faith.

The aim "to lift the entire spirit and purpose of the home" emphasizes that the modern trend to reduce the significance of the home can and should be resisted. In a "Town Meeting of the Air" broadcast on the topic How Can We Strengthen the American Family? one panelist said: "The home of today too often is but a filling station. You come in, blow the horn, fill up, and blow out." No doubt in many communities there is a definite tendency to take the individuals from the home so far as their interests and activities are concerned. But the home is a unique agency of Christian education, imparting to the members of the family the understanding of the Christian way of life. Conrad Bergendoff, president of Augustana College, says in this connection: "Of what avail is the church's preaching in the realm of morality, child welfare, leisure, sexual ethics, etc., if the church cannot exhibit in its own homes a type of home life and personal relationships superior to anything else in all the world? Here is a domain where the kingship of Christ should be so evident that all the world might see and say 'Christian homes are the finest to be found.'"

6. Channels for Helping Parents

The aims of a program of parent education have lined up some of the purposes that a church may have in mind in developing a program of parent education. It is important to consider next by what channels the church can reach parents.

1) A significant channel is the preaching program of the year. The sermon is a basic instrument of adult education, and it occupies the central position in ministering to people. Every sermon can serve the cause of parent education, for hearing the Word of God regularly is basic to keeping our homes in Christian balance. The sermon can be used to present regularly a series of important topics on the home. Incidental references to the home and Christian family life should be included in the sermons throughout the year, but they should not focus on merely one or two applications. While the sermon is basic, parent education cannot be completely handled from the pulpit. An effective program of parent education includes areas involving individuals and groups with special problems, and must make use of the discussion method and personal counseling.

2) A second channel by which parent education can be brought to parents is the nursery department program of the Sunday school. Parents are susceptible to counsel when their children are young. They feel the need for materials which they can use in child training, and feel also the need for guidance in this important area. The nursery department packet and the materials for the nursery roll provide a complete course, for use in church and home.

3) A third channel which can be used for parent education is the meetings of the adult organizations. In their regular program of topic studies some attention can be given to topics which help to better equip parents for their job. Even if only one or two topics a year can be included in the program of the several adult organizations, an impressive contribution to parent education in the local congregation can be made. If topic leaders take time to point to specific problems and to suggest further reading, the

adults in the church can be guided to available resources in the field of parent guidance.

4) A further channel for use in the program of parent education is the church library. More and more congregations are making use of a circulating church library in their work. If such a library contains a representative number of books on the Christian home, child training, and Christian family life, it can make a real contribution to parent education. The church library should, of course, be conveniently organized and well managed. Besides, it should have regular publicity. Supplying reading lists to parents is a simple but effective device. For parent education such a library serves many needs. It offers self-help to parents who have problems that need immediate action. It helps those who may be unwilling to discuss their case with the pastor or teacher, but who will make use of the library. It helps the shy and hesitant person who cannot be persuaded to come to a class, but who may need parent guidance most. It offers help that may not be offered in a course. A reading program on parent education should also include subscriptions for magazines and journals on parent education. These can be preserved in the church library. They provide a wide range of reference materials on problems that may arise in parent education.

5) A fifth channel to transmit parent education to the church is the use of study groups and Bible classes. The church might very well set up special courses entirely apart from other educational agencies. Each year a course of six to ten lessons for parents may be arranged. (See Parent Guidance Series of topic booklets.) Some of the topics that could be considered in such a course are the following:

a. What makes the home Christian?

b. How a child grows spiritually.

c. Discipline and love.

d. Teaching your child to pray.

e. Teaching the Bible to children.

f. Christian home relationships.

g. How to preserve the child from sin.

h. How to deal with the child who has sinned.

i. Training the child in Christian virtues.

j. How to conduct family devotions.

Whether such classes are held during the Sunday-school hour as part of the adult Bible class or separately at another time would depend very largely on the local situation, the size of the congregation, and the facilities available. Sometimes special-interest groups will sponsor such lectures.

6) A sixth channel is the parent-teacher organization, or parent-teacher conferences. Both home and church are engaged in the Christian education of the child. For effective Christian education parents and teachers should have an opportunity to discuss problems of child guidance in education. Whether or not a formal organization is set up for this purpose, the church might well call parents together several times a year for such a meeting. In connection with Bible classes it may be possible to set aside one quarter of the year's work for specific attention to the problems of parent education.

7) A seventh channel that can be utilized is the couples' club. These clubs, which are springing up in many congregations, bring together young married couples for a recreational and educational program. The young married people are a strategic group in the congregation. Many members of this group feel the need for discussing the problems of parent education.

Which of these channels for transmitting the parent education program will be used by an individual congregation will depend on local circumstances. Probably no congregation will make use of all the channels. Certain of them, however, are open to even the smallest congregation.

How to Begin

Parent education is important. If we are convinced of this, we should give attention to the matter of providing an adequate program of parent education in the congregation. The church must help Christian parents quit looking for crutches only and help equip parents for their main responsibilities. Essentially, parent education is not another addition to an already over-crowded program. It is one of the basic responsibilities of the church. As with other phases of Christian education, the work with adults must be functional. It must be home-related. It must meet the issues and the problems which the group finds significant. A sound program of parent education will contribute much to the welfare of our children and youth, and will contribute to the sound undergirding of our entire church program of Christian education.

DISCUSSION QUESTIONS

1. Problems of child training will vary from community to community, and even from family to family, within a given community. What are the most urgent problems in our community and in our homes? How can we solve these problems?

2. The appalling increase in juvenile delinquency in our day may very definitely be related to adult delinquency. Some of this is neglect; sometimes it is a bad example. How can we as individual Christians and as a Christian congregation make a positive contribution to solving these problems?

3. Why is the secular answer to the problems of child training not good enough for a Christian?

4. Which channels of transmitting a parent-education program are needed for our congregation?

SELECTED REFERENCES

Colba, Gladys. *Suggestions for a Parent-Teacher Library.* National Lutheran Parent-Teacher League.

Carter, Jean. *Parents in Perplexity.* New York. American Association for Adult Education, 1938, p. 143.

Christian Family Life Education. Educational Bulletin No. 425. Chicago. The International Council of Religious Education. 1940, p. 64.

Fallaw, Wesner. *The Modern Parent and the Teaching Church.* New York. The Macmillan Co., 1946, p. 228.

Handbook of Adult Education in the United States. Edited by Mary L. Ely. New York. Institute of Adult Education, Teachers College, Columbia University, 1948, p. 555.

Parent Guidance Series Booklets (eight topics in each)
    No. 1. "Your Child and You"
    No. 2. "Making Home Life Christian"
    No. 3. "Happiness Is Homemade"
    No. 4. "Teen-agers Need Parents"
    No. 5. "Guiding the Young Child"
Concordia Publishing House; new booklet to appear each year.

Chapter 15

Leading Parents' Groups

E. H. Ruprecht

DOROTHY CANFIELD FISHER, IN AN ADDRESS to the Harvard Teachers Association, observed that in the old-time homes of a century or more ago there were not only many more brothers and sisters but one or more grandparents, aunts, or great-aunts. In this larger constellation of bygone days there was found a collection of "specialists" and a division of responsibilities for all stages of the development of children. There was opportunity for group living and learning. Such large families exist in only a few places today.

To compensate for a changed family situation, with fewer adults to take on functions once assumed by many, the church itself may be considered the larger family. The various members of the congregation, having a variety of experiences, may well help to provide the training which was once supplied by grandparents, uncles and aunts, and other relatives living under one roof. Potentially, then, we have within the local church a group structure similar to the family of another age. Christians are to be a close-knit group (1 Cor. 12; Rom. 12). One family gives insights, encouragement, and practical assistance to another.

If the local congregation is to capitalize on this opportunity, it will need leadership that understands the needs of parents and can enlist parents and teachers in a program of mutual helpfulness.

1. The Role of the Leader

Good leadership in parent education must supply clear purposes, discover real needs, locate resource materials and persons, and train future leaders.

Generally speaking, there are three purposes to be kept clear, namely, (1) to help the parent, (2) to help the teacher, and

(3) to help the child. Without the daily help of the home, the school and the church cannot do good training. The home without the school and the church cannot supply adequate teaching. The leader might suggest as the purpose of the group "to bring into closer relationship the home and church, that parents and teachers may co-operate intelligently in the Christian training of the child."

Keeping purposes clearly in mind is important. Groups easily lose sight of their main purpose and unconsciously set out to reach secondary goals, such as, raising funds and having fellowship. Parents frequently are exploited by the teaching force, instead of being trained by the teaching force for their role as Christian fathers and mothers. This is a serious weakness of purpose with regard to parents' groups.

Finding the real needs of the parents is next in importance. Every young parent has questions for which he would like to have some answers. What can we do when Johnny has a tantrum? How can we teach our daughter to be truthful? What can we do to get our teen-ager to take more interest in family devotions? How can we control radio and TV in our home? How can we help develop a deeper devotion to Jesus?

Evelyn and Sylvanus Duvall put it succinctly in their book *Leading Parents Groups:* "Parent education starts with the acceptance of the values, interests, attitudes, and anxieties of the group." [1] The leader, therefore, needs to sense the special concerns by private consultation, by personal interview, by home visits, by the considerate exploration of a steering committee, or by using a simple interest finder (which can be a check list of various types of problems and topics), or simply by asking each parent to suggest two or three topics in which he or she is most interested. After a list of problems or topics has been set up, a show of hands can indicate which subjects the entire group wishes to include in the program for the year.

The Duvalls tell of one parents' group that gave to each person present a blank index card and then asked each one to write name, address, and telephone number in the upper left-hand corner, and the age and sex of the children in the upper right-hand corner. The leader then asked each person to put down

---

[1] Duvall & Duvall, *Leading Parents Groups*, p. 24.

the five things which make a good parent.[2] On the basis of suggestions obtained in this way a very profitable discussion can be conducted. Thus at the outset everybody becomes a participant.

In determining the needs, however, it must be remembered that problems of misbehavior, for instance, which appear to be quite the same on the surface may actually be entirely different underneath. A disturbance may be anything from a temporary condition best cured by a little reassurance to the expression of deep-seated personal difficulties.

Having discovered the real needs, the leader's role is to locate resource materials which will help the group meet its felt needs. Such study material may come from the church's headquarters, particularly from its family life committee, which produces a wide variety of materials to help families. A parents' library with an active librarian in charge can be of great service. One church-related parent-teacher league annually gets out a packet of parent-education materials containing the following:

1) Samples of some of the best programs offered by parent groups

2) Aids for leaders: suggestions for the president, the education chairman, the attendance committee, the service committee, the social committee, and the librarian

3) Study materials: the annual study book, a copy of *The Christian Parent Magazine*

4) Books, tracts, films: an annually revised selected book list, selected audio-visual list, some sample tracts and directions for getting them into the hands of the parents of the congregation

It also issues a quarterly newsletter, *Nurture*, which supplies ideas for leaders.[3]

It is not enough to *have* materials. Someone needs to *use* the materials intelligently so that parents may get new insights and knowledge, new attitudes and appreciations, new skills and better ways of training their children. This means the selection of

---

[2] Duvall & Duvall, p. 53.

[3] National Lutheran Parent-Teacher League, 7400 Augusta, River Forest, Ill.

resource persons. In most churches there is much unused talent. Besides the pastor and teachers of Sunday school and parish school, there are physicians, nurses, social workers, educators, psychiatrists. Don't overlook such persons in your community as the judge of the family court or the juvenile court, leaders of boys and girls' work, directors of youth. They have deeper insights, a larger background, and rich experiences to share.

But it is a mistake to use professional leaders exclusively. Every church has fathers and mothers with successful careers of child training behind them.

Often a timid person will be encouraged after you have put into his hands a tract or small book which will arouse his interest, supply the desired information, and lead on to further study. By all means encourage reading by every parent. The job of the leader is to develop growing Christian parents who, in turn, can give wise guidance to their growing children.

Topic leaders should be selected with regard to the subject and should be properly informed. The speaker, for instance, will need to know which parents make up the group, what the ages of their children are, previous reading or study the group has done, the nature of the preceding programs, the follow-up planned, the amount of time the speaker will be given for the presentation, and how the discussion period is to be handled.

The role of the leader also includes training future leaders. Some groups place a husband-and-wife team into each office so that not one person, but two persons, get on-the-job training. Other organizations have for each important task an understudy who, in a year or two, is moved to the leader's position. A good leader keeps himself informed by reading books and a magazine for parents. Parent-guidance courses are offered by universities, public school systems, the social agencies. Special parent workshops are being set up by churches. A good leader gives attention to purposes, needs, study materials, and resource persons. He trains future leaders.

2. Essential Tasks of Christian Parents

In the Christian home the love of Christ is in control. Parents and children are growing up into Christ (Eph. 4:15) in all things. In transmitting a true understanding of the Gospel of Christ, Christian parenthood finds its real fulfillment. To make every home the workshop of the Holy Spirit is the highest goal of Christian parent education. Christian parents become instruments of the Holy Spirit when they carry out what we may term the essential tasks of Christian teaching and training.

ESSENTIALS OF CHRISTIAN TEACHING

1) Giving the child a knowledge of God and His great love for us manifested in our creation and preservation; in God's rule of the universe; especially in the gift of His Son, Jesus;

2) Giving the child an understanding of the Ten Commandments, which show to us our duty to God and to man, and are means through which the Holy Spirit leads the child to a consciousness of sin;

3) Helping the child get a clear knowledge of the way of salvation through faith in Jesus, the Savior, leading to the assurance of forgiveness of sin and peace;

4) Developing in each child an appreciation of Christian character and of the life in Christ — a life of true godliness, justice, mercy, love, service, illustrated first of all in the Christian family;

5) Helping the child acquire a growing understanding of the Bible as God's Word to men, as the source of Christian teaching, and as the guidebook for daily living;

6) Developing in the child an appreciation of the Christian Church as a fellowship of believers, among whom the Word of God is in use, and the Sacraments are administered for the nurture of faith unto life everlasting.

ESSENTIALS OF CHRISTIAN TRAINING

1) Creating and maintaining a home atmosphere favorable to the development of the Christian faith and life;

2) Helping each child develop a Christian view of life and a Christian personality;

3) Giving each child consistent guidance with firmness and love, the type of guidance that will help him discipline himself;

4) Helping each child learn the skills of worship, such as the ability to use the Bible devotionally and to pray; and training the child in the regular practices of worship, in the family and in the church;

5) Helping each child to practice the Christian way of life — a life of love, service, kindness; a life of cheerful obedience and devotion to duty;

6) Developing in each child a concern for all people and for their salvation, and helping each child to take part in the world-wide work of the church.

The apostle's words, "Bring them up in the nurture and admonition of the Lord" (Eph. 6:4), are fundamental in parent education. Equipping parents in the discipline and instruction of children is our task. Christian parent education supplies the important spiritual vitamins which parents, as a rule, cannot get from any other source unless the church comes to their assistance.

When we refer to spiritual instruction and discipline, we must not forget that parents deal with the whole child: body, mind, and soul. In the field of physical growth, in the field of mental health, and in the field of good social relations there are many problems that require attention on the part of Christians. This means that the church should help parents get insights and understandings in those areas, to help each child as it passes through each developmental stage of its life. Robert Havighurst has briefly sketched developmental tasks for six stages of life, from early childhood to later maturity. Being aware of the characteristics of the phases of life through which every human passes will help the parent understand his own stage of life in relation to his past and future. It will also kindle remembrance of phases through which he has passed and will help him to understand what can be expected of his children at any given period of their growth and development. This knowledge helps to fix the "teachable moment" for the major broad tasks which must be mastered if progressive maturity is to be attained.[4] As parents enter upon such a program, they will be more and more convinced that parenthood is the greatest of all vocations. "A family of wholesome, well-adjusted and socially sensitive children is an achievement far more valuable and often more enduring than most paintings or novels or other careers." [5]

---

[4] Havighurst, Robert. *Developmental Tasks and Education.*

[5] Duvall & Duvall, p. 55.

What is more, parents need to understand themselves and how their actions are interpreted by their children. They need to distinguish between symptoms and basic adjustments, and to learn how to manage children well. Their own minds and souls need to be fed. Growing children must have growing parents.

Some parents have sharply limited the number of their children on the plea that they wished to give every advantage to those they do have. These issues were often understood in economic terms: freedom from work and responsibility; having everything done for them; better clothes than other children; special schools, which too often serve to develop snobbery. Instead, parents need to understand advantages for children in terms of security in the love of the home; self-reliance; the development of a sense of responsibility for doing the common tasks of the household; learning to appreciate another person for what he is or he is not, regardless of his color, social class, education, or the size of his pocketbook. Such values as these give stability to parents, children, and the total family relationship. To develop such stabilizing values is an important aim of parent education.[6]

3. Planning a Program for Your Group

In planning a parent-education program you should ask for which parents this program is to be planned: preschool age, school age, adolescent children. How often does the group wish to meet? Do you wish to organize the year's program around a central theme? How give variety? How serve the parents of young children as well as the parents of adolescents? Will the program be developed for all parents, irrespective of the agency which they use — the parish school or the Sunday school? Will there be plans for such parents also who are not yet affiliated with the church?

Plan Your Program for the Entire Year

The planning committee suggests a general theme. It keeps in mind basic and special needs. It utilizes study materials it has gathered. Plans should include: topic for each meeting, the method of presentation, choice of leader or leaders, the audio-visual aid to be employed, the project which is the outgrowth

---

[6] Duvall & Duvall, pp. 55, 56.

of the discussion, the fellowship program. The program is then presented to the entire parents' group for further adaptation to the group's needs. For an example of a year's program see Part VI of this book.

Who Is to Do This Planning?

The program should not be planned entirely by pastors and teachers; nor should it be planned entirely by parents. A well-balanced education committee selected by the group which includes both is desirable.

4. Parent Education Learning Tools

The lecture is good for the purpose of stimulating interest and for providing information, but a lecture should be followed by questions and helpful discussion. The questions of the group will help to eliminate half-truths, focus the information directly on specific problems, aid the entire group in thinking the subject through, and help the group apply the topic to its own needs. The discussion should be guided and not hit-or-miss, or merely the airing of opinions. The best discussion takes place when the group has a similar background of experience, has clearly defined a felt problem, has engaged in some serious study, and, therefore, has basic information.

Leading Discussions

Almost anyone who can think on his feet can lead a discussion. He should be prepared. He should follow an approved pattern.

A. State the topic in the form of an issue or problem.

B. Show the importance of the problem to everyone present.

C. Ask for various solutions and put them on the blackboard.

D. Then ask which solution is Christian and Biblical.

E. Gradually get from the group the main factors and principles.

F. Then ask, "What are we going to do about it?"

G. Close with good motivation for personal and family action.

A Check List of Adult Learning Tools

There are many and varied methods at your disposal to make every educational program effective and fruitful. Choose wisely from the tools listed below a method suited to your topic, aim, available personnel, group.

1) Buzz Groups: Divide large groups into small buzz circles of four or five persons each. Each buzz circle selects its own leader. All are given one question or problem for which to find the best answer. After five or six minutes, each buzz circle reports. Persons remain where they are, simply turning to each other. This may be done with each of the main subdivisions of a topic. It may be used as part of another method of presentation (lecture). Each circle may take a different aspect of the topic (and a longer period of time). Many variations are possible. Get everyone into the act. Ask for brief, one-sentence reports if time is short.

2) Round Table: Group of well-informed persons discusses subject in conversational manner under a moderator. It is then thrown open for audience participation.

3) Panel: A number of persons present various aspects of a topic. Moderator keeps the parts tied together. Panelists ask questions of each other. Audience directs questions to panelists.

4) Symposium: One person for each subdivision of a topic. Together they build up a well-rounded presentation. Moderator then holds open forum, keeps the discussion "on the beam."

5) Interview: An expert, or "authority," is invited. One person interviews him with carefully chosen questions which lead to well-rounded answers, covering major aspects of topic.

6) Role Playing: A certain situation, problem, or activity is selected. Persons are chosen to "impersonate" the people involved. For instance, a parent-teacher conference, a family council in operation, parent-teenager problems.

7) Dramatics: A skit is presented illustrating such things as family worship, home visitation, family-life appeals in evangelism. Some prepared skits are available; or write your own. Educational tableau: in four or five

well-worked-out scenes show the work of so many agencies or classes. Then throw open for discussion.

8) Demonstration: With children demonstrate —
Teaching religion to primary children
Teaching reading
Sex education with sixth-graders in a Christian classroom
Discussion follows.

9) Book Review: Use the procedures of book reviewers to present a book of interest to the whole group. Quotations are given. The book is evaluated, criticized, appraised. Chief lessons applied.

10) Chalk Talks: Someone with skill in drawing (cartoon type) works out the topic by means of concrete "pictures," and talks as he illustrates each point with chalk or crayon.

11) Talent Use: Employing the familiar radio-talent-quest technique, use your children, young people, adults: in opening worship, in presentation of the topic, in social entertainment, in children's choirs, in instrumental numbers, in speech choirs, etc.

12) Field Trips: Take your PTL members on tours: to good schools, new churches, juvenile court, a welfare agency, school for the deaf, new industry, church college, etc.[7]

A family workshop in the local church can be very fruitful. A group of parents meets to explore the nature of children's quarrels and how to deal with them effectively. Other subjects for such special workshops would be: family worship, family recreation, father's part in the teaching-training process in the home, getting obedience, discipline that is constructive and Christian.

FILMS AND FILMSTRIPS

The last ten years have seen the production of hundreds of fine audio-visual aids in the parent-guidance field. They deal with almost any topic of interest to parents, from family worship to sex education and mental hygiene.

Films should be chosen to fit your program aims. They may give the main presentation, introduce the topic, or serve as a re-

---

[7] These are taken from "Suggestions for the Educational Committee." NLPTL.

view. Never use an educational film for mere entertainment. When a film is used, work is involved.

A. The film should be previewed.

B. A good introduction is needed.

C. The audience must be asked to look for something.

D. The projection should be smooth.

E. After the showing there should be a discussion —
with well-framed questions,
with good evaluation,
putting down findings on blackboard,
helping group act on what it has learned.[8]

5. Promotion for Your Parent Education Program

Is parent education the responsibility only of those especially interested, or should it be a part of the program of each adult group in the parish? What place should it have in the existing Bible class for adults? In a parents' Bible class? Is a public meeting with an outstanding speaker necessary to arouse general interest? Is it necessary to get the leaders of all boards, agencies, and organizations in the congregation back of the program? Is a separate parent-teacher league needed? Model constitutions are available for such parent groups.[9]

In their book *Leading Parents Groups* the Duvalls give us this interesting story: The staff of a large church found that their classes in parent education were reaching less than 5 per cent of their adult membership. Larger meetings reached many more, but so superficially as to be of little effect. Therefore they called their lay leaders together and with them planned a total church program. For three months the sermons and all the sessions of adult groups were to be centered on some phase of home and family life. Each group studied some phase of the same topic every Sunday. An extensive program of home visitation was planned. Outside experts were brought in both for consultation and for leadership. As a result, over 70 per cent of the adult members were effectively reached. Such a program was

---

[8] The Family Life Committee each year prepares a Selected List of Audio-Visual Aids. See Section VI of this book.

[9] Write to NLPTL, 7400 Augusta Street, River Forest, Ill.

possible because (1) some members of the church had been studying parent education for years and were ready to be the nucleus of the effort, and (2) larger public meetings had already acquainted a large proportion of the people with its importance and with basic points of view, so that they were willing to give to such a program their endorsement and support.[10]

Naturally, an alert planning committee will make use of the church bulletin and the neighborhood newspaper. It will use, on occasion, some homemade posters, will present brief skits, and will make use both of the telephone and of the mails. In many communities free radio time is available for a well-developed program.

6. Aim for Results

Your parent-education program should do more than talk about a given subject. A successful topic discussion should lead to action. If, for instance, the subject is family worship, there should be demonstrations of the various patterns of family worship. A literature table can display the materials available. Parents should be encouraged to establish or improve the practice.

The parent-teacher league can assist the parish school and the Sunday school in so many concrete and practical ways that dozens of projects will suggest themselves.[11]

There are many problems which even the families of a single church cannot solve by themselves. They can be solved only if these parents unite with all the parents of the community to remove certain threats to Christian family living.

A parents' group should appraise results by such important criteria as (1) parents better equipped for their spiritual teaching and training tasks, (2) children who find a new security in the affection of their parents, (3) children more able to make wholesome adjustments to others in the family and neighborhood, (4) children who are growing in self-reliance and self-sufficiency, (5) children who can take their place in the church and in the world, and (6) children who know and love the Savior and are growing up into Christ in all things.

---

[10] Duvall & Duvall, p. 35.
[11] See booklet on *Service Projects* by NLPTL.

EVALUATING YOUR PROGRAM

Regular appraisal is essential to a good program. Over the coffee cups discuss with your friends the effectiveness of a given program and keep a notebook in which you put down the things you want to do to improve the program.

Ask yourself: Did we reach the people? Did we meet the needs? Are we still reaching our objectives? Did we get participation? Were the people helped? The leader's greatest pay is "to know that God has used him for the building of home and church."

One way to evaluate your meeting is to pass out an END OF MEETING REACTION SLIP

> What did you think of this meeting? Please be frank. Your comments will help us improve future meetings.
>
> What did you like about today's meeting?
>
> What did you dislike?
>
> What improvements would you suggest for future meetings?
>
> On the whole, how do you rate this meeting?
>
> Check one: Poor _____
>
> Medium _____
>
> All right _____
>
> Good _____
>
> Excellent _____

Leaders need to be appraised also. They will help parents approach their task without being frustrated and discouraged. They will remind the group that "there is no such thing as perfection even among Christian parents," that parents' tasks must not be taken so seriously as actually to handicap them in becoming good leaders of their children.

Leading parents' groups is one of the most challenging tasks the church offers its men and women. It involves understanding the role of the leader, focusing on essential tasks, good program planning, using good adult-education tools, adequate promotion, and proper evaluation.

"Those who direct children during their most formative years still are allowed to enter upon their all-important task untrained. We require far more of a beauty parlor operator! But this attitude is beginning to change. Sound child guidance clearly calls for far more than good intentions. More and more we have come to see that parents — all parents — need special training." [12]

Cyril O. Houle, of the University of Chicago, puts it this way: "Adult education *precedes* changes on the elementary level. The education of the young can be greatly improved by education of a few adults." [13]

Wesner Fallaw expresses it this way: "Parents should be the chief concern of the teaching church, not the children only." [14]

To help parents to lead their own children into God's green pastures, to help each child grow, with the Spirit's help, "in wisdom and favor with God and man," becomes one of the main objectives of the church's program.

DISCUSSION QUESTIONS

1. According to this chapter's definition of "the role of the leader," at what points should leadership for parent education be strengthened in your congregation?
2. Compare the tasks of Christian parents set forth in this chapter with similar lists suggested in chapter 14, "Do Parents Need and Want Help," and chapter 16, "Christian Child Training." Then set up your own list (for your own group).
3. In the light of the section, Planning a Program for Your Group, review the program of your parent-teacher organization in recent years and list suggestions for improvement.
4. Check the adult learning tools employed by your group last year. Then discuss the twelve listed in this chapter and their use in your parish.
5. Discuss: Is the basic planning for parent education in your parish sound? What promotional help is needed?
6. Interview a representative number of parents in your parish using the six criteria suggested in section 6 of this chapter.

SELECTED REFERENCES

Lists of Pamphlets for Parents and Parent Education Leaders are available from:

Public Affairs Pamphlets, 22 E. 38th St., New York 16, N. Y.
The Child Study Assn. of America, Inc., 132 E. 74th St., New York 21, N. Y.

---

[12] Duvall & Duvall, p. 9.

[13] Houle, Cyril O., *New Trends in Adult Education.* Chicago University Lecture, November 1948.

[14] Fallaw, Wesner A., *The Modern Parent and the Teaching Church.*

Science Research Associates, 57 W. Grand Ave., Chicago 10, Ill.

Duvall, Evelyn & Sylvanus. *Leading Parents Groups.* Abingdon.

Havighurst, Robert J. *Developmental Task and Education.* Longmans, Green. 1954.

Lane, Bess B., with Foreword by Ernest G. Osborne. *Your Part in Your Child's Education.* Dutton.

Koss, J. Arthur, Editor. *Parish-School-Home Co-operation.* 9th Yearbook of Lutheran Education Association.

Miller, Arthur L. *Lutheran Parent Teacher Organization.*

National Lutheran Parent-Teacher League — annual packet. *Parent Education Materials.*

Simon, Martin P., Editor. *The Christian Parent Magazine.* Highland, Ill.

National Parent-Teacher. PTA Magazine.

Various *Leaders' Guides* of the National Parent-Teacher Congress.

Department of Adult Work, Presbyterian Church in U. S. A. *Parent Education and Christian Family Life in the Local Church.*

Chapter 16

Christian Child Training

Martin P. Simon

IN THE PRECEDING CHAPTER the essentials of Christian child guidance have been presented as being essentially a teaching and training task.

The first concern of believing parents is to lead each child to Jesus and teach him how to live as a child of God. This will be done by interpreting to him his relation to the true God through Holy Baptism (Gal. 3:26, 27); by guiding him to an ever-growing knowledge of the Father, Son, and Holy Ghost; to an understanding of the Ten Commandments applied to life; to a clear understanding of salvation by grace through Christ the Savior; to the practice of daily Christian living; and to a growing appreciation of the Holy Scriptures and of the Christian Church.

Teaching, however, is only half of the task. Training is the other half. The example of the parents, the spirit of the home, daily Bible reading and prayer, regular habits of worship in God's house, the daily conversation, the exercise of consistent, evangelical discipline, in fact, all the experiences of living, be they positive, negative, or neutral, enter into Christian training.

In this chapter we shall show chiefly the procedures, methods, and skills that parents may employ, as part of everyday living, to develop in their children Christian attitudes, Christian self-control, and Christian habits. Parents are to be God's instruments in providing opportunities so that the Holy Spirit may do His work in the heart of each child.

PARENTS ARE TEACHERS

The little girl was hearing her mother tell the story of Samuel, and how his mother dedicated him to God even before he was born.

"You 'decated' me to God, too, before I was born, didn't you?" the girl smiled at her mother. But the smile faded when her mother blushed and said, "No, honey, I'm afraid I didn't."

"Can't you still do it?" asked the girl. "Can't you do it now?"

So mother and girl bowed their heads in prayer, dedicating this little girl to God. Then the girl felt happy again.

The mother not only taught her daughter a Bible story, but she also deeply stirred the feelings of her child. But the mother did it without knowing that she was doing it, did it informally, in her own home, with her daughter on her lap.

Parents are always teaching, though they are not always aware of it. Not all the teaching is good. Parents need to know what to aim for in child training. Once the aims are clear, parents will seek ways to attain them. This chapter suggests four basic aims.

1. We Aim at Right Attitudes

Education is the acquiring of knowledge, skills, habits, and attitudes. These four interact, but the greatest of them is attitudes.

IMPORTANCE OF ATTITUDES

The Pharisee in the temple had more Bible knowledge than the publican, greater skill in teaching. His habits were good. What was wrong? His attitude. What a child *knows* about God is important. How he *feels* toward God is all-important. That's the *attitude*.

Our task is to show parents how to use Bible stories and Bible verses (knowledge); abilities such as making prayers and finding Bible passages (skills); church attendance, daily Bible reading, daily prayer (habits); how to use these to produce right attitudes, as the mother did in the opening story. Knowledge is a tool, not a goal. The devil has *knowledge*. If he only had right *attitudes!*

When the parent tells the story of Abraham, he should not aim chiefly at the memory of such details as how old Abraham was. He should rather aim at the feelings, at creating the yearning in the child's heart, "I want to do such things for God."

CONVERSATION BUILDS ATTITUDES

Bobby came home from school, greatly excited. "There's a boy at our school who comes from Italy," he said. "Then he's nothing but a Dago. Have nothing to do with him," his father said. Was he only making conversation? Oh, no, he was teaching. Conversation teaches.

Virginia also told her folks about the Italian boy.

"Then he's probably having a hard time with so many strange things in a strange land," said her father. "Be extra kind to him."

What did the children in those two families learn from the conversation?

Conversation has immense power. Watch it in your family. Use it for good and for God.

RIGHT ATTITUDES VS. RIGHT ANSWERS

Parents need to look for *right attitudes*, not only *right answers*. Asked, "How are you saved?" the child may answer, "By faith," without knowing what "saved" or "faith" mean. Much of our teaching is verbalism, the learning of empty words. Most parents will remember instances of verbalisms. Even when understood, words profit little unless they set in motion the corresponding feeling and action. Memorizing "God is love" is not yet religion. Through the words "God is love" the loveliness of God must take hold of the child. Stories about Jesus should help the child *feel* the active love of the loving Savior.

"I feel so sorry for the people," Jesus says (Mark 8:2). Many stories tell how "He had compassion." This compassion must not only be translated but also transferred to children. Like the girl in the opening story, they must *feel* it. This is more essential than to *prove* that He loves. Parents should be encouraged in the wondrous art of storytelling as a means toward right attitudes, feelings, and actions.

ATTITUDES ARE NOT INHERITED

"He gets his temper from Uncle Rufus." Perhaps he does if he lives with Uncle Rufus. He does not get it entirely by heredity. Cain was sinful. But so was Abel. Cain had no Uncle Rufus. No doubt Luther rightly traces the cause to the training of Cain. Children do differ at birth, but not as to sinfulness.

Children get their wrong attitudes and habits mostly from the adults. This fact should help parents value their influence.

Good Attitudes Grow Best in Sunshine

Home should be a friendly, happy place. One mother did her "thinking" work (trying recipes, cutting dresses) when the children were at school or asleep. Work at which children could help, or during which she could visit with them (darning, dusting), she did when they were present. That makes a good climate for good attitudes. Another mother sang with her children during the ironing, and told them Bible stories.

Happy parents are better than sour, self-sacrificing ones. Perhaps the best we can do for our children is to be with them, join in their fun, and enjoy them. Whatever we then "don't get done," leave that to tomorrow and to God.

Bible study, devotional periods, meals, and bedtime should be happy events. If possible, there should be no scolding during these times.

Parents should practice habits of happiness: getting up and doing their work with a smile, a prayer, and a song. Children should do likewise. "Count Your Blessings" is a hymn worthy of daily use. Soon parents and children will have the attitude of a happy outlook.

2. We Aim at the Four Securities

The security needs of children may be divided into four kinds:

Physical Security

Each child has the right to protection by way of clothing, shelter, food, and safety. Most parents provide for these needs, though now and then some test shows that some children from good homes are undernourished.

Mental Security

The second security is an honest and true knowledge of the world around us. The mind filled with hobgoblins, fear of black cats, number 13, broken mirrors, fear of policemen, gypsies, lions under the bed, is a worried, insecure mind. The child needs to see itself living in a friendly world, and it should know the "facts of life."

Parents should answer cheerfully and in a matter-of-fact manner when children ask difficult questions, such as sex questions. "From God" is sufficient answer to the little one's question "Where did baby come from?" Until he asks more, such brief answers are adequate. Parents should explain in terms understandable to a child. Details of the mother's or father's part in creating a new life are best left until puberty, unless asked directly. Learning the right names for sex organs is helpful. Parents may explain that sex organs are highly intricate, much as is the eye, delicate and marvelous (Ps. 139:13 ff.). They should speak of sex as a gift of God which is not to be misused. They should talk about the child's sex, not about their own sex.

EMOTIONAL SECURITY

Grandma was right when she fondled her children. Fondling assures the small child of his parents' love. For emotional security the child needs these four: affection, recognition, new experiences, and the security of a good home.

Mother let Tommy put shredded carrots into the jello. That noon he ate "his" carrots without coaxing. After that, Tommy loved to help. The wise mother encouraged him, with surprising results. When seven years old, he insisted on baking her a birthday cake, a good one. This is a true story. All four basic needs were satisfied. Most of our children never use their full capacities, because parents do not recognize possibilities or encourage new experiences.

Not the love which *the parents* feel, but the love which *the child* senses, gives him security. Love must be expressed. The sincere Christian has this advantage: his child knows that his parents will love him because his parents' God wants it so.

Children need love especially when they least deserve it. It is the child who gets poor grades or broke a window, the child in trouble, who needs love. Parents should deal tenderly with a child's fears and troubles. Silly fears and little troubles are neither silly nor little to the child.

For his emotional security the child needs to know that his parents love each other and will stand by him at all times. The promise which bride and groom make at marriage should often be repeated: "forsaking all others, keep thee only unto him." Parents should read frequently such passages as Eph. 5:20-33 and 1 Thess. 4: 1-8 (the latter preferably in the Revised Standard Version); Prov. 5: 15-23; 1 Cor. 7: 3-5 (see RSV). The personal, conjugal union and unity in marriage is reflected in home happiness. Children notice and worry when parents are tense. Quarrels can do serious damage to the children, and can destroy a large part of their security.

SPIRITUAL SECURITY

Children also need spiritual security. Charles Spurgeon, the preacher, and Frances Havergal, the poet — famous children of devout ministers — worried about their salvation for many years; yet they never mentioned it. So do many children today. Parents should talk often about Jesus. Children should know that when they are naughty, they sin. But they should know that God still wants them to be His own. Their sins are always covered by the payment Jesus made for them, so long as they believe in Him as their Savior. Parents sin, too. Caution parents against making a "law" out of the "Gospel" by adding a human condition necessary for salvation, for instance, by saying, "You will go to heaven, IF you stay true to Jesus." The sentence is true, but the IF is law, not Gospel. They should rather say: "Jesus has promised to keep us in faith, so we get to heaven. We couldn't do it alone. That's how much He loves us. He keeps us close to Jesus through the Bible. So let's be sure to read it every day." Spiritual security is the birthright of every Christian child.[1]

3. We Aim at Christian Self-Control

Every home needs Christian discipline.

Perhaps the strongest Bible passage on discipline is Prov. 13: 24: "He that spareth his rod hateth his son; but he that loveth him chasteneth him betimes." Let us apply it to the case of Eli (1 Sam. 2 and 3).

The passage does not say that Eli should have used the rod often. But when Eli "spared" the rod even though he knew that his sons needed it, he failed his children. The parent should be certain that an emergency exists. Then, if punishment is

---

[1] *Safety, Certainty, and Enjoyment,* a tract by Good News Publishers, Chicago, has an extreme statement about David; otherwise it is most helpful on this subject.

needed, he must punish. Children do not resent fair punishment. If they resent it, it probably has been given wrongly (Eph. 6:4). A parent's fairness and love for the child should shine through the punishment.

Parents should be cautioned against the domineering attitude. Rules should be few. It is not fair to forbid normal noise or activity because they annoy the parents. More rules — more transgressions. The consciences of serious children will suffer or be dulled. Obedience is necessary, but sensible Christian parents are necessary too. Obedience is a tool to guide the child.

SIX DISCIPLINE SUGGESTIONS

Discipline is necessary. But if it is to promote the proper development of the child, it should have these characteristics: "(1) It is firm, reliable, and kind; (2) it shows the child what others expect of him; (3) it encourages the child and promotes a feeling of faith in himself; (4) it strengthens the child's skills for better future performance; (5) it does not sever the child's sense of belonging to the group; and (6) it comes from mature, lovable adults worthy of being imitated." [2]

FLEXIBLE FIRMNESS NEEDED

The young child can make his needs known only by crying. Parents should try to anticipate his needs so he does not often need to cry for them, to avoid this connection in his mind: "I cry, they come. I cry hard, they come running." If his needs are satisfied when he is good, he will not learn to enjoy being a nuisance.

One mother would dangle something bright, or otherwise get her child to stop crying. Then she picked him up. The connection thus established probably was: "I smile, she picks me up." There would be exceptions, as when his feeding time was far past. When the child screamed for an object, she waited until he was quiet before giving it. When the child had learned to talk she would say, "There's a magic word which helps us get things." "Please," he would smile. Then he would say, "Thank you."

Some psychologists think children's temper should be encour-

---

2 *When You Marry,* Duvall-Hill, 1953 edition. Ch. 18, p. 371.

aged to explode. They regard temper as a quantity, a "thing" which must come out. But it is rather an attitude which must change. If it is good to "have it out," it is mainly because our attitudes are not well developed. Temper does cruel things. Character warps if children learn to have their way by means of temper.

Parents must be firm — but with a flexible firmness. They must stand like a rubber wall, with enough "give" in emergencies, so no one gets hurt. Parents must also learn noninterference. Gradually children should learn to make their own decisions. "Children, *obey*," says the Lord. Obedience is a basic tool. But in the commandment proper God says, "Thou shalt *honor.*" Obedience gradually ceases as childhood ceases, while honor remains. Through parent control children learn self-control and (because they learn to control themselves by the will of God) God-control. The result is a sturdy Christian independence.

Parents themselves must often learn to control their own tempers and other emotions — for the children's sake. Parents should not "get mad." They should think. They should not get excited. They should look for causes and for remedies. Before you punish, breathe a prayer. The parent must show the attitude, "I love you, but not the wrong you did."

DON'TS AND DOS

Perhaps a few brief rules are helpful, some don'ts and dos:

Don't ignore sin.

Don't punish in anger.

Don't threaten with police, ragman, goblins.

Don't recklessly threaten with hell. Jesus threatened only the hardened enemies with it. Jesus loves naughty children too.

Don't put the child into a dark closet for punishment.

Don't lead the child to think he is "no good."

Don't say, "Wait till Daddy comes home; then you'll get it."

Don't punish for accidents.

Don't punish for first offenses.

Don't punish for a sin that is sincerely confessed.

Don't talk so much, scold so much, nag so much.

Do lead your child to trust God.

Do see things from your child's angle.

Do start the training early.

Do win the confidence of the child.

Do help a child when in trouble by his own fault.

Do praise the good he does.

Do keep your promises.

Do offer the child a choice between two ways of obeying, not between obedience or disobedience.

Do try the family council.

Do encourage the child often.

4. We Aim at Christian Habits

The home needs guidance in developing helpful habits, such as,

FOUR WORD-OF-GOD HABITS

1) *Daily Bible Reading.* Small children love to hear daily Bible stories. Later they will read daily from Bible story books, and from the Bible. These stories should be used in friendly conversation to guide the home life.

2) *Daily prayer.* Children should learn prayers, but also how to pray; how to sum up their reactions to Bible stories in spontaneous prayer; how to give thanks; how to pray in trouble, for guidance, for forgiveness, for strength, for others.

3) *Regular church attendance.* Children should be accustomed to attend, to co-operate with, and support, the church.[3]

4) *Daily family devotions.* A family which prays together, stays together. Parents should use materials which the smallest child present, three years or older, can understand.[4]

WORK, PLAY, AND PAY HABITS

Good habits of work and of social life must be learned, and for this, play is very important in child training. Play also develops action and ingenuity. The play should be mainly in the child, not in the toy.

---

[3] However, "My teacher (or pastor), right or wrong" does not seem an adequate attitude. If a child disagrees with the teacher, he should be helped to see the teacher's side, to be sympathetic and co-operative. But parents should also value independent judgment. Children must learn to think and judge for themselves.

[4] The booklets for family devotions printed by a number of church bodies, show an amazing lack of insight into the needs of the Christian home. Several books of devotions with a vocabulary on the child's level are among the selected readings at the end of this chapter.

Habits of play gradually become habits of work. "Helping mother" should be fun if the wise mother praises the good performance and says little about mistakes. There is always something to praise. Wise parents will expect the young child to be slow, clumsy, inexact, and yet not do for the child what he can do for himself. (See the story under Emotional Security.)

Some children go all the way through high school without knowing what it is to earn their own spending money and church contributions. Even if the pay buys only what otherwise the parents would buy, it is still valuable to have the child earn and handle this money — with some advice from the parents. There are, of course, many other desirable habits.

CONCLUSION

What, then, is the goal of Christian child training? *It is to bring to maturity a person who loves God and desires above all to serve Him; who, therefore, desires to live a useful Christian life of service to others and has achieved a measure of such life by actual practice; who will, through faith in Christ, be in heaven with us.*

Those who work with parents are advised to stress that Christian parents should not be nervously anxious or unduly serious about their duties, but be happy, cheerful companions to their children, knowing that what they cannot do the Holy Spirit can do. Their work is not difficult above their powers. It does take willingness, study, patience, and planning, with much prayer. But if the fundamentals are right, children will survive many mistakes without damage, especially if they feel themselves loved.

God bless our homes.

DISCUSSION QUESTIONS

1. Why do you think the story at the beginning of this chapter touched the little girl's feelings and produced an attitude?
2. If you were to teach the story of Moses, how would you aim? How would you aim in telling the story of Jairus' daughter?
3. Why are attitudes so important?
4. Why is informal home training so lasting?
5. Illustrate from your own experience how conversation builds attitudes.
6. Mention some cases of "verbalism," learning of words without meanings.

7. Which are the greatest enemies of home happiness?
8. Do you agree that a happy parent is better than one who is self-sacrificing? Illustrate your answer.
9. Which are the four securities every child needs?
10. If a child asks about sex, how do you answer?
11. Why need a child be *told* that he is loved?
12. How can you tell if a child knows how he stands with God?
13. What was wrong with Eli's discipline? Why could he help Samuel but not his own boys?
14. List as many DOs and DON'Ts on child management as you can.
15. How do the homes of our church stand in the matter of the four Word-of-God habits, and how can these be strengthened?

SELECTED REFERENCES

Books of the *Parent Guidance Series.* Concordia Publishing House.
1. "Your Child and You"
2. "Making Home Life Christian"
3. "Happiness is Homemade"
4. "Teen-agers Need Parents"
5. "Guiding the Young Child"

Eavey, C. B. *Principles of Personality Building for Christian Parents.* Zondervan.

Ilg and Ames. *Child Behavior.* Harper and Bros.

PART IV
Family Counseling

Chapter 17

Premarital Counseling

Otto A. Geiseman

EVERYONE WHO GETS MARRIED, it is safe to say, has received premarital counsel. Too many, however, have received the wrong kind of counsel from the wrong kind of people. Young men often find their counsel in the alley or receive it at the final stag party a few nights before their marriage. Young brides are likely to get their counsel from silly old women. And the result is that many men and many women have come to their wedding day with horribly distorted views of marriage.

The church, as a loving mother, who is concerned about her children and their happiness, should accept it as a part of her responsibility to provide counsel for those who are about to enter the holy estate of matrimony. It may be said with a measure of truth that the church has always been helpful to its members by way of developing proper attitudes and wholesome conditioning for a happy marital life. Christian teaching and moral instruction imparted by the church to young and old have, in an indirect way, played their part in preparing people for a successful marriage. Hence it is not quite just to condemn the church as though it had never been helpful to its people in this very important matter just because the individual pastor did not always make a point of providing special premarital counsel.

This is not to say, however, that the church should content itself with such help as it provides in its general teaching and preaching. Today so many have such utterly false conceptions of marriage, and the holy estate has fallen upon such evil times, in which separations, divorces, and broken homes are a part of the common scenes of life, that the church must feel itself impelled to make a special effort. The church should extend itself to do its best to prevent the many heartaches presently to be found in homes and families throughout our country.

This is quickly being recognized. Pastors, who during the first decades of their ministry were content to shake the hands of bride and groom and wish them God's blessings for a happy married life, are today reading books, hearing lectures, attending family-life institutes and workshops in an earnest endeavor to learn how to offer premarital counsel helpfully.

1. Approaches and Techniques

Approaches and techniques employed in premarital counseling may vary widely. Some pastors base their counsel on the text of the wedding ceremony itself. They analyze constituent parts of it and interpret their meaning. It is not difficult to see that this might well be a very helpful and apt way in which to gain and hold the interest of the prospective bride and groom while the counsel is being given. If the marriage ritual contains a number of the more important statements which the Holy Scriptures have to make on the subject of marriage, the marriage form immediately provides a good foundation on which to build sound pastoral counsel. Even though much can be said for this method, it is not here commended as the best unless it is used merely as a starting point. Otherwise there is a danger that the counsel be limited to the major points set forth in the marriage form. If other matters are spoken of, they may have to be drawn in by special effort.

Some pastors touch only on the spiritual aspects of marriage when giving premarital counsel. They are of the opinion that the physical and the economic sides of marriage had best be dealt with by a doctor and other professional family counselors. Even though it is quite obvious that a doctor's knowledge of the physiological aspects of marriage would be greater and more detailed than that of a pastor, and even though marriage counselors associated with family associations might be somewhat better versed in the economic aspects of marriage, there is still a great question whether it is wise to omit these matters from pastoral counsel. It is very doubtful whether young couples will take the time and go to the trouble of appealing to such people for information and advice. If the pastor does not speak to them about these matters when they come to make arrangements for the marriage ceremony, it is highly probable that they will receive no worthwhile assistance from any other. What is more, we ought never lose sight of the fact that the church must teach its people to view all aspects of marriage in the light of Biblical truth. Hence, the pastor ought not be reluctant to discuss every important phase of the marital relationship. Not only should he discuss it, but he should approach the entire subject in a completely frank and forthright manner so as to put his counselees completely at ease. He should make them realize from the very manner in which he deals with the subject that he regards every part of it as something sacred, natural, and exceedingly important.

Here we recommend that the pastoral counselor follow approximately the following pattern in submitting premarital advice.

2. Marriage, a Divine Institution

First, it should be impressed upon bride and groom that marriage is not, as many of our day suppose, an institution which has resulted from human experimentation with various arrangements in the relationship of the sexes to each other. The truth is that marriage was instituted by God when He created man. He said, "It is not good that the man should be alone." This is so obvious that it hardly requires elaboration. Man by himself does not even have the capacity to propagate his own kind. Besides this, he lacks certain qualities which are essential if life is to be at its best and most beautiful. Hence God created a woman and endowed her with certain qualities lacking in man. He gave her to man so that she might be a complement to him, filling out that which was wanting. God intended that this relationship should be regarded as holy and that it should endure for life. Because of the careless views held by many on the subject of divorce, this matter should be dealt with in a clear and unmistakable way.

3. Duties of Husbands and Wives

When the proper foundation has been laid and the bride and groom have learned how to view the holy estate of marriage, the pastor should explain to them what God intended their respective duties to be in the capacity of husband and wife. It should by no means be taken for granted that prospective brides and grooms are familiar with the principles of God in this matter. So many persons seem to feel that they are perfectly competent for marriage because they have attained majority age, have enough money to buy an engagement ring and a wedding ring, and are able to procure a license from the state. The divorce courts of the land provide eloquent testimony to the fact that this is not true. The church should, therefore, take time and put forth the necessary effort to lay upon the consciences of brides and grooms the duties which go with entrance upon marriage.

Young men who come to their day of marriage with complete confidence that they know all that needs to be known and can do all that needs to be done successfully to fulfill their responsibilities as husbands, particularly if they have a good weekly income, should be reminded of the Lord's enjoinder, "Husbands, love your wives even as Christ loved the church and gave Himself for it." Any husband, whether young or old, who thinks that he is capable of measuring up to this ideal must indeed be possessed of capital conceit.

Brides, too, should be reminded that it takes more than a pretty face and an alluring figure and a high-school course in home economics to fulfill the divinely imposed obligations of a wife. Newspaper advertisements are inclined to place so much emphasis on the physical attractiveness of a wife that this has come to be thought of as the one factor about which a woman ought to be most concerned. However important it is for a wife to keep herself neat and attractive, it is vastly more important for her to understand the injunction of the Holy Scriptures: "Wives, be subject unto your husbands even as the church is subject unto Christ."

These words require interpretation, particularly in this day of Biblical illiteracy. Brides must be told that the church is subject to the Savior in a spirit of love and gratitude and that this should characterize their relationship to their husbands. They are not to be slaves, but they are to be grateful, and they are to respond to affection with affection. They are to regard their husbands, not as a convenient meal ticket but as the one person in this world whom they should strive particularly to make happy. They should also understand that they will never be quite satisfied with their marriage unless their husband is the kind of man whom they can look up to as the head of the house.

4. Weaknesses and Frailties

When the pastor has discussed these aforementioned basic principles, he will do well to remind the prospective bride and groom that no two persons are capable of fulfilling perfectly the duties that are theirs. Because of their individual weaknesses and frailties it is very probable that they will both make mistakes and fall short of the divine ideal. Because of this fact it is important for them regularly and daily to join their hearts and hands in earnest prayer and to give God regular and frequent opportunity to build them into stronger and more mature spiritual beings by feeding their souls with Word and Sacrament.

At this point the pastor will find it natural and easy to ask about the religious affiliations of both the bride and the groom, should one or neither of them be members of the church. If either the bride or the groom is affiliated with another church, the pastor will do well at this point to try in some gentle and careful way to discover how serious his or her past church affiliations may have been and how thoroughgoing the training was which the individual received. This will enable him to evaluate the better how to handle this particular situation from that point forward.

The pastor will do well right at this time to explain how important it is for the two hearts to be united in a common faith and for both of them to sit in the same pew and kneel at the same altar. He should explain that this will become increasingly true when their union is blessed with children. We have found it profitable to inform such men or women of the procedures of the church by which they can become familiar with its teachings so that they can intelligently decide whether they would like to affiliate with the church of their spouse or not. Often such individuals respond with a great deal of interest, whereupon their names can immediately be placed on a prospective list of adult catechumens.

If neither the bride nor the groom is affiliated with any church, the importance of their spiritual life should be discussed with them at greater length, and every encouragement should be given to have them come to divine services and to special classes for adult instruction. This can often prove a very fertile ground for successful mission work. If the bride or groom is marrying an unchurched person, he or she should at this point be reminded of the particular responsibility to be loyal and faithful so that under God the unchurched spouse may be attracted to the church and its message. The average pastor will know from experience that faithfulness on the part of a Christian member in a marriage often serves to win the unchurched person. He also knows that carelessness and indifference on the part of the churched spouse almost without fail will prove an insurmountable barrier to the winning of the unchurched individual.

5. The Economic Side of Marriage

After the pastor has laid down the fundamental Biblical principles governing marriage, he must proceed to show how these apply in a practical way to the economic side of marriage. Many marriages are ruined because of difficulties which arise in the dollar-and-cents areas of life. The pastor should explain how important it is for the success of their marriage that they use good judgment in observing a budget. Every experienced pastor will know that even some people of mature years, who have had ample opportunity to learn better, still do not know how to make ends meet. They habitually spend more than they take in, with the result that many heated arguments arise on the subject of money.

The matter of unselfishness should also be stressed. Some men seem to think that they are responsible to no one but themselves for the manner in which they spend their money. They seem to think that the family has no right to expect more than they give for its support, however small a part of their income this might be and however lavishly they may spend money on themselves. Women, by the same token, often prove themselves utterly unreasonable in the demands which they make on their husbands. Some men are almost hopelessly encumbered by debt because their wives must have every household gadget and every kind of modern electrical household appliance the American market affords. Beyond this there are women who demand clothes, entertainment, and other items of luxury to a point where the husband's spirit is broken.

Even though a pastor may not be an expert economist, he does know enough about the moral and spiritual aspects of life to teach brides and grooms that a marriage cannot be successful when such selfish attitudes as the aforementioned prevail. The principle here, as in all other matters of marriage, must be: each for the other.

Modern life poses a special problem from an economic point of view. Rents are so high and household furnishings so costly that few young men are capable of bearing the total load of establishing a home. Hence many young women, if they want to be married at all, find it necessary to continue in some position of remunerative employment. The pastor should make clear that he would in no wise criticize such an arrangement, for he is sympathetic toward them in the particular economic situation in which they find themselves. But when he has said all this, he must also go on to explain that there are certain psychological dangers inherent in a marital arrangement in which both husband and wife are remuneratively employed. The truth is that every man would like to be the one who provides the home and the full support of his wife. While he may, on the one hand, admire his wife for her readiness to lend a helping hand and to contribute weekly earnings to the family exchequer, he nevertheless at the same time instinctively resents the fact that this is true.

The wife, by the same token, may be completely willing to hold a job and to make her contributions to the family till. This does not mean, however, that she does not instinctively rebel against the situation. Since she was a little girl, she dreamed about the day when she would be married and live in a house provided by her husband which she would do her best to convert into a happy home.

Young couples may often find themselves growing irritable with each other without quite understanding why this is so. Often we may be sure the reason for it is to be found in the fact that neither one of them is altogether satisfied that both of them should hold paying positions. If the pastor will make this clear beforehand, he may save a new bride and groom from many an unhappy hour.

6. The Sex Relationship

The divine principles underlying the relationship of husband and wife to each other must also find their application to the conjugal relationship of man and wife. Just why pastors should shy away from the discussion of this particular side of married life is difficult to see, for certainly God in His Holy Book saw fit to speak quite frankly on this matter.

The pastor, in discussing this subject, should explain that the sex relationship is not to be thought of as something filthy. He should show that the very thing which God condemns as adultery and fornication outside of marriage is a divinely intended act inside of marriage. A bride and groom should understand that this relationship is to serve several important purposes.

First, this is God's way of carrying on the propagation of the human race. The Creator is ready to honor husbands and wives as His co-workers in the production of new human lives. No man or woman can create a child, but they can have the glory of being used by God in the creation of a child. Prospective brides and grooms should be warned that any malicious endeavor to circumvent the plans of God and to avoid the responsibilities of parenthood are wrong and bound to rob them of the happiness which God intended them to have.

It should also be explained that the sex relationship between husband and wife is to serve the further purpose of giving them an opportunity most intimately and completely to express their love for each other. A special word of caution should be addressed to the groom at this point, reminding him that any selfish behavior on his part in this important matter might have serious consequences for the future of their marriage. Hence the husband should always prove himself thoughtful and considerate of his wife's feelings in the matter.

The pastor should also remind both bride and groom that the sex relationship in marriage is to serve as a divinely intended safeguard against all sexual aberrations. That is why both husband and wife should be made to see very clearly that they should be genuinely interested in each other's happiness also from the sexual point of view.

If the pastor deals with this subject in a simple and frank manner, he will open up the possibility for the bride and the groom to discuss the entire subject between themselves in the same wholesome way. This can be extremely helpful and can enable them to make such mental, emotional, and spiritual adjustments beforehand so that they can come to their wedding day with the spirit of balance and equanimity.

7. In-laws

Often it will also be important for the pastor to show how the divine principles underlying marriage apply to the whole question of in-laws. Since so many families of yesterday had only one or two children in which an imperious father or mother could attain to a lordly dominance over the child's life and in which that poor lone child could readily become almost helplessly attached to, and dependent on, a father or a mother, it is important that the pastor should make it plain that a husband should leave his father and his mother and cleave unto his wife, and they shall be one flesh. Obviously this should also be applied to the wife, especially in a day when so many girls so easily and quickly make up their minds to leave and go back home to mother when little difficulties arise within their marriage.

CONCLUSION

Every pastor will find occasion, as the individual needs of different couples present themselves, to adjust his counseling comments to those needs. It is clear that a young couple which has been reared in the church, with both being married for the first time, are faced with a given situation. By the same token, a couple in which the one or the other has been previously married and then has lost the spouse either through death or through divorce is confronted with some additional problems which call for special counsel. Because of this the pastor should never become stereotyped and mechanical in presenting premarital advice. The couple to whom counsel is being given should be able to feel that the pastor is addressing himself to their particular situation and that he is trying to apply the principles of God to the kind of problems which are likely to arise for them, and to life situations such as theirs very probably will be.

If the pastor will take enough time and show enough interest to provide special premarital counsel, he is likely to discover, with the passing of the years, that many will be genuinely grateful for the help that was given.

EDITOR'S NOTE: There are many helpful tracts, forms, and pamphlets available in this area. These the pastor may use himself or give to his counselees, such as those on mixed marriages and various premarriage inventories or forms. For one example of an inventory see Part VI of this book.

DISCUSSION QUESTIONS

1. For what reasons is marriage counseling so necessary today?
2. What are the advantages of a "topical" approach over the "marriage ceremony" approach?
3. In view of much common knowledge of sex today, why should the church and the pastor discuss these matters?
4. What important spiritual skills should the Christian marriage counselor recommend to the newly married?
5. How should the pastor handle questions asked by the counselees regarding child spacing?
6. What reading materials should the pastor recommend in his counseling program?

SELECTED REFERENCES

Adams, Theo. F., *Making Your Marriage Succeed.* 156 pp. Harper. $2.

Amstutz, H. Clair, *So You're Going to Be Married.* Herald Press. 82 pp. 50 cents.

Geiseman, O. A., *Make Yours a Happy Marriage.* CPH. 78 pp. $1.25.

Peters, Clarence, "Premarital Counseling." 25 cents from the author.

Duvall and Hill, *When You Marry,* 1953, chs. 1, 6, 10 to 15.

Manikam and Highbaugh, *The Christian Family in Changing East Asia,* ch. 3. Intern. Missionary Council, Philippine Federation of Christian Churches, Manila.

Wood, L. F., *Premarital Counseling.* NCCC.

Wood, L. F., *Harmony in Marriage.* Round Table Press. 75 cents.

Chapter 18

Succeeding in Marriage

Oscar E. Feucht

FAMILY HAPPINESS AND A SOUND MARRIAGE are closely related to each other. "Marriage is the foundation of the family structure. The togetherness of man and wife, meaning their entire relationship to each other, becomes the framework within which the family exists. Whatever the family is, depends largely upon what the marriage is."[1]

It is chiefly for this reason that the pastor's concern goes beyond the wedding ceremony. He is not only an officiant of the church in the founding of a home but wants to help make each marriage succeed and grow in value and significance with the years. He serves not only in premarital counseling but also in postmarital guidance.

One pastor, being informed that a couple which had lived together many years had decided on a divorce, chose a unique approach. He selected five couples of the church who were successfully married and asked them to make casual calls on this couple, each on a different night. After the last couple had made their visit, this man and wife gave up their divorce plans and said, "If they can make a go of marriage, so can we."

By the grace of God marriages can improve with the years, as romantic love grows into married love and is sanctified by Christian love. Yet many couples need help in this matter.

To give such help, marriage counselors and pastors have drawn up lists of significant points which are factors in successful marriage. They differ greatly and represent various points of view and scales of values.

---

[1] Marjorie Louise Bracher in *Love Is No Luxury,* p. 94.

Mair Waters suggests Ten Rules for Happy Marriage:

1) Look before you leap.
2) Don't leave in-laws out of the picture.
3) The wedding is just the start.
4) Don't let little things become big things.
5) Be sure to have financial teamwork.
6) You always pay for life — children.
7) Don't let romance die.
8) Make your home a place of refuge.
9) Share your religious life.
10) Marriage is a life undertaking.[2]

G. Ray Jordan develops thirteen points:

1) Spiritual foundation
2) Married for life
3) Mutual high regard
4) Christian graces
5) Understanding each other
6) Forbearance
7) Strong character
8) Bond of religion
9) Democracy in home
10) Good humor
11) Kingdom concern
12) The Golden Rule
13) Commitment to Christ [3]

Selma Giving in the *Lutheran Herald* lists:

1) Self-giving love
2) Good health
3) Self-sufficiency
4) Common background
5) Common faith

---

[2] Waters, Rev. Mair A. J. *Ten Rules for a Happy Marriage* (mimeographed). First United Church, Victoria, B. C., Can., 1949.
[3] Jordan, G. Ray (from a tract).

    6) Ability of self-support

    7) Fulfilling one's role

    8) Good character and training [4]

Sociologist Evelyn Millis Duvall suggests:

    1) Love is only the start.

    2) You are partners now.

    3) Settle the money question.

    4) Meet your problems.

    5) Right attitudes to in-laws.

    6) Time out for play.

    7) Recess for rest and diversion.

    8) Share the housework.

    9) Be affectionate.

    10) Seek advice when needed.[5]

Others, speaking in more general terms, have mentioned: Christ's presence, praying for each other, loving as Christ loved, faithfulness, forgiveness, becoming "one flesh," re-emphasis on "obey," and the family pew.

In this chapter we shall develop a few of the more important factors in a successful marriage. Each marriage is as different as the personalities involved, and any "formula" can only be a general guideline.

1. Religion Is Vital

It is most significant that various studies have emphasized the role which religion plays in marriage success. Judson T. and Mary G. Landis, in their book *Building a Successful Marriage,* say that religious orientation is fundamental to personality structure and the key to personality patterns. Burgess and Cottrell, in *Predicting Success and Failure in Marriage,* show that where both husband and wife attended Sunday school after age ten and regularly worshiped in church, the adjustments in marriage were favorable. Terman concluded that "unfavorable attitudes toward religion characterize more of the unhappy men.

---

[4] In *Lutheran Herald,* February, 1947.
[5] *Building Your Marriage.*

Happily married men are a distinct majority among those who like Bible study and . . . who believe it is essential that children have religious instruction." A study of 25,000 marriages showed three times as many marital failures among those with no religious affiliation.

These studies also indicate just how religion helps. It (1) serves as a family bond; (2) gives security midst changes, problems, crises; (3) supplies an integrating philosophy; (4) cultivates considerateness, love; (5) teaches self-discipline; (6) gives confidence, a set of values, eternal destiny; (7) develops responsible parents. Religion gives meaning and purpose to all aspects of family life and is a source of wisdom, insight, and power. (See diagram in *When You Marry*, Duvall and Hill, p. 398.)

A common faith gives to marriage the necessary undergirding. It is related to marriage as the keel is to a ship. A man may, despite his membership in a church, live chiefly for his business, money, or position and honor; while his wife is deeply spiritual and has a different set of goals in life. Dr. George Crane, a psychologist and newspaper columnist, advises bride and groom: "Join a church and become an active member. Nothing in society will give you greater protection in your marriage."

Praying together to the same God; confessing the same creed; communing at the same altar; living, working, and giving for the same causes — these things establish a spiritual basis for life together. Family prayers and regular worship in God's house keep the fires of faith alive and glowing.

Fifteen-year-old Elizabeth, her younger sister, and her brother were spending a vacation with their grandparents. In connection with the evening devotions grandfather made a remark that religion is the cement that holds marriages together. When Elizabeth asked more questions he explained: "There was a time when we did not get along very well. Then one day I overheard grandmother telling God what she couldn't bear telling me. I quietly went upstairs and knelt down beside her, and told God my side of the story. And from that day to this day we have never had a problem that wasn't solved when we took it to the Lord in prayer."

Yet pastors find many couples who never pray together at home. In counseling we should help couples in trouble seek the help of religion, make use of their Christian faith, and practice the virtues which flow from it.

2. A Christian Interpretation of Sex

Although sex is not always the chief cause of difficulty, those dealing with marriage problems find that many marriages do suffer because there is no Christian view of sex as part of God's creation.

Sex is viewed differently by different people. To those who live by the worldly philosophy of "eat, drink, and be merry" or "wine, women, and song," the indulgence in sexual gratification belongs to the "rightful" pleasures of living. This "cult of pleasure" seems to be on the increase. It is fed by moral laxity and a false so-called freedom.

The very opposite view we call Puritanism or Victorianism, which veils sex in secrecy and keeps people in ignorance. Sex is tolerated as being only evil, something about which to be ashamed. This view is rapidly giving way to better understanding.

In our scientific age sex is regarded by many as a biological phenomenon, merely the operation of glands. The studies of Dr. Alfred Kinsey have overemphasized this view and have tended to divorce sex from morals and religion.

In the history of the church many views have been held. Augustine and Tertullian regarded sexual desire as sinful in itself. This contributed to the idea that the celibate life was superior. The Roman church developed the view that the sex act is good only when the intention is to have children. In the Middle Ages the idea that both the human body and the world are evil greatly influenced views on sex. Puritanism and pietism accentuated a new legalism, which reversed the teaching of the Reformers, namely, that sex belongs to God's order of creation and is, therefore, essentially good, not evil. "It is not nature that is evil. It is man's sin which perverts nature."

Nor is the function of sex in human beings like the function of sex in animals. "Animals have no sex life apart from procreation, which is seasonal and entirely outside their conscious control" (Bracher).

Marjorie Louise Bracher, in her book *Love Is No Luxury,* gives this brief summary of a Christian view of sex.

1) Man and woman complete each other (Gen. 2:18, 24).
2) The sex act itself makes them one flesh (Matt. 19:6; 1 Cor. 6:16).
3) This union or oneness cannot be broken and is not to be violated (Matt. 19:3-6).
4) It is a function involving the whole body, the entire person (1 Cor. 6:15-20).
5) It is a function given us for the duration of life in this world (Matt. 22:30).
6) Physical union is at once a duty and a right, equally for the man and for the woman (1 Cor. 7:3-5).

"Sexual desire, as it exists in human beings, is God's provision for binding man and woman to each other for their mutual benefit and for the development of their child." [6]

A careful examination of both the Old and the New Testament will support a wholesome, positive view of sex, as a gift of creation, to be properly used *within marriage,*[7] for the welfare of mankind and the glory of God.

It is this Christian view of sex that the church should stress to straighten out marriages that are in distress.

3. Emotional Maturity

Fundamental for a good marriage is the ability to make good social and emotional adjustments.

All people have a physical age, a mental age, and an emotional age. A person may be chronologically twenty-one but emotionally more like a child of ten. Marriage counselors, therefore, ask, "Are you old enough to marry?" meaning "Are you mature enough? Can you stand on your own feet? Do you face problems like an adult?"

Emotional age is illustrated by a moving picture which shows different groups of college-age young people who are going on auto trips. Each car runs out of gasoline out in the country far away from a filling station. Drivers and occupants react differently. Some are completely frustrated and let their tempers

---

[6] For a more complete treatment, see Chapter VII, *Love Is No Luxury,* by Bracher.

[7] The Bible throughout makes any infraction of the law of purity (the Sixth Commandment) a sin (Matt. 5:28). Also see ch. 19.

flare up. Others meet the situation with reason and composure. They illustrate the emotionally mature person. Marriage is such a test — but far more complex.

In marriage two persons are brought together in the closest, most intimate, most demanding of all human relationships. It should be remembered that emotions are part of every human being and need to be expressed in a constructive way. Emotions restrained at work are likely to explode at home. However, a person who easily feels slighted, can't control his temper, resorts to putting the blame on others, or otherwise doesn't act his age, is immature. In many studies of divorce, investigators have found that immaturity is the most frequent basic cause.

Good emotional control shows itself in such matters as meeting problems instead of evading them, ability to look at both sides of a problem, patience in dealing with another person, avoiding sudden outbursts of anger, starting and closing each day with pleasant conversation, focusing on a problem rather than on the mistakes of your mate, keeping tensions from building up.

One Christian mother with a large family attributed the success of her children's marriages to the fact that she had trained each child to assume responsibility very early in life. As each child advanced in age, he developed also in good judgment, dependability, and happiness in performing well his assigned tasks.

Much depends on the kind of persons that are brought together in the marriage union. They both should have "good wearing qualities" — traits, attitudes, and temperaments that make living together easy.

To help couples practice self-control and make good adjustments is to help them succeed more and more in their marriage. The Christian religion supplies that help. Love, joy, longsuffering, goodness, gentleness are gifts of the Spirit (Gal. 5:22). People who practice Christian virtues are mature.

4. Ability to Deal with Differences

The romantic idea of marriage played up by the movies and modern fiction has done much harm. Young people get a false idea of what marriage actually is. There is some conflict in every marriage. Perfect matching of personalities doesn't happen, and some disillusionment is inevitable. There is bound to be discord as two family patterns flow together in a new home, and as two egos assert themselves. Each new task or area of activity may become the subject for differences.

Differences have a way of growing. Little things that irritate have a way of assuming significance that is altogether out of proportion. Fatigue, annoyance, a slighting remark, bad habits, loss of work, poor housekeeping, some burnt toast, unwise spending, the care of the baby, and the like, may be sources of conflict.

The most smiting words — the hardest they could choose — are often used to add injury to insult. The tongue gets into the act and sets up new fires of animosity. Tensions greatly disturb the normal functioning of the family. Sometimes they last for the duration of the marriage.

What strategy should be employed? (1) "Explode and get it out of your system," says one school of thought. (2) "Calm down. After a cooling-off period discuss both sides of the problem," say those who advocate conciliation. (3) "Establish who is right and who is wrong, and make truth triumph," is a procedure long used — but not always with good results. (4) "Go out for a walk, or work off your feelings outside the house" is the advice others would give. (5) "Avoid trouble at all costs. When you feel anger rising, postpone action," is the theory of some who invite trouble tomorrow. (6) "He who is wise gives in to keep peace in the family" is the advice of an old German proverb.

Christians should follow the example of Jesus and be forbearing and forgiving. They should realize that men and women are weak, sinful beings subject to common failings. They should have the love by which faith works, and the patience that exerts self-control. Daily they will repent of weaknesses, unkind words, and mutually ask for forgiveness. They will accept the assurance of God's forgiveness and start each day in the new strength God supplies. All these are a "plus" that for centuries have helped Christian marriages succeed.

Yet even Christians are not perfect. Consequently they quarrel at times. We all need to learn the techniques of reducing friction. Marriage demands adjustments — learning better ways to get along, and unlearning old habits over all the years of married life. We need to distinguish between destructive quarreling which attacks the person and does serious injury (belittling, alienating), and constructive argument which discusses issues and not persons, and tries to solve problems to keep them from coming up again. Even in moments of difference and painful quarreling the permanence of love, and concern for the other mate, should shine through. As the quarrel subsides, the offer of peace should be made to release tensions. Many allow their hopes and dreams to be shattered too quickly by family spats. Actually they can serve a helpful purpose like the safety valve of a steam engine. Even where the problems lie deep and the situation seems hopeless, couples can get help from professional marriage counselors. They need not go on in unresolved conflict the rest of their lives.

Differences are to be expected. The important thing is what a couple does about them. Husband and wife should find a way of removing friction — experiment with problem-solving approaches until they find one that helps, instead of letting each successive quarrel further deteriorate the marriage. They should agree on the next step toward solution; pray for wisdom and patience; focus on the problem, not on the mate; and try not to allow tensions to build up.

There are Christian couples who read 1 Cor. 13 once a month as part of their procedure, who use their wedding anniversary "day" (each month) for a frank discussion, who make it a policy never to close the day angry with each other, who think of each other every time they pray "And forgive us our trespasses as we forgive those who trespass against us."

To help marriages succeed, we must be able to give practical help for dealing with conflicts constructively and as Christians.

No marriage is well established where there is not good communication between husband and wife. They need to understand each other, what they expect of their marriage and of each other. Every couple needs moments of leisure, rest, and relaxation in which the affectional relations are built up.

5. The Question of Money

Because of the frequency of the problem of finances in marriage, this deserves some attention here.

It is harassing worry over financial problems, or constant

nagging about the inadequacy of the pay check, or drinking up wages that should go for food, that are such a serious strain on any marriage.

We live in an economy which demands a regular cash income. The cost of living has risen steadily. The standards which young people set for themselves in the way of housing, furniture, a car, recreation, and social entertainment are quite high, far exceeding those of a generation ago. Often military service keeps the income on a bare subsistence level. Two-income family living is quite common. As of 1955, 30 per cent of the labor force (in the U. S.) was made up of women. Shall the wife work? Under what conditions should she refrain from working?

These are only a few of the questions and factors related to money. What shall be classified as a necessity? What is considered a luxury? How much of the income should be put into housing? Into food? Into clothing? How much should be spent? How much should be given to church and charities? How much should be saved? What is wise spending? How is one to avoid costly mistakes? Who should be the family bookkeeper? What is really wise stewardship? Children's work and allowances play a part as well as "do-it-yourself" repairs and improvements. Agreeing on a household budget can be a most helpful device.

Husband and wife need a similar sense of values before they can really agree on spending the income in a manner pleasing to both. The marriage partnership includes earning, spending, saving. It has been said that it takes one wise earner and two wise spenders to make marriage a success. The wrong attitude toward money and its wrong use has ruined many a marriage. There is no virtue in poverty, nor is wealth a guarantee of happiness. Happy couples have settled the money question. Christian couples do not permit money to become all-important. Money is good only if used for worthy ends.

6. Other Factors

(1) *Mutual High Regard.* — Love and honor are not far apart. We cannot long love one whom we do not admire. Respect and admiration go hand in hand. We like to be in the company of those we admire. Let each continue to achieve and grow — in old and new projects — along with the cooking of a better meal, furnishing a room, doing the work on the farm, at the office, in

the store, delivering a talk, or painting a picture. Honest performance of daily work — inspires. As husband and wife encourage each other to do their best, their mutual high regard grows. So does their sense of security in each other.

(2) *Good Family Relations.* — The Christian couple has a great advantage in a common faith. This is strengthened if they also have a common cultural background. For in marriage two families are drawn together as well as two individuals. Your relatives on both sides of the house are important. You need their love, their goodwill. In many instances their economic help is needed, e. g., to help put in the first crop on the farm or to make a down payment on a house.

Much has been written with regard to the interference of in-laws, some of it true but much of it exaggerated and misleading. Parents need to remember that young folks are usually happier when they live separately and assume full responsibility for themselves. The Bible emphasizes this separation as a new generation is begun (Gen. 2:24). Parents, too, have an adjustment to make. It is often said that "your son's your son 'till he gets him a wife, but your daughter's your daughter all her life." Family reunions and frequent gatherings in both parental homes cultivate good relations. Yes, in a sense you *do* "marry the whole family." Good relations must be cultivated.

(3) *Balanced Living.* — Life is many-sided. Four things are needed for balanced living: religion, work, study, play — the spiritual, mental, physical, social. Health of body and mind is essential. Good health demands that there be time for relaxation, entertainment, and play. A sense of good humor has saved many a marriage. A good laugh and an evening where a person is at ease and understood, revive our spirits and are ingredients of a good marriage. Variety is the spice of life. Couples should be encouraged to take time for leisure activity in house and yard, for play and recreation, for concert and baseball game, for a good book or play. Balanced living calls for a rounded-out life of many experiences — work, play, study, and worship.

(4) *Marriage a Partnership.* — In marriage, independence is to be exchanged for interdependence. Each one needs to accept his role — husband as breadwinner, wife as keeper of the home. Each must be able to stand on his or her own feet, and wrestle

successfully with life's problems and realities. Life is not a dream. Home is not a fairy castle. Making a living is not riding a magic carpet. The sturdiness of the oak is needed to weather storms. *A manly husband and a courageous wife, with the hope of the pioneers in their blood, will each do his or her share without complaint and will take responsibility.* This creates strength and cements the union.

In marriage each partner must be willing to go all the way — which Christian love dictates — rather than half the way.

While it is God who blesses marriage, husband and wife must, first of all, be willing to work at creating a successful marriage. Contrary to popular opinion, marriage includes the pleasant and the unpleasant, happy moments and unhappy ones, hard work and the commonplace, a heap of everyday living, and some experiences of ecstasy. The happiness factor should not be overemphasized. Help couples to prepare for the realities of life and increase their skills in using their Christian resources, and you will help people to succeed in marriage.

The wedding doesn't make a successful marriage. It's only the starting point. Romantic love must grow into mature, married love, in which the love exemplified by Christ (Eph. 5) more and more changes selfish love into unselfish love.

DISCUSSION QUESTIONS

1. What are the reasons why religion plays such a vital role in a successful marriage?
2. In the light of this chapter's section on sex, what revisions in thinking should you make to have a Christian view of sex?
3. Discuss desirable and undesirable emotions. List the things you would like to remember and practice in order to develop better emotional control.
4. Which of the six strategies of dealing with differences would you choose as being most promising of beneficial results? Why?
5. What additional techniques that are particularly Christian would you suggest?
6. What do you consider a sound, objective approach to money matters for a Christian couple?
7. Evaluate from the standpoint of practical usefulness the factors, (1) to (4) under point six.
8. Reviewing the entire chapter and especially the lists of significant factors for success in marriage (at the beginning of the chapter), draw up your own list of what you consider "the first ten."

SELECTED REFERENCES

Bracher, Marjory Louise. *Love Is No Luxury*, ch. VII. Muhlenburg. Press. 1951.

Duvall & Hill, *When You Marry*, chs. XI, XII. Heath. 1954.

Wynn, John Charles, (Ed.). *Sermons on Marriage and Family Life*. Abingdon Press. 1956.

Duvall, E. M. *In-Laws, Pro and Con*. Association Press. 1954.

Duvall, E. M. *Building Your Marriage*. Public Affairs Pamphlet No. 113.

Landis & Landis. *Building a Successful Marriage*. Prentice-Hall, 1948.

Terman, Lewis M. *Psychological Factors in Material Happiness*. McGraw-Hill. 1938.

Burgess, Ernest W. & Cottrell, Leonard S. *Predicting Success or Failure in Marriage*. Prentice-Hall. 1939.

Chapter 19

Preventing Divorce

Oscar E. Feucht

IN THE UNITED STATES 400,000 divorces are granted each year (in 1946 there were 610,000!). To this must be added 22,000 annulments, countless separations, and a large but unknown number of desertions. Our divorce rate is five times that of Canada, three times that of France, six times that of England and Wales. In 1870 there was one divorce for every thirty-four marriages; in 1948 it was one for every four new marriages. From 1940 to 1949 United States marriages increased 40 per cent, but the number of divorces increased 100 per cent.

But this is only part of the total picture. Thousands of couples live in an armed truce or in almost unbearable anguish of heart. They refrain from divorce out of one or more of the following considerations: children, property, business, need of support, moral or religious reasons, fear of publicity, and inability to pay the court costs. When we take these unsuccessful marriages into consideration, we see how large our problem at its base really is. For altogether too many couples "holy wedlock" has become "holy deadlock."

Society's relaxed view of divorce has also affected the churches. There is now one divorce for every twenty-five (new) Roman Catholic marriages as compared with one in ten for all Protestants. In The Lutheran Church — Missouri Synod as of 1951 there was one for every twenty (new) marriages. This compares to one in four for the entire United States. In 1953 our church had 1,218 divorces, in 1952 there were 1,298, and in 1951 the number was 1,280. All studies show that there is a high correlation between active church membership and marital stability.

This is one of the reasons why the church and its ministers

have a great responsibility. The church has access to the individual at most significant points in life. Eighty-nine per cent of all marriages are solemnized by clergymen. The church is the chief guardian of morals and the repository for the life-changing Gospel of Jesus Christ. It is in the best position to give the kind of preventive as well as remedial help needed. It has an educational program. Improvement will come as society guards the entrance to marriage rather than the exit.

The Christian minister holds the key. The Christian faith has relevance to all of life. The church is best fitted to give guidance, since religion is the key to marriage success. The pastor is better fitted for the job than the doctor of medicine or the lawyer or the justice of the peace. Parents, by and large, fail to prepare youth for marriage. If the church will not do it, it will, in most cases, not be done at all. The Word of God has much to say to couples entering marriage (1 Peter 3:7; Eph. 5; 1 Cor. 7, etc.).

The question then remains: What can the church do?

1. The church can be more concrete and practical in its program of instruction, with greater attention to the development of Christian faith and character.

Marriages fail because people fail. And people fail because they live without God. Where, on the other hand, man and woman have a deep respect for God's will as revealed in the Scriptures, and a proper regard for self and the neighbor, their marriage has a solid foundation.

This means that the churches should intensify indoctrination, giving each boy or girl, each youth and maiden, each man and woman, a good, practical understanding of sin with the Ten Commandments illustrated by life today, and a clear understanding of the grace of God in Christ, of forgiveness, and the new life which flows from Christian faith. Sound doctrine and unadulterated Bible teaching are imperative to develop convictions that are anchored deeply. For it is genuine Christian manhood and womanhood that is the best preventive of divorce.

The church can and must build up also the psychological "background factors" that predict success in marriage. Psychologist Lewis M. Terman gives us the following list on the basis of much research:

a) Superior happiness of parents
b) Childhood happiness
c) Lack of conflict with mother
d) Home discipline that was firm, not harsh
e) Strong attachment to mother
f) Strong attachment to father
g) Lack of conflict with father
h) Parental frankness in matters of sex
i) Infrequency and mildness of childhood punishment
j) Premarital attitudes toward sex that were free from disgust and aversion.[1]

Generally speaking, these points are closely related to what Christians teach and should practice. In its work with children, youth, adults the church can strengthen each one of these factors.

Solid Christian character is decisive. This calls for a maximum, not a minimum of Christ-centered and life-related teaching and training by church and home. Judge Paul W. Alexander, of the Domestic Relations Court of Toledo, Ohio, says "marriage failure is rooted in character failure."

Not only should every church intensify its teaching of basic Christian doctrine, but it should weave family-life education into its entire program of teaching and activity so as to reach effectively all age levels with such guidance as each may need. Special courses should supplement the regular program on the teen-age, young people, young adult, and adult levels. The resourceful leader with awareness in this area can do much.

2. The Church can give a positive view of sex as a gift of God.

Children, young people, and adults are constantly exposed to sex stimuli as never before in our history. The sex movie, magazine, comic book, radio program, and television show are the main — and very potent — sources of present-day sex education.

The information people receive will fit into one of three conceptions of sex: (1) as the subject of ribald jokes and hidden pleasure, (2) as a thing that is "dirty" and always sinful, (3) as

---

[1] Terman, Lewis M. *Psychological Factors in Marital Happiness,* p. 372. McGraw-Hill.

belonging to God's creation and essentially good. If the church does not counteract with Christian conceptions of sex the wrong information that comes from lurid booklets, untold damage is done. It is necessary to take sex out of the gutter and put it into the realm of the Spirit.

The church, however, can teach a one-sided, negative view of sex, so that the child or youth puts the label of "sin" upon it for life. It must distinguish between wrong desire (lust, concupiscence, Matt. 5:28; Rom. 7:8; Col. 3:5; 1 Thess. 4:5) and the right desire, namely, conjugal love within marriage (Gen. 2:24; 1 Cor. 7:3-5; Eph. 5:28, 29).

It should be noted that Luther emphasized the chaste and decent life in his positive explanation of the Sixth Commandment, "Thou shalt not commit adultery." There are many opportunities to teach sex as a gift of God. In the wider sense sex means everything related to male and female.

Sex may be treated not only in connection with the Sixth Commandment; it belongs in the First Article of the Apostles' Creed (creation), in the Third Article (sanctification), in the Fourth Petition (pious spouse . . .), and in every Bible story where God Himself has put it. The birth of John the Baptist and of Jesus speak of sex with a simplicity and a purity unequaled in any other literature.

To help develop a proper view of sex, the church teaches that man and woman are the "masterpieces of creation," that human personality is to be respected at all times, that God has given the moral law for the observance of all people, and that believers honor the body as the temple of the Holy Ghost (1 Cor. 6:19, 20).

It is conceded by all marriage counselors that right attitudes toward the other sex and the function of sex in our lives are all-important. Knowledge of sex without due respect for God's moral code is disastrous.

Who but the Christian home and church can supply the Christian attitudes so essential in a right view of sex as a gift of God?

The church should stop debating the subject and should do something constructive in closest co-operation with parents, devoting its best energy toward equipping parents for this task.

3. The church can set up an effective program of premarital guidance and counseling.

Too frequently the church's help has been too little and too late. As has been said, it is better to guard the entrance of marriage than the exit. Christian counseling should become a standard procedure in every parish. It is encouraging to learn how many pastors have made a start and are developing skills for the task through more experience. The writer had no difficulty in introducing the practice. As a rule, every marriage was performed in church before the altar. In every case there was a short address or sermon with a personalized message. Premarriage counseling, separate from the wedding arrangements, was part of the preparation. Every couple showed interest; all couples responded with genuine gratitude for the insights and the practical guidance given. Properly done, marriage counseling is most fruitful for the home and for the church.

Much helpful material on marriage counseling has been written and is available to the pastor. Roughly, the procedures fall into three categories: (1) following the marriage ceremony (interpretive discussion), (2) using a topical approach (discussing the principles, purposes of Christian marriage and giving guidance with practical problems, emphasizing the spiritual), (3) using a premarriage inventory (as the basis for discussing problem areas and guiding toward success).

The first procedure, if unwisely used, may become very routine and rehearse what Christian couples already know. The second procedure is likely to become a bit "preachy" unless a good interview technique is employed. The third procedure may emphasize the social and physical at the expense of the spiritual.

Personal aptitudes differ. Any pastor can master all three. He will find it easy to begin with the first, develop his technique with the second, and eventually achieve most success with the third, improving his method with each new experience.

For an ideal program (not always attainable) we cite the one developed and used by a pastor in the Northwest. It consists of three group guidance sessions with his young people and three counseling sessions with couples before their marriage. The group discussions are on (1) dating, (2) choosing a mate, (3) engagement. The premarital counseling sessions are devoted to (1) getting into the subject with Westberg's "Premarital Counseling Guide" (an inventory in Part VI of this book); (2) the permanence of marriage, using the marriage ceremony as a guide; (3) becoming one flesh, the development of mature love and good relationships.[2]

4. The Church can give guidance and counsel to the married to help them succeed in their marriage.

This has been treated in some detail in another chapter. Here we should like to emphasize that the church's main work should be preventive rather than remedial. But frequently couples wait until divorce proceedings have been started, or until the problems are very deep-seated and require the attention of the expert social-welfare worker or professional marriage counselor. Churches should know what community agencies and services are available and make referrals to these when cases demand this.

Great Britain seeks to save its marriages with a complete system of counseling. The government set up a committee to investigate the situation. It made four proposals which have been put into operation: (1) to make available a sufficient number of competent persons to give advice, and see to it that their availability is generally known; (2) to encourage young people to seek competent advice in preparation for marriage; (3) to encourage married couples to seek competent advice as soon as serious conflicts arise; and (4) to attempt reconciliation whenever a break has occurred. This service was set up on a civic basis but in close co-operation with the churches.

Adult groups in the local church should offer at least one general topic discussion or activity a year in the area of successful marriage. Such books as *Love Is No Luxury* (Bracher) or *Making Your Marriage Succeed* (Theo. Adams) will prove to be the most helpful, not only in the hands of the topic leader or teacher but in the hands of adults themselves.

Because counseling is a skill, it is learned chiefly by practice. Every pastor should have read and studied one or two good books on marriage, for instance, *Facts of Love and Life,* by Duvall, and *When You Marry,* by Duvall and Hill.

Premarital counseling is a "must" today, and the pastor holds the key.

---

2 May, Rev. Edward C., Portland, Oreg.

5. The church can inform and warn its people, especially its young people, in regard to mixed marriages and divorce.

Divorce has been called "the unhappy opposite of a wedding." It is the legal ending of what began legally with the marriage ceremony and the getting of a wedding license. Divorce is the evidence of unhappiness, not the cause. Divorce is not a solution but a retreat or escape, with attendant circumstances that are seldom agreeable or wholesome.

Consider the alternatives to divorce. Individuals must ask: What lies ahead? Will a second marriage be better? Will divorce really bring happiness? What is good about the existing marriage? Are the bad things improvable? Are they bearable? Have I done my part to make marriage a real partnership and a working enterprise? Is it love for another or mere infatuation that has suggested a divorce? Have I consulted a marriage counselor?

Divorce will create some new problems. "I must live with myself and my conscience. It will mean making a living by myself. Can I keep up payments on the house? It will mean making new friends. People will look askance. Both I and my husband will suffer emotionally for some time. Can I endure the new loneliness I'll experience? Can I live a chaste life? How will relatives act toward me? What attitude will the church take? How will Jesus look upon the step we are taking?"

And what will it do to the children? In the Detroit study by sociologist Goode and journalist Wittels,[3] it was learned that 1,000 children were involved in the 425 Detroit cases under study and that 300,000 children are semiorphaned each year by divorce in the United States. The report said: "Death does not divide loyalties and create bitterness like divorce. Divorce sears children for life." It has been proved that children of divorced parents are more likely to become divorced themselves when they marry. The Family Service Association of America found that 53 per cent of juvenile delinquents studied came from broken homes. These are facts that need to be made known, to overcome the trend toward divorce.

The permanence of marriage is to be stressed. One general survey showed that 33 per cent of young married couples enter-

---

[3] Reported in the *Saturday Evening Post*, January 21 to February 18, 1950.

tained the thought "If our marriage doesn't work out, we can get a divorce."

George W. Crane [4] gives this pithy advice:

a) "Vaccinate" young people early against divorce.

b) Don't rush into marriage.

c) Get married in church.

d) Plan the financial operation of your home.

e) Plan for two or more children.

f) Play your role of *wife* (divorces don't begin in the kitchen).

g) Work daily at making your marriage succeed.

h) Both become active in the same church.

This informing and warning can be done in many ways. It should be done tactfully and discreetly, backed up by Scripture, and motivated with the Gospel and the new life in Christ. There are many effective tracts, pamphlets, films, and filmstrips available to aid you in your program with youth.

Practically all churches are warning against religiously mixed marriages. The Maryland Youth Survey (1938) indicated that there is a definite relation between broken homes and the absence of religion in the home. Highest marriage casualty rate was for homes where neither husband nor wife was church-affiliated. Only slightly lower were homes where one mate was a Roman Catholic and the other a Protestant. In such homes religion becomes an area of conflict, often with tragic results. Thus practical experience favors marriage between persons of the same faith and avoiding marriage where there are serious differences. We owe all young people guidance with the facts that are apparent from the reading of the Roman Catholic Ante-nuptial Contract.[5]

6. The church can work with the courts; it can serve on, and set up, marriage councils and clinics.

Most marriages can be saved with the right kind of therapy. Many domestic relations court judges realize that treatment (not a court trial) is needed. Christian lawyers usually are ready

---

[4] Ph. D., M. D., Northwestern University, in his syndicated newspaper column.

[5] See such materials as *To Sign or Not to Sign*, Mayer, and *If You Marry Outside Your Faith*, Pike.

to work with the church and welfare agencies to keep marriages intact. But they hesitate to work with pastors who are not equipped for marriage counseling and lack experience or training. Pastors must show their concern, reveal their competence, and make themselves available. Jurists who understand the problems best believe that up to 50 per cent of the couples asking for a divorce could keep their homes together if they received proper help in time.

There are marriage councils in many cities. The panel usually includes a social worker, an attorney, a clergyman, and one or more well-informed businessmen. The case is presented by the client. The problems involved are analyzed. One or more solutions are suggested. They are constructive steps to close the breach. Religion, it is recognized, plays a vital part. More and more persons are equipping themselves as professional marriage counselors who respect the place of religion.

The marriage council is workable by a group of congregations which pool their best talent, or by a single (large) congregation. Thus, for instance, St. Peter's Lutheran Church of Joliet, Ill. (Dr. Erdmann W. Frenk, pastor), has an Advisory Council to guide persons in trouble. It is made up of the pastor, a woman social worker, a lawyer, several members of the church council, a physician — all members of the congregation. Such councils are a possibility in many localities. They pool the experience of many professions to give aid on a Christian basis. More such action is indicated if more homes are to be rehabilitated.

7. Christian citizens can also work for sound, uniform divorce laws and for constructive procedures.

The American Bar Association has been working for many years to improve divorce laws. Its committee reports many disturbing facts. It admits that "marriage laws are a travesty of justice." Most causes submitted in court are only partly true. In a high percentage of cases there is collusion. Usually one of the parties is not in court to contest the case. The present practice, says Judge Paul W. Alexander, head of the committee, "puts a premium on vindictiveness, vilification, exaggeration, and fabrication." Often not a shred of evidence is presented. The average hearing-time for a divorce case in Detroit, according to one study, was six minutes. Judges are overwhelmed by the number of cases to be processed. One judge disposed of forty-one cases in a single day. Goode and Wittels, describing this phase of divorces in 1950, titled their article "Perjury Unlimited." [6]

As everyone knows, there is no uniformity in either marriage or divorce laws. They vary from state to state. Many states vie with one another to get most of the shady divorce business. In many places some municipality offers marriage licenses without any precautions and actually encourages elopement. Clandestine affairs likewise go on without any curbs.

Determining the real causes of divorce is basic to good remedial action. But such causes are difficult to determine. In the 425 divorce cases studied by Goode and Wittels in Detroit the main causes seemed to be the following:

a) Emotional immaturity (insecurity of character and temperament)

b) Modern industrial civilization (wife and children are not as economically necessary as in the past)

c) Romantic love (the error that this alone is a sufficient basis for a lasting union)

d) Parental disapproval and mother-in-law trouble (in 62 per cent of the cases one or more of the parents had objected to the marriage)

e) Differences in background (this included religion)

f) Finances and lack of housing (strangely enough, there are more divorces in prosperous times)

g) Jobs for women (to the neglect of children and homemaking)

h) Ambition (either on part of the man or the woman)

i) Infidelity (moral laxity and unfaithfulness)

One is surprised not to find in this list drinking, gambling, cruelty, sex relationship, incompatibility, and desertion. The authors explain that most authorities believe these are symptoms or end results rather than causes. "Obviously a happily married, emotionally mature man doesn't drink or gamble to excess, beat his wife, or desert his family. Nor does a happily married, emotionally mature woman neglect her children and home, run

---

[6] *Saturday Evening Post* series, January 21 to February 18, 1950.

around, or nag her husband to distraction. The causes of the breakup of marriages lies not in what people do, but why they do them." [7]

Social workers and jurists are still debating whether adultery is a basic cause of divorce or a symptom of a marriage that has gone wrong somewhere. In so many cases it is impulse, pride, anger, stubbornness, and basic misunderstandings (all closely related to emotional immaturity) that led couples into divorces, which they didn't really want as they probed more deeply in their own hearts. This in no way minimizes the offense of marital infidelity. The Toledo Domestic Relations Court found that, contrary to the charges brought up in court, 46 per cent of the husbands had been unfaithful and 21 per cent of the wives; and Dr. Goode found a high percentage of actual infidelity.[8]

Polls taken with different groups show that clergymen will name as major causes such things as adultery, hasty marriages, lack of religion, drinking, desertion; judges may list sexual degeneracy, neglect, low mentality; psychiatrists will trace divorce mainly to emotional disease. Similarly, the laity will have opinions based on hearsay or subjective judgment. There is no doubt that the word "incompatibility" has been overplayed and indicates a symptom rather than a cause.

It is significant that the "secondary" causes trumped up in court are often "artificial padding" and that the real causes lie in the failure of individuals. It is precisely at this point that the church gives its help — help no other organization can give.

The American Bar Association advocates a single code and uniform procedures: (1) good domestic relations courts, (2) judges specifically trained for this job, (3) using the aids of psychological and sociological services, (4) social service workers attached to each court (for remedial therapy).

Some judges believe, as has been said, that half the marriages could be saved by constructive therapy. This means two million divorces might be avoided in ten years and that 1,500,000 children would in that time have their home preserved for them. According to this plan, people could not apply for a divorce but

---

[7] Goode and Wittels, *Saturday Evening Post*, January 21 to February 18, 1950.
[8] Ibid.

for treatment. A case worker would be assigned to make an analysis and work with the family for six months or a whole year on a constructive basis. Only when all efforts have proved to be fruitless would the case be allowed to come to court. This is treating divorces as sick marriages.

Surely, Christian citizens and the church as such are interested in such an approach and have very much to contribute. Unfortunately, progress even on so good a plan has been slow. How well-informed are you as a pastor or a church worker on the *status quo* in your community with regard to preventing divorce?

Should not the church, too, study its procedures? Is it true that there is rarely a really innocent party when all contributing factors are taken into consideration? Has the church also been too legalistic? Is its main task a disciplinary one, or should it take the lead in reconstruction? It is the church which stands for reconciliation — with God and with man. The church deals with sick souls. The Gospel of Christ is the most powerful transforming power the world knows. Let the church increase its training of competent counselors, work with the community, realize that better laws are necessary, and play its spiritual role with courage, and the divorce tide will recede.

Harold Kildahl gives us food for thought and action when he writes: "Because the churches have assumed an attitude of passive protest, other groups have undertaken to do the work the churches have neglected."[9]

DISCUSSION QUESTIONS

1. What are the major reasons why the church should be active instead of passive in preventing divorce?
2. In what way does Christian teaching "build up" Terman's "background factors" for happiness in marriage?
3. Set up a lesson unit on "the Christian view of sex" for a class of high school seniors.
4. What major discussion subjects would you select for premarital interviews?
5. What arguments can you give to support the assertion that "divorce is usually not the remedy" for sick marriages?
6. How can pastors establish good working relations with the courts and give assistance in preventive therapy?

---

[9] *Family Affairs.* Augsburg Press.

7. How important are happy marriages in relation to the family? In relation to God?

8. Make your own list of basic causes for divorce and a parallel list of symptoms (outward expressions).

9. How can Christian citizenship help in the development of better divorce laws?

SELECTED REFERENCES

Duvall and Hill. *When You Marry,* Association Press. 1953.

NCCC. *Marriage Troubles Can Be Overcome* (leaflet).

Pike, James A. *If You Marry Outside Your Faith.* Harper and Bros., 1954.

Terman, Lewis H. *Psychological Factors in Marital Happiness.* McGraw-Hill. 1938.

Schmieding, Alfred. *Sex in Childhood and Youth.* CPH. 1953.

Mayer, F. E. *To Sign or Not to Sign.* CPH.

Chapter 20

Parents and Children in Trouble

Marjorie Stolzenburg

A GREAT MANY CHURCH PEOPLE think almost always of normal, typical families in which everything runs smoothly. For that reason also they may not understand why the church should engage in family-life education. There are a great many households where things are not in good order and where parents and children are in distress. All church workers should see some of these problem families as social case workers see them.

One church-related welfare agency [1] during a recent year cared for 500 children and dealt with the families from which they came. And this was only one half the number of children that needed help. Others were referred to agencies in the community for day-nursery care, counseling, and housekeeping service, according to the problems they represented.

At the end of the year this agency, analyzing all cases, looked for the causes behind each family breakdown. In the order of frequency, they were:

a) Unmarried motherhood

b) Mental illness or emotional instability

c) Marital difficulty

d) Desertion and/or neglect

e) Death of one parent

f) Behavior problem of child

---

[1] Lutheran Child Welfare Assn., Addison, Ill.

1. An Unwed Mother

Seventy-three unmarried mothers were given service in a recent year; two thirds were under twenty-five years of age and one third were from fourteen to twenty years old.

Let us consider the case of Marion, age eighteen. She was a member of a church. Her only brother was a soloist in the choir, and both parents were active members. Her parents had come from Central Europe. The father of Marion's child was an American boy of Irish descent. Marion was very much in love with him, but her parents had objected to her marrying him.

We further learned that Marion's mother had been a deprived person in her own youth. Her attitude was reflected in her statement that she never thought she would have to go to her grave bearing the sin of her child. There seemed to be no allowance for the sinful human heart or for the grace of God. The mother, who did housework before her marriage and had suffered an injury, was an exacting housekeeper and frequently would get into quarrels with Marion over petty things.

Marion's father was a short, slight man under five feet in height. He swore profusely about Marion's situation and bitterly maligned the father of the child. When our worker visited the home, the father said he was disgusted and shortly left the room to let his wife carry on with the problem. He was employed as a janitor of the building in which they lived.

In the course of Marion's interviews she said she could remember friction in the home, particularly when she was about seven years old, and financial difficulties had been so great that her mother was at the point of divorcing her father. However, at his request the mother had stuck with him through the crisis.

The home was a three-room apartment on the second floor of a large apartment building. The furniture was worn and of poor quality, but neat and very clean. There was only one bedroom in which there were two double beds, one for the father and son and the other for Marion and her mother.

Marion's mother said that she could never accept Marion's boy friend, since he was of a different culture, and because his nationality and customs were too different from theirs. After her daughter had become pregnant, however, she had agreed to the marriage, but then the boy disappeared. Her father told Marion that she could not go out with boys from now on for at least four years. The mother has insisted that she remain unmarried until she is at least twenty-seven, if then. The outcome of the situation with regard to the baby is that Marion kept it, bringing it home to this crowded, emotionally torn family, because her mother willed it.

CONCLUSION AND LESSONS

Marion's family had practiced the outward forms of religion; they attended church, were active in organizations. Yet family life at that home was not Christian in some important aspects.

Some of the conflicting situations were: the infliction of Old World ideas on a young girl being educated in American ways of living; the housing factor, which has so many implications beyond the mere physical one; the over-protective element; the lack of privacy; the complete thwarting of any individualization. Then, too, we see the inconsistency with which this girl was being trained. She was told she should know better than to get herself into this kind of situation, though she had received no sex education, and at the same time she is going to be further infantilized by being told to remain in the home and not to marry. Here a neurotic mother is holding on too closely to her child to overcome a personal frustration. We cannot help but also think of the infant who will be brought up in this home, no doubt as a constant reminder of Marion's sin.

We need to get closer to the families of the church to help them use their religion in their daily lives, and, if they have problems, to come to their assistance before the crisis is reached.

2. Unstable Parents

The next-largest category of reasons for children having come to the agency last year was emotional instability or mental illness. Although we list this rather glibly as the reason for the child having had to be placed away from his home, actually the illness was only symptomatic of the underlying causes. We found that in most of these cases the father himself was immature and emotionally disturbed. Unfortunately, we so often find two immature people getting married, each wanting to lean too dependently on the other, only to find neither can "take it." Then a breakdown occurs.

Let us look in on the Smith family, which was referred to us by their pastor. When we came into the picture, the mother was being committed to a mental institution. The family service bureau had been helping the father, dealing particularly with his feelings in the entire matter; the pastor was aiding him as his spiritual counselor; a lawyer had also been called to the aid of Mr. Smith, who wanted legal assurance that everything was as it should be for his own and the children's protection. As we became better acquainted with Mr. Smith, we saw a well-meaning father, deeply concerned about his children. He held a steady job and was always conscientious about his work. However, he was quite insecure. His custom was to surround himself with a panel of specialists who were to do the thinking for him. So it was in placing his children with our agency. All his "consultants" had to express approval before he could go ahead.

Mrs. Smith, on the other hand, had come from a closely knit family, where the children had been over-protected. She married a dependent type of person and then had five children in quick succession and was overwhelmed by the responsibilities. This all added to her final breakdown.

Through the time of her illness she has put the blame for it on Mr. Smith. Although she is quite ill and a long term of treatment will be needed to help her to recover sufficiently, she writes to the children that she blames their father, telling them not to listen to him and that she will soon be back to care of them. At the same time the father visits the children regularly and is helping them align themselves with him. We, who see the children in the interim between the father's visits and the mother's letters, see the disturbed reactions of the children, and we know what the cost of this broken home means not only in dollars and cents but in the emotional and mental health of the children. The oldest girl is showing signs of needing intensive case work and possibly psychiatric treatment.

Lessons for the Church

In situations like this we can only deplore the fact that in the church we do not have premarital counseling as a part of every parish program; that two people as unprepared for mature, adult responsibilites as the Smiths are not helped before marriage to see what they will face later. The results of good counseling would either have discouraged them from entering into a marital relationship or would have prepared them to use available resources when the first problems arose, perhaps saving the situation before a complete breakdown occurred.

A family breakdown, whatever its cause, is always painful to children. What can we do about it? How can we help before things pile up to the breaking point where separation of the child from his own home is necessary? All this only supports the need for family life workshops where preventive measures are being developed.

It can be done. When the laymen, the teachers, and the pastors of the church join hands with us, families are rebuilt. Many children are returned to their own homes after a one- or two-year period. Unfortunately, children have to suffer separation from home, where all their security lies, in order that parents might be re-educated. How much better if we could have had parent education so that separation would not have become necessary.

3. A Sex Delinquent

Sex delinquency is on the increase. It is a major concern of our crime-prevention forces, our juvenile courts, our social agencies. It is disturbing to parents. Like all other types of misbehavior, it is closely related to home influences and neighborhood environment.

Janice, age thirteen, had been referred to us by the Juvenile Court on charges of sex delinquency. She was held in the detention home for several weeks until the court hearing. At the hearing the girl's pastor and our case worker were present and, with the consent of the court, the responsibility of helping the parents and the home situation was left up to the church. The girl was returned to her own home, but under the supervision of our agency. At present she is receiving intensive case work from our worker while remaining in her own home.

Looking back into this family situation, we see a foreign-born father, aged thirty-nine, who became a church member soon after his arrival in this country in the 1920's. The mother is an American-born woman, aged thirty, of German parentage. There were five children, and a sixth is due at any time. Again we see children being born in quick succession, with the mother fearing each pregnancy. This, in turn, has begun to cause marital friction between the parents. Besides, the family income and the housing are unable to keep up with the rapidly increasing family. This family of seven, soon to be eight, resides in a five-room flat on the third floor. Housekeeping is good, and the rooms appear clean; but the inevitable noise of too many people in too small quarters would quite naturally cause tensions and fan small flames of anger into serious fires. An added tension is caused by the fact that the father works at night. He wants the home somewhat quiet for daytime sleeping and has little time to devote to his children. His relationship with Janice has been almost totally ineffectual.

Being the oldest child, Janice had been given too many responsibilities too early in life. She still needs to be dependent on adults. Instead of experiencing a normal, gradual development, she has been pushed off into an independent state before she was ready for it. Added to this, she is a tall, thin girl — taller and larger than most of the other children in the seventh grade, where she has chosen companions older than herself; in fact, her friends are boys of high-school age. She is not very attractive in appearance. Not having had too much attention, she has not had too much self-respect. When tested psychologically, she had average intelligence, but by the transfer to another school she had lost a whole grade, which has made her more self-conscious.

During interviews with her she has confided to our worker concerning her sex experience and has revealed that she had not received the benefit of sex education. Janice was quite confused about boys and has found all sorts of excuses to justify her sexual misbehavior. She also has frightening dreams at night and wakes up screaming. She was a very greatly disturbed child who needed intensive case work treatment over a long period of time.

The mother, having now become somewhat aware of the girl's problems, has recently asked for books on sex education which she might give Janice to read, since she herself feels incompetent to discuss this with the girl.

How the Church Helped

Again, on the surface, this family and the children have attended church as often as possible; the children attend the parish school, and Janice verbalizes about how much church and school mean to her. On the other hand, some of the simple but satisfying pleasures in life have been left out, and only the monotony of facing ever-limited finances and increasing tensions remains.

Since the church was charged with doing something for this family, the members have joined hands and have started a program of helping them. The pastor called together a group of men and women and discussed the family with them. The women take turns inviting the mother out to their own homes for a social evening. At other times they take the smaller children out on excursions to give the parents a resting period. This, incidentally, allows the parents time to give Janice the extra attention she needs. The men have encouraged the father to become interested in the men's club at church, and they are taking him out bowling. For Janice herself the school has put forth special effort to give her added attention. She has been made responsible for duties which have given her standing with the other children, and recently she was given a prominent part in a dramatic effort in which she did exceptionally well.

There is a long way to go in helping this family readjust sufficiently so that Janice may feel her rightful place in the home. With a helping hand, however, the parents may feel their burden lightened enough to be willing to take time to give Janice more of the attention, love, and affection she needs.

It might be added that in the comparatively short time we have known the girl, her appearance has markedly changed. She has taken an interest in herself. Her hair is well groomed, and she has been wearing more attractive clothing. Lately she also seems more self-confident and poised.

Summary

We see that problems of children are inseparably related to the problems of parents. Crises come in the best marriages.

We of the church should be willing to lend the helping hand. But we should study to learn how best to give that help. We should not take the job away from families, but we should rather help them to help themselves. When the task is too great, then it is time to call on your church-related welfare agency and to use specialists who are available in the community.

In our preventive work, the parent-teacher association can give helpful guidance. We all have a great deal to learn about the growth and development of the normal child. But we also need to learn about the deviations from normal behavior which occur in even the best of Christian homes. Stealing, untruthfulness, nail-biting, hair-pulling, and other types of undesirable behavior on the part of children are frequently symptoms of nervousness and tension and should be treated from the viewpoint of causation.

We should also attempt to get to the parent of the preschool child when many early symptoms of behavior clearly indicate a need for help and interpretation.

All of us feel the need for guideposts along the way to help in establishing better family relationships and constructive ideals in our children. We in the church recognize at the same time that these are only aids toward a higher goal: that of making Christianity a living force in people's lives. In the truly Christian home problems are handled prayerfully; children are accepted as a gift from God, and parents look to Him for strength and guidance. We ourselves must, first of all, be examples of integrated Christian personalities. By our example we can help other families make Christianity something more than a Sunday-church-attending routine. Christianity must be a dynamic force to all of us in our day-by-day living.

DISCUSSION QUESTIONS

1. How can we train parents, teachers, pastors to detect children's problems?
2. How can teachers help to develop Johnny's whole personality?
3. Of what use can the parent-teacher association and other adult organizations be in helping parents understand child and family problems?
4. How can we best use welfare agencies for people with problems?

5. Why is a preventive program so essential? What is your church doing? What should a program include?

6. What guidance is your church giving toward Christian sex education? Parent education?

SELECTED REFERENCES

Spock, Benjamin. *Baby and Child Care.* (Can be obtained in a pocket edition.)

Children's Bureau Publications. *Guiding the Adolescent, The Child from One to Six, The Child from Six to Twelve, Infant Care.*

New York City Committee on Mental Hygiene. *Some Special Problems of Children* (aged 2 to 5 years). Series of eight. 105 E. 22nd Street, New York 10, N. Y.

Chapter 21

Christian Mental Health

Edgar F. Witte

WE ARE BECOMING INCREASINGLY CONCERNED with the problems people are facing in adjusting to the complexity of life in an atomic age. A sense of insecurity and anxiety, of futility and frustration, of rejection and loneliness, is engulfing an ever-growing number of individuals. Many are cracking up under the strain, mental illness is on the increase. Emotional disturbances in terms of physical ailments, of socially unacceptable behavior, and of delinquency are becoming commonplace.

1. Insights Through Psychological Science

The First World War and the years that followed focused attention on these problems. Deepening knowledge was gained as psychology struggled to attain the status of a science, as psychiatry developed, and new insights resulted from the work of Freud and others in the psychoanalytical field. Under the leadership of Clifford Beers the mental hygiene movement began to pull these threads of knowledge together and to impress upon all who were concerned about the proper development of human personality and social relationships, the importance of feelings, emotions, and attitudes of individuals as these reflected their repressions and conflicts, their inner struggles and frustrations. His book, *The Mind That Found Itself,* directed the attention of the general public to the importance of sound mental health and the role of emotional disturbance in wrecking the life and happiness of people.

Dr. Adolf Meyer, whose death occurred in March 1950, gave currency to the term "mental hygiene." We are thus dealing with a comparatively modern development when we turn our attention to the many articles appearing in the public press and to the great number of books dealing with the treatment of behavior problems and the prevention of mental illness.

The principles for which mental hygiene stands and which it seeks to inculcate, however, are not new. Philosophers from Socrates to William James, dramatists from Aeschylus to Shakespeare, poets from Homer to Milton, in bygone generations gained insights into human personality and behavior and charted the course of human development which today is being validated in many instances by the experiments and observations of modern scientists working in the field.

2. Insights Through Holy Scriptures

Even deeper insights have been given to us through revelation by the writers of the Bible. The keenest of all are those which our Lord Jesus Christ brought to light in His dealing with people and, especially, in the principles which He laid down for our guidance in human relationships and the directives He gave to govern behavior.

Too few people, however, have been familiar with the writings of philosophers and the great men of literature, yet even such failed to apply the precepts they had learned to the problems of everyday life. It remained for modern psychologists and psychiatrists to point up this wisdom, to popularize these insights by rediscovering them through their own research in the realm of human behavior or testing them through the techniques of scientific method. This pattern is even more pronounced with respect to the teachings of Christ. His admonitions to love one another, to turn one's cheek to the smiter, to walk the second mile, to bless them that despitefully use and persecute us, have been rejected as impractical and utopian until modern psychology discovered that "instead of a cultural luxury, loving has become a scientific necessity — even a scientific imperative" (O. Spurgeon English, M. D., *Marriage and Family Living*, Vol. XII, Winter, 1950, p. 3). Speaking in general about the role of religion and religious precepts in the lives of people, Dr. Carl Jung, in *Modern Man in Search of a Soul* wrote:

"Among all my patients in the second half of life — that is to say over 35 — there has been not one whose problem in the last resort has not been that of finding a religious outlook on life.

It is safe to say that every one of them fell ill because he had lost that which the living religions of every age have given to their followers, and none of them has been really healed who did not regain his religious outlook."

It is indeed a sad comment on our age that, whereas in times past men judged the truth or falsehood of a statement or the worth or unworthiness of an act according to whether or not it agreed with, or had the approval of, the Bible, today the acceptance of a Bible statement by many people depends upon whether or not it is in agreement with the latest, though not necessarily the last, assured result of science. We are, of course, happy when the findings of any branch of scientific knowledge reinforce a Biblical truth; but our reason for believing the Bible is not because we can find scientific proof for its statements. Rather, we are everlastingly testing the Bible because we believe it.

We are pleased, therefore, that discoveries in the fields of psychosomatic medicine and psychiatry are bearing out many of the teachings of the Bible. Not that we need this proof, but it suggests that the mental hygiene movement is not antagonistic to Christianity but an ally which can both help Christianity and be helped by it to the benefit of mankind.

While we seldom think of Christianity in terms of developing human personality, of helping people achieve emotional maturity, and as an aid in treating neuroses, it can, we believe, be demonstrated that Christianity is helpful to people in achieving these goals. As people "grow in grace and in the knowledge of Jesus Christ," they attain those ends in personality development which mental hygiene has found desirable and by the very means that authorities in this field advocate. Christianity makes its contribution especially in two areas: by aiding people in achieving maturity and by helping people to overcome their fears and anxieties.

3. Mental Maturity

One of the significant discoveries of scientific psychology is the demonstrated fact of human differences. People differ in intelligence, for example, and they mature intellectually at a rate and at a time different from their physical maturation. Through the work of Binet and Terman and many others, tests and scales were developed which enabled a measurement to be made of the native intelligence of an individual and to express it in a quantitative measurement known as the intelligence quotient — the well-known IQ. Through the use of these techniques it was discovered that while certain individuals might mature physically, their minds stopped growing at the juvenile or adolescent level, and they never progressed beyond the mentality of childhood.

For some years it was thought that the solution for the world's ills had been found in these discoveries. Hope was held out that if we could weed out the mentally deficient and retarded, prevent them from marrying, or at least from having children, we would have a superior race, an aristocracy of brains to replace that of inherited social position or wealth. This was the stage when, as Dr. Harry Overstreet points out in *The Mature Mind,* things were not judged in terms of good or evil but of knowledge or ignorance.

The world, however, could not shut its eyes to stubborn facts, to the obvious truth that people of superior intelligence could be guilty of the most heinous crimes, as was true in the case of the brilliant Chicago University students, Loeb and Leopold; that men would use their intelligence to exploit their fellow men; and that the most vicious and depraved as well as the most unhappy people in the world frequently were people of brilliant intellect. The answer to the riddle of human personality and behavior, evidently, was not to be found in education and intelligence testing.

4. Emotional Maturity

At this point psychiatry came forward with its concept of functional disorders of the nervous system. People acted queerly, suffered from neuroses, harmed themselves and others, not because they were mentally retarded or deficient, not because of brain injuries or disease, but because, on account of emotional disturbance or emotional immaturity, their minds did not function normally. As further studies were made, the emotional life in contrast to intellectual aspects assumed a place of dominating importance. It led to the recognition on the part of many people of the role played by the family and by religion in molding the life of the individual and in developing normal personalities.

Teachings of Christianity, generally forgotten or held up to ridicule, assumed a new importance.

The first step was the realization that just as individuals mature physically and mentally at different rates and degrees, so they also grow to emotional maturity at different rates and in some cases fail to attain the adult level of maturity. Some of the most stubborn personality and behavior problems, it was discovered, arise out of the circumstance that while a person might be an adult in years, he may still be a child in emotional development. It takes but little imagination to picture the havoc wrought by a person who wields the power of an adult but is as willful, as ruthless, and as lacking in emotional control as a little child.

Denis Diderot stated that every child is born into the world a potential criminal. The task of rearing a child thus is to turn raw human nature into character. A little child is aware only of itself, its own desires, its own comfort. The process of developing into maturity is one of becoming increasingly aware of the needs, desires, and rights of other people. This proceeds normally in family living, in the give-and-take between brothers and sisters, children and parents. Gradually children become aware of people outside the family; they establish relationships with members of the opposite sex; they grow up to respect the rights and privileges of other people and take on responsibilities for the welfare of an ever-widening circle of their fellow men. Thus they attain maturity.

Many people, however, do not reach the end goal of this process. Somewhere along the line their emotional growth is arrested at an infantile or juvenile level. They remain so self-centered that they never become aware of the rights and desires of other people. Others never get beyond recognizing the rights and privileges of their own family or their own immediate social group. They have progressed beyond the infantile level of emotional development but have never gone beyond the adolescent stage. We speak of these people as being emotionally immature, incapable of assuming adult responsibility, of taking into consideration the wants and needs and desires of people in whom they have no personal interest. This results in selfish and self-centered living in utter disregard of the rights of others and in a total lack of concern about the welfare of those that make up the community; it leads to family breakdowns, marital difficulties, delinquency, antisocial behavior, and community disorganization.

5. The Teachings of Christ Help Us Mature

It need not be pointed out to the Christian that the teachings of Christ, if followed, not only reinforce this process of maturing which we have described but are the specific for attaining emotional maturity. We have been speaking of emotional maturity in terms of becoming aware of the wants, needs, desires, rights, and privileges of others. This will be recognized as the hard core of what the Bible calls love, whether it is parental love, conjugal love, romantic love, love of our fellow man, or the love of God. Love is not maudlin sentimentality or the pleasure of sensuality; it is the ability to place someone else ahead of ourselves, the willingness to put the will and the need of other people ahead of our own will and our own need. "Greater love hath no man than that he give his life for his friend." "God so loved the world that He gave His only-begotten Son."

By definition, self-love is the negation of love. It is no love. Real love — love powerful enough to overcome innate selfishness — we believe, must be created. It is not the natural and inevitable product of family living, as experience has amply proved. We believe further that the only power great enough to lift individuals out of their self-interest and the self-centeredness with which they were born is the love of God manifested in Christ. Without this constraining love emotional maturity can scarcely be attained. This is Christianity's greatest contribution to mental health and emotional maturity.

We have spoken previously of love being a necessity. Until now we have been thinking of love for others as essential to our emotional growth. We also have the need to be loved. All that has been said about the necessity of being concerned about others is reversible. We are the beneficiaries of love received as well as love given. To be loved, to be held in esteem, is essential to our happiness and to our normal development.

6. The Christian Emphasis on Love

Child psychologists assure us that a frequent cause of behavior problems in children is the feeling of rejection, of being unloved and unwanted. Love is difficult to feign, and often parents actually reject their children, although they will not admit this to themselves. Frequently they seek to compensate for a feeling of rejection by over-indulging a child, showering it with attention, gifts, and advantages. The child instinctively senses the true attitude of the parents and reacts with hostility, aggressiveness, and other patterns of wilful behavior. How important, then, is the role of Christian love in the family in the development of well-rounded, mature personality! The home where children are regarded as precious gifts of God rather than the unwelcome penalty of "love's" pleasures, where parents, constrained by the love of Christ, place the well-being of their child above their own convenience and pleasure — that home provides for the emotional needs of the child which are so necessary to its development as a happy and useful adult. With love child-dren can learn to co-operate, to work with one another, to be happy and helpful. Without love they become quarrelsome, destructive, and delinquent.

Family life saturated and permeated by love does not come of itself. Its spring is the love revealed to the world in Christ. "Ye husbands, love your wives even as Christ loved the church." Those who would share this love of Christ and enjoy its blessings must faithfully use the means through which it flows into human lives. All that is said elsewhere with respect to family worship at home and in the family pew is applicable here. These activities are advocated, not to create a specious piety but because thus one learns the fundamental laws of life and how to live life so that one has it more abundantly. The laws governing life and happiness are not something apart from Christianity. The same God who gave us the Bible created the laws that govern our life and the development of our personalities. As we learn more and more of these laws, we discover that they are of the same fabric with the precepts laid down in the Scripture for our guidance. One can discover this by a simple experiment. Put the Scriptures to a test. Make Christian love the basic ingredient of family living, and see the results in the well-rounded development of children who reflect the love that enfolds them.

7. Faith and Prayer Allay Fears

Another area in which Christianity makes an important contribution to the creation and preservation of mental health is in the allaying of fears and anxieties. Fear serves a useful purpose in the lives of men. For one thing, it keeps people from placing themselves needlessly in jeopardy. Fear of danger leads them to avoid situations which may be harmful to them. Then, as Dr. Walter B. Cannon points out in his study *Bodily Changes in Fear, Rage, and Anger,* fear places the body in a state of readiness to meet emergencies, to fight an approaching enemy, or to flee from an impending danger.

The havoc is wrought in the lives of modern men by the fact that many of the things he fears are intangible. He does not face an enemy he can attack or a danger he can flee. Yet his body is, by his fear, placed in a state of readiness, of nervous tension. Denied an outlet for this pent-up energy in action, man turns to substitutes for action, to worry and anxiety. In many this develops into a state of chronic anxiety, resulting in a long list of physical ailments which rob them of their peace, health, and happiness.

The Christian faces these fears with faith. He can say with David: "The Lord is my light and my salvation; whom shall I fear? The Lord is the strength of my life; of whom shall I be afraid?" (Psalm 27.) Thus the Christian has a sure cure for fear. Armed with the shield of faith, he can ward off the attacks of fear or, succumbing to it for the moment, can soon cast it out.

Christianity also provides another means to counteract fear. A Christian is never at a loss to do something constructive about his fears. He need not resort to worry as a substitute for action in time of fear and anxiety. He can pray. Prayer, of course, is not a magical device by which we control God or summon Him to do our bidding, like Aladdin rubbing the lamp to call the genii to obey his will. Prayer is a channel through which the power of God flows into our lives, enabling us to bear our burdens, conquer obstacles, and overcome our difficulties. It is also a constructive activity which discharges the nervous energy pent up in our system; it restores our bodies from a state of excitement to a calm which permits us to act intelligently rather than emotionally. It is the certain cure for worry. Modern psychology has developed some useful techniques for getting rid of worry, but for thousands of years Christianity has delivered believers from the torments of worrisome fears and anxieties. Try it, and see.

8. Christ's Forgiveness and the Sense of Guilt

Space does not permit entering into a discussion of all the causes of fear and anxiety, their nature and treatment; nor are these necessary to our present purpose. We do wish to point out, however, that the basic cause of fear, regardless of what the precipitating factor may be, is a feeling of insecurity in the universe. This is due to a lack of trust in God; it arises either out of unbelief or from a sense of guilt. He who does not believe in God as the Author and Creator of life and as the Creator and Preserver of the universe but thinks of the world as an accident brought about by the interaction of blind mechanistic forces can hardly have any sense of security in this world beyond that which man with his puny powers can create. Even he who believes in God but is convicted by his conscience and realizes that, having disobeyed God, he is rightly not the object of God's love but of His wrath finds scant comfort in the thought that God is in control of the universe. He feels that he is outside the protecting circle of God's love. It is significant that almost the first words Adam spoke after his disobedience were: "I was afraid."

To these Christianity comes with the message of redeeming love, assuring them of forgiveness through the atonement on Calvary, convincing them that now nothing can separate them from the love of God (Rom. 8). They have security all-encompassing and absolute because God is now their loving Father, whose protecting hand is ever over them, who is "with them when they pass through the deep waters, who has graven their names upon the palms of His hands."

These, then, are some of the contributions which Christianity makes to mental health and which permit us to speak of Christian mental hygiene. It brings us to the acceptance and understanding of the dynamic power of Christian love, the kind of love which, when received, brings about a well-rounded personality and, when given, brings the individual nearer to maturity. The faith and trust it inculcates in God as a loving Father bids anxious fears subside and delivers the believer from the turbulent waters of worry and fear into the calm of peace and real security. "Godliness is profitable —," "Scripture is profitable —" also for mental health and emotional maturity (1 Tim. 4:8 and 2 Tim. 3:16, 17).

DISCUSSION QUESTIONS

1. In what way has modern psychology refocused attention on the teachings of Scripture?
2. Why is mere mental brilliance or knowledge alone not enough for human well-being?
3. For what reasons is emotional maturity as important as a sound body and an intelligent mind?
4. How is good emotional health valuable in family living? In husband-wife relationship? In child care?
5. In what ways is genuine Christian love the key to good personality development?
6. Just how do faith and prayer help us meet fears and conquer them?
7. Why is the assurance of forgiveness essential to true happiness?

SELECTED REFERENCES

Beers, Clifford. *The Mind that Found Itself.* Doubleday. 1953. 394 pp.

Overstreet, Harry. *The Mature Mind.* W. W. Norton. 1949. 295 pp.

Public Affairs Pamphlet. *Mental Health is a Family Affair.* No. 155. 28 pp.

Preston, George H. *The Substance of Mental Health.* Rinehart. 1943. 147 pp.

Chapter 22

The Pastor and the Family

Otto A. Geiseman

THE TITLE ASSIGNED FOR THIS CHAPTER assumes that it is a part of the pastor's life to be helpful to family life in his parish. Such an assumption rests on solid fact, as might be apparent from experiences in the ministry on a single day — experiences that are samples of what goes on in the practical life of a pastor throughout the year.

Yesterday the mothers of three new babies were visited. One mother was a Christian from childhood on, another was a very recent convert, and the third was an unchurched woman whom we hope one day to gain. At 5:30 p. m. a young couple appeared at the study to receive counsel in preparation for marriage, the girl a Lutheran, the husband of Baptist background. From 9 p. m. until midnight we counseled with a woman, a recent convert to the faith, and her hard-drinking unchurched husband, with the hope of bringing some semblance of peace into their home. Every pastor will find that his concern for happy family life within his congregation will constantly call for his interest and energies. The question is: How can he be most helpful to the family?

1. The Example of the Pastor's Family

One might begin by saying that nothing the minister does in the congregation to help family life is of much greater importance than the example he provides through his own home. The relationship of the pastor to his own wife and to his children, the relationship of his wife and children to himself, and the impression of his home gained by the parish and the community, have a very important bearing on the family life of his people. The language of example is still very effective and powerful. All who know the facts will agree that the family life of Protestant pastors has been an incalculable blessing to countless people. Because this is so important, and because we all have reason to be exceedingly humble when we consider how far we fall short, we can only pray God that He might help us through His Holy Spirit to make our own family life more beautiful and thus to set a better example for those entrusted to our spiritual care. Unhappiness in the parsonage has often not only served to embitter the members of the pastor's family but also to work havoc in the life of an entire parish.

2. Gain the Confidence of the People

If a pastor wants to exert a wholesome influence on the family life of his parish, it will be necessary for him to take a warm and vital interest in all his people — fathers, mothers, and children alike. The father's job, the mother's health, the children's progress — all should be matters of interest to him. There is no other way in which one could gain the confidence of the people more fully and quickly than by taking an interest in them. We are going to be of interest to our people if we are interested in them.

3. Apply the Gospel to Family Life

The minister should serve the best interests of family life among his people by teaching what God has to say on the subject of home, marriage, and family life, and by showing how the law of love finds its first application in the relationship of spouses, of parents and children, of brothers and sisters. Almost every sermon gives us a chance to show men and women, boys and girls, how Christian love should express itself in various family relationships. Such witness and testimony may well be used by the Spirit of God to work out finer and nobler concepts in the hearts of our people concerning their own family life. We can never take for granted that such preaching is not necessary.

Nor need the application of the Gospel to family life be limited to messages delivered from the pulpit. Bible classes, confirmation classes, meetings of the various church organizations, sometimes afford us excellent opportunities for speaking helpfully about marriage and the family. Sometimes, as a matter of fact, such meetings make it possible to speak with greater frankness and directness than would be possible from the pulpit.

4. Make Practical Suggestions

Suggestions of a practical and specific nature for the improvement and beautifying of the home and family life are also in order. The pastor may help the families of his parish reach higher spiritual levels by encouraging them in the conducting of family devotions, in the reading of the Holy Scriptures, and in the use of prayer and family discussions of spiritual matters. Experience has taught me that sometimes a great deal more of this is being done in Christian homes than one would be inclined to surmise. It is equally true, however, that the conditions of life under which our families must operate often make it extremely difficult for the family as such to worship together. They arise; they eat; they go to work and return from work at different hours. They have such different schedules as to leisure-time pursuits that it is sometimes impossible to get the members of even small families together with any degree of regularity at one time.

5. Do Pastoral Counseling

Family counseling presents another large area in which the pastor can, under God, be very helpful. This requires, to be sure, that he be able to sense and understand at least to some extent the heartaches and worries which fill the hearts of many. It will also require that he be sufficiently human so that the people will count him capable of entering with sympathy upon a consideration of their problems. If people think that their minister is going to be terribly shocked when they tell him of their troubles, and if they feel that he is much too far above them to recognize the significance of the things by which they are troubled, then they are likely to avoid him rather than consult him. This is where a long ministry in one parish pays rich dividends. People come to know you and to have the necessary confidence that you will enter wholeheartedly upon an earnest consideration of their difficulties.

Family problems are by no means easy of solution. Sometimes a pastor may have to expose himself to misunderstanding and bitter condemnation by espousing the cause of righteousness. All this, however, dare not cause him to shrink from the opportunity to be helpful in the preservation and improvement of family life.

6. Sources of Family Strife

One who must counsel with people in family matters will do well to remember that certain things serve as most fruitful factors of disturbance in the home and family life. Nothing is more common than *selfishness*. Families are not always disrupted by some terrible and catastrophic event. Much more often family life is destroyed by an endless series of small things which reveal the selfishness of husband or wife, parents or children. By the process of accumulation a multitude of little things soon add up to something formidable.

Unsatisfactory adjustments in the physical relationships of husband and wife also are a common source of irritation and family strife. Although the pastor will not be professionally equipped to deal with difficulties arising from physiological factors, he can impart light and guidance from the moral, spiritual, and psychological point of view. Many a woman has been frigid because she has thought of the marital relationship as something shameful and unclean. Proper instruction can remove this psychological block and thus contribute to a happier home and marital relationship. Various kinds of perversions are apparently becoming more and more common, with the result that unhappiness follows out of such degrading practices. Certainly a pastor imparting appropriate Biblical instruction concerning these matters can afford real help and thus be instrumental in saving homes and families from disruption.

Many homes are made unhappy because of difficulties which arise from *money matters*. Sometimes families land on the rocks because they have too much money. They become so engrossed in the pleasures of this life and this world that they lose their moral and spiritual equilibrium, destroy their own souls and therewith their capacities to live a happy Christian family life.

Sometimes there is strife in the home because of *limited financial resources*. When one considers how much personal experience most pastors' families have had in operating homes on painfully limited budgets, it would seem that every pastor could qualify as an expert in the guidance of those who encounter difficulties because of their economic limitations.

The *interference of in-laws* also frequently serves to disturb family peace. Sometimes it requires a high degree of courage and fearlessness to cope with such problems because the father-in-law or the mother-in-law in question may be, respectively, the chairman of the congregation or the president of the women's society. It always remains true that each couple and each family is entitled to live its own life and to enjoy happiness without officious interference on the part of others, however closely related they might be. Frank and fearless counseling can often serve to correct situations which otherwise might lead to tragic ends.

Families are sometimes broken up by a *lack of common interests.* Where this is the case, a pastor can be helpful by suggesting various areas of life in which a mutuality of interests might be successfully cultivated.

Jealousy, a demonic thing, frequently contributes to the destruction of family happiness. Since jealousy springs so largely from selfishness, it should not be too difficult for a pastor to shed at least such light as is necessary for the troubled individuals to recognize their problem and then to work, under God and with God, toward a happy solution.

7. Serve the Total Person

The pastor who would afford counsel in family matters as well as in all problematic situations will do well to remember that each human being has a body, a mind, and a soul. These three constituent parts do not exist separate and apart from one another but are rather most intimately integrated with one another. If something goes wrong in the area of the one or the other of these three, repercussions are likely to be felt in the other two. Hence the pastor who would counsel his people wisely and helpfully will do well to try to determine from what source the chief difficulties arise in a given situation. Are the causes of a spiritual, a mental, psychological, or a physiological nature? Once this has been discovered, the necessary steps can be taken one by one toward an effective elimination of the difficulties.

DISCUSSION QUESTIONS

1. How does a family-centered ministry help build up a congregation? Make preaching more concrete? Improve evangelistic outreach?
2. Which topics can be handled more satisfactorily in topic discussions, panel discussions, and lectures than in the sermon?

3. Make a list of practical subjects related to family life a pastor may take up in house calls.
4. What are the chief sources of family strife in your congregation and community?
5. What steps should be taken to increase your ministry to families?

SELECTED REFERENCES

Oates, Wayne E. *The Bible in Pastoral Care.* Westminster. 1953. 127 pp.

Hulme, Wm. E. *How to Start Counseling.* Abingdon. 1955. 157 pp.

Anderson, Stanley E. *Every Pastor a Counselor.* Van Kampen. 1952. 111 pp.

Knubel, Frederick R. *Pastoral Counseling.* Muhlenberg. 1952. 102 pp.

PART V
Helping Families

Chapter 23

A Parish Family Life Program

John P. Uhlig

1. The Family-Centered Parish Program

EVERY CONGREGATION HAS SOME KIND of an activity program designed to meet the needs existing in the parish and in the community. The ideal parish program is family- and people-centered. It follows the pattern of Jesus, who said that He came, not to be ministered unto but to minister.[1] Such a program has the loving heart of Christ, bent on helping and healing; it has the loving eyes of Jesus, tenderly focused on individuals to detect their varied needs, both spiritual and physical; it has the loving hands of Jesus, determined and ready to serve. The ideal parish program is designed to minister to families and to people. Roy A. Burkhardt maintains that "no local church truly conceives its task that overlooks the venture of helping families find the greatest possible fulfillment."[2] A personal ministry of Christ-like service is the ideal. "The pastor who misses the chance to work with his families in the solution of their problems and in the celebration of their victories is not in the fullest sense a pastor."[3]

2. Discovering the Needs of Families

The needs of families come to our attention almost daily in magazine and newspaper articles, in the meetings of welfare organizations, city councils, and parent-teacher organizations — even in social gatherings.

---

[1] Matt. 20:28.
[2] Wood, Leland Foster. *What the American Family Faces*, p. 103.
[3] Ibid., p. 107.

Commenting on the origin of existing family life programs,[4] Evelyn Millis Duvall says that "they were demanded by the folk who are already living in families and who wanted some of the help and guidance that could be gleaned from the professional fields of religion and law and sociology, and the many other sciences and arts that have grown up with real contributions to offer family life." [5]

Here are the needs as the workshop held in River Forest in 1949 saw them:

1) Both parents and the church need to realize that the home is the most important factor in training the child for total Christianity. The home is "the school of Christian living," "the most fundamental institution in the world," "the nursery of every generation," "the college of life," "the training-ground for the child." One writer says: "There is no agency that can compare with the family for promoting the normal emotional expression of the child, and for the forming of personality patterns." [6]

2) Families need conditioning to withstand the social evils of the day — materialism, individualism, and self-interest. The church dare not underestimate or ignore the tremendous impact which the pressures of our times are having on our people.

3) Each member of the family needs training in the personal use of the Bible. The family exists for this very purpose, to foster such growth in grace.

4) Each member of the family needs training for a life of communion with God in prayer. "Families that pray together stay together."

5) Parents and children need training for leadership in family devotions, for the discussion of religion in the family circle, and for mutual Christian admonition.

6) Parents need the assistance of the church in carrying out

---

[4] Agencies functioning locally and nationally in the field of education for family life include: the National Council of Churches of Christ in America, the United Council of Church Women, the National Conference of Family Relations, the National Congress of Parents and Teachers, YMCA, the Child Study Association of America (N. Y.), the American Institute of Family Relations (Los Angeles), the Association for Family Living (Chicago). *What the American Family Faces,* pp. 98, 99.

[5] Ibid., ch. 4, p. 98.

[6] Ibid.

an effective program of child training in the home. It should include living together in love, growing together in grace, and serving others.

7) The home needs to be enlisted and more closely integrated into the church's program of Christian education. "The church needs the home as an outgoing laboratory in which all that it stands for is lived out in intimate human relations, and the home needs the church and a continuous contact with it to keep its own religious devotions vital and its spiritual fires burning." [7]

8) Young adults need guidance and direction for growth in Christian living and preparation for marriage. The young adults have been termed "the lost generation," the "no-man's land of our churches," "the ripe and inadequately harvested section of the adult education field," because they are often left to shift for themselves.

9) Young people need counseling on the many problems which confront them — conduct during courtship, choosing a life-partner, engagement, the relationship between husband and wife, between parents and children, stresses and strains of marriage, crucial experiences of home life, religion in the home, and others.

10) Each member of the family needs training in co-operating with the family, church, and community. This involves an understanding and appreciation of why God has made the individual what he is and why He has placed him where he is.

3. Are Our Churches Today Meeting These Needs?

Are our churches today meeting the needs of families? A survey taken at the Family Life Workshop (River Forest, 1949) revealed that the situation is not altogether satisfactory. This survey covered thirty-seven congregations, twenty-five urban and twelve rural, ranging from 200 to 1,000 or more souls. In the majority of the parishes family visitation is conducted chiefly by the pastor. This visitation includes new families which have moved into the community, those received by transfer, those where a newborn babe has arrived, those where sickness and bereavement have entered, and the indifferent families of the parish. Some congregations use special committees or the usual

---

[7] Ibid., ch. 5, p. 101.

congregational organizations for this work, but in most instances it is the pastor who carries out the visitation.

The survey also showed that not much specific, constructive counseling takes place in most of these visits. It revealed the important fact that the average congregation has no specific program for strengthening and nurturing Christian family life. Family life education is carried on in a more or less incidental way by means of the Sunday sermon and in the meeting of the ladies' aid, the youth society, the PTA, the couples' club, and others. In the thirty-seven congregations represented by the poll, only one congregation had a family forum, eight observed a family week, twelve had family nights, four held conferences with parents, two maintained a parents' library, and four conducted mothers' clubs. Furthermore, while several pastors did some pre- and postmarital counseling, none conducted regular classes in family-life education.

Although this survey gives us a picture of only a few parishes, it nevertheless indicates that, by and large, congregations are not meeting the needs of their families as adequately and completely as they should.

It is perhaps not too difficult to account for this. The average congregation has been functioning with a church-centered, instead of a family-centered, program, with the emphasis on service by the layman to the church, on giving and working for the church.

Family needs, however, call for more specific services on the part of the church to people. Almost every member of every family in the average parish today faces problems, difficulties, and trials, many of which are distinctively characteristic of our generation and were almost unknown a generation ago. They face moral issues and questions for which they have no answers; or they have wrong answers. A realistic church program today must be different from the average parish program of a generation ago. It must aim not only at getting service *from* people but also at giving service *to* people. It must pattern itself after the motto of the Master: "The Son of Man came, not to be ministered unto but to minister." Where the church comes with a service program to the homes and offers types of helps which every family needs, the church returns to its basic function as a means to an end, and not as an end in itself.[8]

4. What Some Churches are Doing

Here are some churches which are conscious of family needs. A simple cataloging of their programs will suffice: family forums to discuss family life, family-life workshops using four Sunday evenings and featuring sectional meetings on five age levels, Wednesday-evening family night, a one-day family camp for families which cannot afford to go away to a summer conference, one church service a month to serve families with children, family institutes with outstanding persons of the denomination or community as leaders, publication of a regular bulletin to develop parent participation in Christian training, short-term courses for parents and young people, Bible classes which devote time to Christian family life, a forum on courtship.[9]

Some churches feature courses for young people, for young adults, and a school for parents. Others have set up libraries on family life, enlisting the co-operation of the local public library. One parish has regular working committees: a group of young women to help the socially maladjusted girl, a group of married couples to help counsel young couples, a group of physicians to help with premarital and husband-wife relations.[10] These instances show what is meant by a program of family-life education in the local church.

5. What a Balanced Program Should Include

The church which sees the need of family-life education will desire to formulate a definite program to meet this need. The question is: What should a balanced program include? The River Forest workshop developed a blueprint for an adequate family-life program, suggesting eight things which can be done to help families.

1) Thorough indoctrination of young and old is certainly the starting point in any program of the church, with special attention given to the sanctity of marriage and the Bible basis for

---

[8] Feucht, Oscar E. "Inaugurating a Family Life Program." *Lutheran Education,* January, 1950, p. 219.

[9] Ibid., p. 220.

[10] Wood, Leland Foster, pp. 104, 105.

Christian family living. The church's first task is still Christ-directed, life-related Bible teaching for young and old, so that they may be Christian in all relationships of life.

2) Family-worship guidance is a second essential. In a discussion on family worship a lay member of a District board for parish education remarked that while he believed in family worship, he did not know how to proceed in order to make it effective. Undoubtedly such cases are numerous. Much practical help is needed in this area. (See Chapter 11.)

3) Adoption of a Christian home standard which sets forth those factors that help to make a home Christian, enables families to evaluate their home as to purpose and function, and serves as a constant reminder to strive for the attainment of its standards. (See Chapter 3.)

4) Inaugurating a home visitation program, one purpose of which would be to offer systematic aid to families — new families, homes which have a new baby, the average families, families in distress, the spiritually indifferent families. The co-operation of the homes in the church's program must be solicited. Christian education should be conceived of as a mutual endeavor between parents and the teachers of the church. (See Chapter 13.)

5) Offering a counseling service which will include pre- and postmarital counseling so that the Bible's guidance can be applied competently and comprehensively to the specific family problems. (See Chapters 17 to 22 for details.)

6) Establishing a nursery department. "Child evangelism begins at birth, and the church which is first on the scene may have the inside track," says one writer.[11] The chief value of a well-designed nursery department of the Sunday school is not merely the early enrollment of the child but a program of service to the parents. (See Chapter 12.)

7) Offering study courses with units on courtship, marriage, and child training. These may be offered in the Bible classes, youth, adult, parents, couples organizations as a part of their program, or they may be special study groups. (See Chapters 14 and 15.)

8) Developing Bible classes, discussion groups, activities for

---

[11] Feucht, Oscar E. *A Family Life Program for the Parish.*

young married people (couples' clubs), and for older adults (senior citizens), such as church-related golden age clubs.[12] (See Chapters 25 and 26.)

This is only a blueprint, but it shows the wide range and scope of family life education in the local parish. It can serve as a guide in setting up a comprehensive program that meets parish needs.

6. Use of the Profile Form and Check List

No two congregations are exactly alike. In one congregation there will be many families of young couples with small children. In another church the typical family with school-age children will predominate. In a third church the majority of adults will be over forty, with many retired folks in the sixties and seventies. You can get the family complexion of your church by classifying your families according to a few standard categories, and then with a bar graph you can visualize the family pattern of your parish. A special family profile form has been prepared for this purpose.[13]

Because congregations differ in make-up, family life programs will also be different, if they are to meet the needs of the families of a specific congregation.

Another device that will help you see your potential service to families is the check list: "What Is Your Church Doing?" [14] This list will greatly help the pastor, the board of elders, the board of education, and the educational leaders of all agencies and age levels in seeing new opportunities to "minister" as Christ ministered.

7. The Right Approach is Fundamental

The key to a people-centered ministry and a family-conscious church is the right attitude. Before we can have a family life program, there must be some family life thinking; there must be the sympathy, the compassion, and the alert eye of the Lord Jesus, the great Good Shepherd.

The program must grow out of a "spirit of service." It dare

---

[12] This program has been slightly expanded since 1949. See ch. 4.

[13] *Family Profile Form.* See Part VI of this book.

[14] *What Is Your Church Doing to Prepare Its Constituency?* See Part VI of this book.

not become mechanical or merely organizational. It must issue from "a feeling of concern" for families and must be built on the love of Christ. "The love of Christ constraineth us." [15]

There are two institutions which are based on love and where love works out in practice — the home and the church. They are thus bound together and must reinforce each other. Says Leland Foster Wood: "The church has a particular solicitude for the family because the family and the church are so definitely based upon a set of values which arise out of the same roots, namely, love and fellow-feeling." [16] The church which is close to the heart and mind of Jesus, who Himself is love, will reflect this divine love by staying close to families.

The family life program should not be considered as something "new" or "extra." Serving families has always been the work of the church. It is a part of the regular preaching and teaching ministry. It is one phase of the pastoral care of a congregation.

It should be merged with what already exists. It should be a part of the program of the men's club, of the ladies' aid, of the youth society, of the Sunday school, of the parish school.

This program deals with, and must involve, all age levels from birth to death; for the goal is "the development of the individual through the family for the glory of God."

A family-life-education program involves not only all ages and all agencies but also all types of programs — formal and informal, devotional and instructional, recreational and social. It demands curriculum changes so that the whole "climate" is conducive to Christian family living.

8. Implementation of the Family Life Program

A good family-life program is developed gradually, usually over a course of years. But procrastination should be avoided. One author advocates: "Start right away. Don't say this and that won't work in my church. Of course, the program of another church won't work, but the principles will. Even a humble beginning is a sound approach." [17]

---

[15] 2 Cor. 5:14.

[16] Wood, Leland Foster, p. 237.

[17] Wood, Leland Foster, p. 247.

Here are some steps in implementing and inaugurating such a program:

1) *Fix the authority.* The congregation, recognizing that a family-guidance program is its responsibility, should authorize the setting up of an adequate program. If there is no committee on Christian education, one should be appointed. If it has restricted its influence to the school-age child, a corrective provision could be added to the constitution like this: "To advance the Christian nurture of all persons committed to the congregation from infancy to adulthood, particularly also to foster a constructive program of Christian family life education." [18] Fixing the responsibility is one thing; getting someone actually to implement a program is another. That is why the next step is

2) *to get a committee working* to set up the program. This can become the work of the board of elders or the board of education (or a subcommittee of one of these boards). The committee must be given the vision and trained in family life work.[19] The pastor naturally must supply good leadership. The next step is therefore

3) *to survey local needs.* The committee will study what has happened and what is happening to the American family today, the changes to which it has been subjected, the crisis which it faces. It will analyze the needs of the community and the parish. It will determine the present extent of family guidance in the parish. It will discover the weak areas which need strengthening. This will take time and should be done thoroughly. The pastor and the committee are now ready

4) *to plan the curriculum and develop the full program.* This should be done with the people of the parish. It is to be a people's program. Consult with the teachers of children, with leaders of youth and adult groups, and with parents. This advisory group could serve as a planning council. Be sure that the program is not merely remedial, but preventive and constructive, offering definite aid to families. Be selective; do not include too much at the start. Develop a long-range plan.

5) *Enlist the support of others* in carrying out the program. "Too many pastors, parish school teachers, and Sunday school

---

[18] *Lutheran Education.* January, 1950, p. 221.

[19] Utilize the family life training courses and workshops offered in your home community or nearby communities.

superintendents want to do their work single-handedly. They are depriving the Church of Christ of valuable services. Blessed is the minister of the Word who has learned leadership from his Lord, and likewise has chosen his "twelve" and his "70" and his "120." [20] Choose capable persons who can help with the program, professionally trained persons in the congregation, Bible class and Sunday school teachers, organizational workers, public school teachers, doctors, nurses, and the like. Become acquainted with, and utilize, the resources the community has for family assistance.

6) *Plan to make a library available* to parents and families. Such a library should include "some general guidance material, various study courses, guidance for conducting family worship, tracts, pamphlets which meet specific problems and needs, and materials for on-the-job training of leaders, materials for young people and children, for those entering marriage, for young parents, for parents with adolescent children, and for the aging family." [21]

7) *Move into action* by making definite recommendations to the congregation to gain official sanction. The matter should then be presented to all groups of the congregation. These presentations should be made as dramatic as possible, using audio-visual aids, radio skits, panel discussions, and the like.

9. Regular Evaluation and Appraisal

To keep family life education vital, self-perpetuating, and truly recreative, someone must put new life into it and give it the spark of fine Christian leadership. It should not be routinized and become dead and cold; that is the best way to lose it. Accordingly, each year the program should be evaluated from the standpoint of whether it served the congregation, strengthened its members, and helped its families. Improvements should be based on such an appraisal and on new information, guidance, and instruction gained by reading, observation, and conference.

Such a family life program in the local parish will truly help the Lord build the church by building Christian families.

---

[20] *Lutheran Education.* January, 1950, p. 224.

[21] The Family Life Workshop at Concordia Teachers College, River Forest (1949), compiled a list of over 300 books and pamphlets and a listing of some seventy audio-visual aids.

DISCUSSION QUESTIONS

1. What is the difference between a church program that is chiefly church-centered and one that is also family-centered?
2. By what means may the actual needs of the families of a given congregation be ascertained? List them.
3. How much specific family life education does your own congregation now have? For each age level? As to quantity? As to quality?
4. Name the chief types of teaching and training which you believe belong to a balanced family life program.
5. What approach to your congregation will be effective? How will you make it evangelical? How will you make it Christ-motivated? How can you convince church members that this program is God-pleasing?
6. What are the main steps for the proper inauguration of a planned family life program in your church?

SELECTED REFERENCES

The Bible, chiefly the ministry of Christ in the four Gospels.

Feucht, Oscar E. *A Family Life Program for the Parish.* Board for Parish Education.

Lutheran Education. January 1950. Concordia Publishing House.

Wood, Leland Foster, Editor. *What the American Family Faces.* Eugene Hugh. 1943. 254 pp.

Fallaw, Wesner. *The Modern Parent and the Teaching Church.* Macmillan, 1946. 228 pp.

Chapter 24

Home and Church Co-operation

Remus C. Rein

IN RECENT YEARS pastors, politicians, and educators have become increasingly convinced of the need for a closer co-operation on the part of the home in the process of education. State, school, and church are rediscovering the truth that the home is the first, and potentially the most important, educational agency and that parents are the real teachers.

1. Whose is the Child?

Much of the failure of education in the past must be attributed to the faulty answers given to the question: Whose is the child?

Imperialistic and authoritarian governments answered this question by taking the child into their custody to educate and train him according to their will. Their philosophy was that people exist for the state. The rights of individuals, especially those of parents, were ruthlessly brushed aside.

The school, too, often acted as though the education of the child were a responsibility that had been exclusively entrusted to it, and that the only duty of parents was to see to it that the child would attend and that he would fit himself into the program of the school. When it became apparent that the school alone was not sufficient to provide all the education the child needed, the home was often ignored. Instead of calling on parents to give the needed assistance, social agencies were established to supplement the efforts of the school.

Nor is the church wholly innocent. While the church has always been the champion of the home, it has frequently given the impression that the home exists primarily for the purpose of helping to promote the church's program. Instead of helping parents fulfill their obligations, the church has often assumed the role of acting as a substitute for parents.

This practice of ignoring the home and placing the growing child more and more in the care and keeping of all sorts of agencies, including the church, has been termed "the unforgivable error of modern life and of the modern Protestant church." [1]

To be sure, the sovereign authority and responsibility for the child rests on the parents, who bring the child into the world. Human life starts in the home. Nor is there any potentially greater agency than the home for giving educational guidance. But while the state, the school, and the church must be faulted for their part in ignoring the home in the education of the child, the fact remains that many parents must also be blamed for willfully neglecting their duties and for encouraging others to assume obligations that rightfully belong to them.

2. The Home and Christian Education

In God's creative plan the home is not only the first but also the most important institution in the world. The child's first world is his home. His parents are his first teachers. Moreover, parental influence continues even after the child enters school. If this influence is truly Christian, the home becomes the most effective agency for the Christian training of children. But if this influence tends toward evil, it is not only very difficult but next to impossible for all other agencies to counteract and set aright what the home has done amiss.

Some churches refuse to enroll children in their educational agencies unless they can enroll the parents at the same time and thus assure the church of the co-operation of the home. We do not agree with this extreme view; for the Holy Spirit can change the heart of a child through the Word of God without the help of parents. Yet it must be said that unless God works a miracle, the child will go the way of the home (Prov. 22:6). [2]

3. The Church and Christian Education

The home bears the first responsibility for the spiritual training of the child. The priesthood of believing parents cannot be

---

[1] Fallaw, Wesner. *The Modern Parent and the Teaching Church.*
[2] Fallaw, p. 21.

transferred to others (Deut. 6:6-9; Eph. 6:4; 1 Peter 2:9). However, we no longer live in a simple society. The heritage to be passed on to every new generation of children increases greatly each year. Our economy does not supply the leisure for the instruction of the young which existed in a more agricultural era. Few parents have the time, the ability, or the inclination to give their children a full education and training. God in His wisdom has, therefore, charged the church to assist the home in this important but difficult task (Matt. 28:19, 20; John 21:15, 16).

The task of the church is not only to give additional instruction and training to children but, especially, to educate parents so that they can better discharge their obligations in the home. In other words, the church is to supplement the efforts of parents, not to supplant them. Moreover, it is a tragic mistake when parents suppose that the Christian instruction and training which the church offers is all the child needs. The process of education is continuous. The child's entire life is in need of supervision and guidance. Nor is anyone in a better position to provide this than the parents.

On the other hand, parents should not ignore or disdain the help the church offers. Since it is God's will that the church should assist the home, parents should acknowledge gratefully the help the church offers and should make the fullest use of its educational agencies both for themselves and for their children.

There are no age limitations in the Savior's great commission to His church to teach all. The church must, therefore, direct its educational program to the needs of all members of the family. More than this, the church should concern itself with the family as a unit and not merely with its individual members; for it is in the family that human personality finds its highest development, and it is in the family that Christian traits which the church seeks to cultivate find their highest expression.

4. Home and Church Need Each Other

Since both home and church have their God-appointed functions, and since both are concerned with reaching the same objectives, it follows that both can best accomplish their purpose when they work together. "It is not a question of the church calling upon the family to help put over the church's program. Nor is it a question of the family calling in the church to make up for failures or to take over a difficult part of its task. Rather it is a relationship of complete mutuality. The family finds its richest self-realization in the larger community of Christian families. The church finds its noblest fruitage in the love and community of family life. Together they seek to develop each person to his fullest spiritual capacities and to extend that love and community to encompass all mankind as children of one Father." [3]

Home and church need each other. The church needs the help of the home in achieving its goals of Christian living and Christian service; the home needs the help of the church to assist members of the family, as individuals and as a group, to develop to the fullest degree their capacities for such Christian living and Christian service. The church needs the help of the home to reinforce its objectives; the home needs the help of the church to familiarize itself with its God-appointed duties and to guide it in carrying out these obligations. To offer such mutual help, it is necessary for home and church to come together so that they may discover what each has to offer, what their limitations are, and what each needs to do in order to fulfill its sacred task as teacher.

5. The Church Serving the Home

The first task of the church is to provide those specialized phases of the program of Christian education that can best be carried on in and by the church. To fulfill this task the church must provide suitable educational facilities and must strive to enroll every member of the family in one of its educational agencies.

An efficient nursery department with well-trained teachers, home visitors, parent-teacher study groups, and, if possible, a weekday Christian kindergarten, can offer the best help to parents with preschool children.

Elementary school children can be served effectively through such agencies as the parish school, Sunday school, Saturday school, vacation Bible school, weekday classes, and confirmation classes.

---

[3] Quoted from "Christian Education Today." International Council of Religious Education, 1940.

High school students, young people, and adults can be served through Bible classes, society meetings, and study groups. The young people's society, ladies' aid, mission society, men's club, married couples' club, parent-teacher meetings, and similar organizations within the church, can be utilized as teaching and training centers.

In addition, the church can direct its pulpit program to the needs of families. It can arrange for family programs in the church. And it can provide helpful reading and study materials, both tracts and books, adapted to the interests and needs of the various age groups.

As the church enlarges its program of service to families, it will feel an increasing need for training more volunteer workers through such media as conferences, Bible institutes, and Sunday school associations.

The second task of the church in working with the home is to offer guidance and inspiration to parents in carrying out those phases of Christian education which can best be carried on in and by the home. To fulfill this task the church must carry on an effective program of home visitation.

The groundwork for home visitation is laid when the pastor utilizes house calls to strengthen Christian marriage and family living. He gets a new opportunity to serve the home at every birth, baptism, confirmation, wedding, illness, funeral.

Teachers can offer guidance and help to parents by visiting the home immediately after the child is enrolled in one of the educational agencies of the church. Through further visits in the home, teachers can learn more about the child's environment and can bring about a feeling of friendliness and helpfulness.

When the child has reached the age for confirmation instruction, a special visit to the home by the pastor will prove helpful in impressing on the parents and the pupil the meaning of this important step in the child's life.

"Sponsors" can be appointed for each new family to extend friendship, to cultivate Christian fellowship, and to help integrate them into the life and work of the church.

A special committee working with the extension department of the Sunday school can be assigned the task of visiting sick and delinquent pupils each week. Besides bringing comfort and cheer, these visitors may also go over the lesson the pupil missed in the church school.

All families need help, but not all families need the same kind of help. Rather than rely solely on the help of social agencies, the church will do well to have a family committee to consider special cases and to render every possible assistance.

6. The Home Serving the Church

The home can co-operate with the church by becoming thoroughly familiar with the aims and objectives of the church's religious, educational, and social program, and by endeavoring wholeheartedly to carry out this program as individuals and as a family group.

Parents, at the time their children are baptized, should pledge themselves to establish the family altar and to nourish the Christian faith and life of their children by teaching them to pray, by guiding them in reading the Bible and memorizing Scripture, and by training them to share their joy of salvation with others. Above all, parents can best train their children by the example they set in their own lives.

Members of the household can discuss the sermon, the lesson, the educational topic in the family circle and then earnestly endeavor to put God's will into practice in the home, in the community, and in all relationships in society.

To keep their children under Christian influences, parents can provide wholesome literature, recreation, and entertainment in the home, and can arrange for association with other Christian families for Christian fellowship. Family-at-home nights are perhaps as important as family-at-church nights.

Every member of the family can take an active part in the church's classes, societies, and organizations. Those possessing the necessary qualifications can offer their services as teachers or leaders; all can offer their help, and all can contribute generously for the work of the church.

7. Involving Parents as Teachers

Fortunately Christian education is coming into its own. Not only is it reaching down to birth and up to old age, it is also outgrowing the four walls of a schoolroom. Education is as wide as life. Still great majorities — in their thinking — restrict it to "church and school." Our task is to restore to the home its inalienable duties as well as its rights. How can this be done? How can we get parents to do their duty as teachers?

The church can take the initiative in a number of ways.

1) It can make use of a twofold approach to the child: directly in the classroom, indirectly through the parents in the home. When a child enrolls in a church school, a chain reaction should be set off, by means of which contact with parents is systematic, purposeful, very practical, and helpful. The aim of Christian evangelism must reach the mother and the father of every child in the church school. A sincere and persistent program to enroll the whole family in the Sunday school will pay rich dividends.

2) Lesson assignments should be directed to parents as well as to pupils. When parents get challenging requests from their own children — or from the teachers — to help Johnny read a Bible chapter with understanding, to make up his own prayers, to practice helpfulness in the home, then parents will identify themselves with the spiritual training of their children and will themselves feel a need for the church's instruction to equip them to help their children. This is the deeper significance of Deut. 6: 6-9, which is addressed to fathers and mothers. Spiritual truths must be first *"in thine* (parents') *heart"* before parents can teach them diligently and effectively to their young.

3) We have the custom that teachers send a progress report to parents on the achievements of their children. What would happen if this were completely reversed? Let parents be asked quarterly to report on the help they have given their children, on the spiritual knowledge, attitudes, and habits they have helped inculcate. Ask for a report on behavior improvements observed, and many indifferent parents will be aroused from their sleep. Surely, this is a telling yet practical way to get home co-operation.

4) Out of such tactics there will develop quite naturally a desire for parents to talk to teachers and vice versa. Quarterly conferences between teacher and parents in connection with, or separate from, formal parent-teacher meetings should be arranged. Let the church-home team discuss aims for the quarter's lessons, projects to be carried out at home, attitudes that are

to be built, and habits that are to be developed. Then the downright practicality of the church's teaching program will be discovered by parents, and they will be enlisting themselves.

8. Church and Home Working Together

While both church and home have their respective responsibilities, it is essential that they come together for co-operative planning. The most effective way of doing this is through parent-teacher meetings. Fortunately, more and more congregations are setting up such meetings. They are more essential than most churches seem to admit. They are needed just as much where a congregation has only a Sunday school as they are in churches that have Christian elementary schools. All parents need to be involved in such meetings.

Moreover, these conferences must be purposefully directed toward studying and planning the respective duties of both the church and the home. The program for these conferences should be carefully planned in advance, and printed copies should be mailed to all parents. Such subjects as the following might be considered for the meetings:

> How the church can work with the home
> How the home can work with the church
> Understanding and guiding children
> How Christian growth takes place
> An explanation of our Sunday school lessons
> Family worship in the home
> Building the Christian home
> The power of the parents' example
> The importance of Christian companions
> Purposeful Bible reading.

A completely new series of parent-guidance booklets is now appearing on the market annually, each with eight topic-discussion outlines especially designed for Christian parent-teacher meetings.[4] Their scope is best seen by glancing at the titles and table of contents of Volume I.

---

[4] Concordia Publishing House, St. Louis, Mo.

Your Child and You
Basic Needs of Children
Building Right Attitudes
Discipline That Is Constructive
Problems of Adolescence
Enlisting the Home
Fostering Spiritual Growth
Mental Health and Your Child
Seven Problems in Sex Education

Equally challenging are the topics in the other volumes of this series that have appeared. (See end of chapter.)

Just as the National Parent-Teacher Congress has provided for public school PTA's splendid resources for many years, so now there are available similar resources for church-related parent-teacher groups. These include a quarterly newsletter, entitled *Nurture,* and a packet of program helps for the leaders.[5]

Christian educators, Sunday school superintendents, and pastors will be surprised at the number of helpful books that have recently appeared for Christian parents.

Parent-teacher conferences offer a splendid opportunity for parents to consult with teachers on questions relating to themselves and to their children. These meetings present an occasion for Christian fellowship and permit parents to discuss their problems with other parents in the larger family of the church. The informal character of such meetings, in contrast to the more formal church service, also serves as an inducement for unchurched parents who have children enrolled in the school.

There are many varying factors in large and small, in urban and rural churches. Not every church will find it possible or practical to adopt all the suggestions offered in this chapter. The important thing is for all churches to recognize that, while the primary obligation of giving religious guidance rests on the home, the primary responsibility for helping Christian homes rests on the church. The problem of adequate Christian education for children is primarily a problem of educating parents. The solution to the problem of Christian education in general lies in educating the whole family.

---

[5] National Lutheran Parent-Teacher League, 7400 Augusta, River Forest, Ill.

DISCUSSION QUESTIONS

1. Why is the home such a powerful teaching force? What opportunities and advantages do parents have which teachers do not have?
2. In what respects must the home have the church for the Christian nurture of children and adults?
3. How can the church enlist parents as teachers of religion in the home?
4. What topics for parent-teacher meetings would you suggest to a planning committee?
5. Why do you regard parent education so important for the church? For the nation?

SELECTED REFERENCES

Fallaw, Wesner. *The Modern Parent and the Teaching Church.* Macmillan.

Home and Church Work Together. Division of Education, National Council of Churches of Christ.

Home, School, Church Co-operation. Lutheran Education Association Yearbook. 1952.

Grevenow, George. *The Application of Lutheran Teaching in the Home* (mimeographed).

Wynn, J. C. *How Christian Parents Face Family Problems.* Westminster. 1954.

Parent Guidance Booklets. CPH:
  "Your Child and You"
  "Making Home Life Christian"
  "Happiness is Homemade"
  "Teen-agers Need Parents"
  "Guiding the Young Child"

Nurture. National Lutheran Parent-Teacher League, 7400 Augusta, River Forest, Ill.

Christian Parent. Highland, Ill.

Chapter 25

Helping Young Adults

Arnold F. Meyer

THE AGE GROUP which we call young adults has been in existence as long as there have been people. The only difference is that formerly they were not called by that name, and the church, as a general rule, did not consider it necessary to provide special programs of study, activity, and service for them. Usually the term includes the age group between the years of twenty-five and thirty-nine. In this chapter we shall deal mainly with married young adults.

1. Where Are the Young Adults?

You will find them wherever you go. Some have just been married and are fortunate enough to be living in their own home, or have taken over the home place, or farm. Others are renting a few rooms, an apartment, or are living with their in-laws while both husband and wife are working until they can find or afford a place they may call their own. Still others are living in trailers and government housing while they continue their schooling or complete a term of military service.

But where are they in the program of the church? Visit one of our Sunday schools some Sunday morning, and you will find all age groups represented from the nursery class, ages two and three, to the adult Bible class, up to the age of eighty. Very seldom will you find a department for young adults. If we should ask the young people's group where the young married couples are, the answer would be that they are with the adults. The same question asked in the adult class would bring the answer that they are in the senior class of the young people's department. As a rule, there will be few in either one of them.

Look at the calendar of a congregation's organizational activities. There you will find listed the activities of the men's group, the various women's societies, the youth societies, even boys' clubs and girls' clubs, but only rarely a young married couples' club; [1] and still this age group (twenty-five to thirty-nine) constitutes more than one fourth of the population of our country which is fifteen years of age or over.

The fact of the matter is that in the Bible-study program, as well as in the service and recreational activities of the congregation, there is a distinct corridor, a vacant gap, between the young people's department and the adults. Consequently, there is a good reason to ask: "Where are the young adults?"

2. How Are Young Adults a Responsibility and an Opportunity?

Wherever they are, it is becoming increasingly apparent that the church must find a place in its program for this age group, with its vast potential for service in the Lord's kingdom. This should not be a difficult task; for among them you will find many young men and women with ability, initiative, and an eagerness to work out their ideas. They want and need to make "test flights" and in that way discover their own capabilities.

The church would be the loser if it failed to discover, tap, conserve, and use the energy stored up in these young people. If it fails to provide guidance and direction for them, this does not mean that these talents will not be used somewhere; but they may be misused, dissipated, or put to use exclusively outside the church.

From this age group comes the leadership for the congregation in the immediate tomorrow and even today. It should be remembered that most of the men and women on our home mission frontiers are below the age of thirty-five. So are the men and women to whom we entrust important work in our foreign mission fields. Without a doubt most of the disciples of the Savior belonged into this age classification. These were the people to whom Jesus said: "Go ye and teach all nations, baptizing them in the name of the Father, and of the Son, and of the Holy

---

1 In 1952 there were about 800 married couples' groups in our 5,000 congregations.

Ghost." "Ye shall be witnesses unto Me" is addressed also to young adults of today. In our own experience we know of a number of congregations that have presidents, secretaries, treasurers, and financial secretaries between the ages of twenty-five and thirty-five.

"The field is the world," says Jesus. Usually we have thought of these words in terms of geography as though they applied only to people who lived in "far-away places with strange sounding names." It should be emphasized that they also have their application in the field of sociology, covering all the various strata of society, the rich and the poor, the learned and the unlearned. In the area of chronology they include all age groups, particularly also the large sector of young adults.

The church needs these people, and it needs them *now*. A church with only the wisdom of age accomplishes little. The vibrant enthusiasm of youth, tempered by sage counsel, can do much for the advancement of the cause in God's kingdom.

It is apparent, however, that the church can never be satisfied only to *take* from these people; it must also *give* something to them. A way must be found by which it can work with its young adults. The answer is to provide a program of Christian training and an opportunity for growth and maturity in faith and in life.

Such a training program will bring many blessings to the people in whose interest it is being offered.

1) It will increase their spirituality. In connection with their special "life situations" it will help to re-awaken a religious consciousness and deal with their particular religious problems.

2) It will help to build the right kind of church-home relationship. If any program of church-home relations is to be established, it should be attempted first on this age level. Success with this group will set the pace for the entire congregation.

3) Opportunity will be afforded for counsel in family relations. Not only will the pastor have an opportunity to lay solid foundations for some new homes, but capable Christian couples who have successfully overcome problems themselves can counsel in what may be called informal marriage clinics.

4) Training may here be provided for the future leaders of the church. This involves the welfare of the entire congregation. By training and leading the young adults, a congregation is enabled, humanly speaking, to place its future into competent and trained hands.

5) Missionary activity will be encouraged. Where a husband or a wife are of another faith, or unchurched, group activity of the young adults will serve as a valuable connecting-link between the church and the husband or wife not affiliated with the congregation. Family unity with regard to religion will be encouraged.

6) Finally, it will provide fellowship for those of one age group. These people are seeking the fellowship and companionship of others of their own interests, temperament, and age. Here we may provide this wholesome fellowship and sociability with such as are "one in hope and doctrine, one in charity."

Lives thus guided will be substantially enriched and will enrich the church in which they hold membership. In short, to use the language of the community chest, "everybody benefits"; the church which looks after its young adults will be benefited, as will those who participate in the program.

3. What Kind of Program Will Meet Young Adult Needs?

The program must be suited particularly to the special needs of young adults. Ordinarily this group will not be happy with the pattern handed down from the adult department. Neither will they be satisfied with a revamped youth program. They may take some good features from both, but the young-adult program will not be an exact copy of either of them.

A good rule to follow is to have the program start where the people are. Their drives and interests should be taken into consideration. This period of early maturity is for most men and women the busiest time of their lives. They are setting up their own homes, the children arrive, the pressure of the daily grind at home and at work is continuous and heavy. For the majority of them there is a taxing financial strain. Disappointments and disillusionments are almost inevitable as these people face life in its realities.

In his book, *Church Group Activities for Young Married People,* Dr. George Gleason enumerates ten basic wants inherent in young adults. These are:

1) Security in obtaining food, shelter, clothes, and avoiding pain
2) Friendship and fellowship
3) Activity and rest
4) Recognition and praise
5) Thrills and adventure
6) Sex expression
7) Cultural growth
8) Freedom for self-expression
9) Opportunity to serve
10) Feeling of at-oneness with the universe and its Creator.

While it is not the function of the church to meet all these demands, the leader will recognize their existence and will direct them into the best channels. A Christian young-adult program must fulfill the purpose which God has given to the individual and to the church, while taking into consideration the basic human drives.

The content of the program should offer the following: Bible study, Christian fellowship, worship, family-life education, my church, discussion of Christian doctrine, applying the Bible to daily living, applying the Bible to current events, the topics of the day, and Christian service.

The major factor in determining the specific nature of the program and the methods should be the wishes and desires of the group. These desires can best be ascertained by means of interest finders. These will help you decide, for example, the method to be used in Bible study, the particular areas in which the group feels the greatest need for help — in worship, in family life education, in the use of the Bible for daily living. Such interest finders will also be an aid in giving guidance to leaders in applying the topic discussions, Bible-study sessions, projects, worship, fellowship. They will also tell the leader the type of presentation preferred, such as guest speakers, home talent, panel discussions, forums, quiz programs, visual aids, book reviews, and others.

In the matter of fellowship and recreation, interest finders will give information as to the kind of play or social activity in which the members of the group are interested, such as party games, photography, music, picnics, dramatics, table games, and so forth. They will help you in suggesting to young adults service projects within the congregation and the community. Such projects may be teaching Sunday school, singing in the choir, serving as ushers, participating in a neighborhood missionary canvass, helping with the enlistment of prospects, working in the church office, taking part in a congregational home visitation or every-member stewardship canvass, offering your service to the trustees in repairing, cleaning, and repainting the church property, helping the institutional missionary, giving a party for orphans.

4. How Shall We Organize the Young Adults?

On the basis of what has been said up till now, it is obvious that the organization of this group is becoming more and more of a necessity; but the question is: How shall we proceed?

Here a note of warning is in place. Do not begin by issuing a general invitation in the Sunday bulletin to all the young adults of the congregation to come together on a given evening and "organize." There are always a few successful exceptions, but in most cases this would be a good way to risk failure and get the whole movement off to a bad start.

A far better way would be to arrange for an exploratory meeting to which a few interested individuals have been invited with the express purpose of discussing the need and demand for a special adult group in the community and congregation. In this way it could be determined what the young adults are thinking and what they would like to see happen in the church. More such meetings may be called if necessary to "talk things over." In the course of time this may lead to the appointment of a steering committee to "get the ball rolling."

If there is sufficient interest as a result of these discussions, it may be well to obtain consent from the congregation, if that consent is required.

Now we are ready for a possible list of prospective members.

These may be gathered from confirmation classes, adult classes, marriage records, baptism records, missionary-prospect lists, and other church lists. The marriages performed by the pastor provide a continuous list of additional prospects.

After this preliminary work has been done, the time has come to call a meeting of all interested prospects, chiefly through the couples already interested. Several couples have been appointed in advance to plan a complete program for the first meeting. When the group gets together, it should discuss, and decide on, plans for future meetings and adopt a tentative schedule and program.

At this point questions will arise as to the type of organization which is desirable. In a small congregation a single unit may serve the purpose. In the larger churches the group could divide itself into neighborhood or interest units. In all cases it is recommended that the organization be kept quite informal and definitely related to the home.

It is a good thing to proceed slowly with the setting-up of a permanent organization and the drawing-up of a constitution. Also the selection of a suitable name might be postponed for several months until the group is well established. Those present may decide on procedure from one meeting to the next. The usual officers may be elected temporarily. Some groups have found it desirable to elect a couple for each office, instead of an individual.

Eventually a constitution is prepared, although it may be possible to get along without one. If it is decided to have one, this should be the outgrowth of the wishes of the membership. Experience has proved that it should not be too elaborate. In the course of time the group will want to choose a name. This should be a distinguishing name, which fits the group. A few names that have found favor are Married Couples Club, The Wedding Ring, Concordia Club, Young Adult Fellowship, etc.

Committees should be appointed as needed. A membership committee is a "must." This committee should arrange to call for new prospects and take them along to the meetings. A program committee arranges for the devotional opening and the educational features. The social part of the program is best handled by a rotation of couples.

The time of meetings may vary according to the wishes of the group. Some meet every Sunday morning as a Bible class and then arrange for occasional week-night social meetings. Others use Sunday evenings, weekday evenings, or the evenings when the entire congregation is gathered for church night. Since this is the busiest time in the lives of these people, meetings should not be held too frequently.

Outward organization is not nearly as important as the program itself. The group which maintains the proper balance in the matter of Christian education, fellowship, and worthwhile service projects has a much better opportunity to continue than one which goes off the deep end in one of the three directions. Keep the program Bible-centered, service-conscious, home-related, and tied together with the bond of Christian fellowship, and your young adult group will be a valuable aid in the work of His kingdom.

DISCUSSION QUESTIONS

1. Since 31 per cent of the average community of persons over fifteen are young adults, it is not difficult to compute the young adults in your church. What is 31 per cent of your congregation's communicant membership?
2. What provision does your parish now make for young married people (twenty to thirty-nine), in the Sunday school's Bible classes, in the age-group organizations?
3. How many good reasons for serving young adults in the church can you give? Why don't the purely adult groups (men's club, ladies' aid) appeal to young married people?
4. How does a congregation increase its ministry of the Word when it has both Bible study and fellowship for young married people?
5. What are the best ways to build a program that meets the needs of this age group?
6. What guidelines for organizing young adults are suggested?
7. Why is the number of young married adults increasing in America? Why are married couples groups increasing in our churches?

SELECTED REFERENCES

Gleason, George. *Church Group Activities for Young Married People.* Assn. Press. $1.00.

Gleason, George. *Single Young Adults in the Church.* Assn. Press.

NCCC. — Div. Ed. *Young Adults in the Church.* 15 cents.

Committee on Young Adult Work. *Young Adults in the Church,* a complete handbook. United Church Publishing House, Toronto, Can.

Chapter 26

The Aging Family

Oscar E. Feucht

LARGELY BECAUSE OF ADVANCES in medical science, improvement in nutrition, and a better national economy, the American's life expectancy is expanding. The average life span in the days of Julius Caesar was twenty-two. By the year 1900 the span of life for Americans averaged forty-eight years; but by 1930 twelve more years had been added, raising the average age to sixty. In the next twenty-five years it rose again by seven years to sixty-seven years.

There is also a difference between the life span of men and women. In 1930 the average for men was fifty-nine while that for women was sixty-three. Today women live at least five years longer than men, speaking in terms of general averages. Some experts believe that we can expect more and more people to reach the age of eighty and ninety.

In the first half of the twentieth century the population of the United States doubled, but the number of persons sixty-five and over quadrupled. Thus we get the following distribution of the United States population of persons over sixty years in 1950:

Age	Population	% increase since 1940
60—64 years	6,059,475	28%
65—69 years	5,002,936	31%
70—74 years	3,411,949	33%
75—79 years	1,503,982	39%
80—84 years	774,391	48%
85 plus	576,901	58%
Total	17,329,634	33%

It is estimated that within another generation the number of persons over sixty will reach thirty million in the United States alone.

One of the experts at the Institute on Aging held at Washington University, St. Louis, Mo., in April 1953 said: "A society that supplies only economic security for its aged, while leaving other insecurities untouched, is doing only a surface job. Now that medical science has added more years to their lives, it is up to us to add more life to their years."

Uncle Walter is a lonely man. He looks lonely when you see him sitting expressionless in the shadow of the dark little box he operates — an elevator. What will society do, what will the church do for Uncle Walter? What can he do?

And the church is definitely involved. It has its portion of persons sixty-five and over. Congregations vary greatly, as will be revealed to anyone who takes the trouble to make a "family profile" of the individual parish. In most suburban areas of our metropolitan centers there will be a high percentage of young couples, and the average age (children and adults) may be in the lower twenties. In one of our smaller communities in Southern Illinois we have a congregation of 519 communicants, of which one hundred are sixty-five or over.

In its aging families the church sees not merely a problem but a new opportunity for service.

1. A New Approach to Old Age

Fortunately, our generation has developed a more constructive and hopeful view of growing older. Adult education has focused attention on the fact that we learn at fifty and sixty, or even at seventy, almost as well as we learn at fourteen and fifteen. Popular books have been written to show that we may get a fresh, new start on life at age forty or sixty, or even eighty. Evidence has been gathered that has changed our opinion with regard to the later years of our lives. A pastor who retired at sixty-five in Kansas City entered upon a very successful new mission project in California and surprised everyone with his second career in the ministry. Winston Churchill became Prime Minister of England for a second time at age seventy-eight and did some of his greatest writing at the age of eighty. Albert Schweitzer, at eighty-one, is a musician, a philosopher, a theologian, a naturalist, a doctor, a surgeon, a writer, and an organ builder. He could have made a great name for himself in any of these fields; but he preferred to bury himself in the African jungle, there to minister to the bodies and souls of the natives.

Musician Arturo Toscanini, exceptional in his genius, is also exceptional in his vitality at eighty-nine, as displayed in many ways. Marie Beynon Ray, in her book *The Best Years of Your Life,* cites many more examples. Radio and television programs are emphasizing "life after eighty." A Cornell University professor at ninety is known as the world's most indefatigable horticulturist. Gladstone, Benjamin Franklin, Galileo, Titian, Booth Tarkington, Helen Keller, and a great host of men and women for many generations have proved how much can be accomplished in the later years of life.

> IT IS TOO LATE! Ah, nothing is too late
> Till the tired heart shall cease to palpitate.
> Cato learned Greek at eighty; Sophocles
> Wrote his grand *Oedipus,* and Simonides
> Bore off the prize of verse from his compeers,
> When each had numbered more than fourscore years.
>
>   · · ·
>
> Chaucer, at Woodstock, with the nightingales,
> At sixty wrote the Canterbury Tales,
> Goethe, at Weimar, toiling to the last,
> Completed Faust when eighty years were past.
> These are indeed exceptions, but they show
> How far the gulf streams of youth may flow
> Into the Arctic regions of our lives,
> Where little else than life survives.
>
>   · ·
>
> For age is opportunity no less
> Than youth, though in another dress.
>
>   (From *Morituri Salutamus,*
>   by Henry Wadsworth Longfellow)

People at seventy or eighty need not resign themselves to the front-porch rocking chair and complain of the bitterness of life and the burden they are to society. Our senior citizens are a remarkable resource to the country and to the church. But someone will need to guide them into this new attitude toward old age. Someone has put this new approach to old age thus: "Old people should not be *retired* but *retreaded* for a new phase of life and service."

2. Physical Problems and Their Solutions

Caring for the aged has been a problem since the beginning of civilization. Some of the treatment accorded them is only another example of "man's inhumanity to man." It is encouraging, therefore, to note the progress that has been made under the influence of the Gospel in ministering to the aging. Old folks do have problems, but those problems are not insurmountable. Let us look at a few of them.

The economic side of old age: Fifty years ago two thirds of our old people lived in rural areas, with many things to do in the garden or about the farm. Today two thirds of them live in the city, where early retirement has become the rule. "Only 2 out of 5 men over 65 are employed (in 1955) as compared to 4 out of 5 in 1870." [1] It takes a lot of money to support a couple after retirement, as the administrators of our homes for the aged will tell you. Undesirable housing, present-day mobility — with relatives living hundreds of miles away — ill health, and senility add to the economic problem.

To increase the economic security of old folks, the community needs to promote the employment of older persons. Industry and business are taking some commendable steps in that direction. Outlet shops for marketing arts and crafts and other products of men and women in later life are needed. The community can provide vocational guidance for the aged to help them cash in on their talents and hobbies. It can review retirement practices and work for better old-age-assistance programs.

The problem of housing: Only one fourth of the people over sixty-five are entirely self-supporting. The statistics of the American Bankers Association tell us that of one hundred men (starting at the age of twenty-five) only one will be really wealthy at sixty-five, only four will be in comfortable financial circumstances, only five keep on working, fifty-four will be dependent on family or public assistance, and thirty-nine will have died. The bearing of all of this on the housing problem is quite apparent.

To meet this need for home security, Elizabeth Breckinridge, executive director, Community Project for the Aged, Welfare

---

[1] "Aging, A Community Responsibility and Opportunity," U. S. Dept. of Health, p. 6.

Council of Metropolitan Chicago, suggests: "Providing suitable living arrangements for older population, community planning and promotion, such as public and private housing projects, welfare services available to persons in such housing, providing ways and means so that old folks may stay in their own homes as long as possible, providing other necessary types of shelter." There is some completely new thinking with regard to housing old folks on a community basis: individual, convenient apartment units in the home community rather than an institution.

The matter of health: People will continue to grow old, but they will not look like old men and women of three generations ago. Nor need they all be confined to the rocking chair. Medical science is providing special services to the older folks. One physician who specializes in health for the aged (geriatrics) was able to move fifty-five people out of one county home back into active society through his health rehabilitation program. And, what is more, he helped three hundred others remain active in the home community, outside an institution.

The kind of help needed by aging families is varied and includes a health-education program for the aging and their families, expanded clinic and hospital facilities, interim personal-care programs, help with marketing, housekeeping, and such other services as are offered, for instance, by the Family Service League of America.

Mental and emotional health: Psychiatrist Jack Weinberg says: "Rigidity in the aged is a defense against anxiety and is therapeutically reachable." He is saying that undesirable social characteristics in older persons are frequently the results of emotional insecurity and that proper treatment and personal attention can remove many of the causes and lead to good adjustments.

This calls for a program of education of the aged and of their families, development of leisure activities, use of community agencies and resources. Such a program will also help Christian people to retire *to* something rather than merely *from* something; it will give them new insights, skills, and a much more wholesome attitude toward growing old. Community psychiatric services for the aged would be a very great help.

The treatment of the whole person is involved: Body (health), mind (emotions), and soul (spirit). The problem of dependency will involve, as a rule, all three, and solutions will depend on attention to the soul as well as to the body and the mind. So the church is also involved with regard to the physical problems.

3. Preparing for Your Later Years

Seward Hiltner, of the University of Chicago, has outlined a number of things that people need to do in their forties and fifties if they are properly to get ready for, and enjoy, the later years of life. Let us review these very practical suggestions.

1) *Think about old age before you get there.* Many old people still connect old age with negative thoughts of fear and anxiety. Suddenly they find themselves old and their bodies unable to respond to the demands of the mind. A different attitude will result if people will look squarely into the future, anticipate some of the dangers and difficulties, and really talk about the later years and how they will use them profitably. Unless they think, plan, and talk about these years, they are not really prepared for old age.

2) *Take an inventory of your health.* Older people should have regular medical checkups. They should be on friendly terms with a family physician who can give them counsel, educate them with regard to what they may expect, help them with proper diet and good advice, and make suggestions with regard to physical and mental work. The illnesses of old age, if detected in time, can be handled much better.

3) *Do some long-range financial planning.* Today most people have insurance policies. They need to learn how much will be available to them in terms of pensions and social security payments. Some adjustments will be needed with regard to housing, food, and clothing. Many old people can become much more self-reliant and satisfied by being almost entirely self-supporting in old age if they will plan their financial future (where to live, how to live) and seek the counsel of those who really have competence in financial planning.

4) *Prepare now for a change of pace.* Many persons have become so attached to their lifetime jobs they are very unhappy once this type of work ceases, and they are suddenly "put on

the shelf." Much of this difficulty can be avoided if there is
a plan for easing out of a vocation and if arrangements are made
for a change of pace. Plans should be made to stay on the job
on a limited-service basis, or to semiretire to new work or to
a hobby. The famous French physician Alexis Carrel said: "The
aging man should neither stop working nor retire. Leisure is
more dangerous for the old man than for the young."

Herbert Hoover left the White House at fifty-eight; but he
entered upon a most exciting period of his life, as fruitful as, or
more fruitful than, his career as President. Older folks should
think of working six or eight months instead of twelve months,
three or four days a week instead of five or six days, half days
instead of whole days. We still get much more out of life if we
stay happily at work, helping ourselves and helping others. Here
the church particularly can lift the vision of its old people and
help them invest their later years in Kingdom service. Your lifetime work can be a hindrance to your retirement if you can think
of life only in terms of your vocation and have not developed
broader interests and avocations.

5) *Develop a healthy mental and spiritual outlook.* This
makes the selection and further development of hobbies, crafts,
and other activities in the forties and fifties very important.
Seward Hiltner, therefore, says: "Put your job where it belongs.
If our attitude toward it tends to produce ulcers, the job can
hardly be said to glorify the Lord." He suggests that emphasis
should be on making a life that pleases God and serves man
rather than making a living. This asks for a Christian sense of
values. It means that your job, however high you have esteemed
it in the past, should not control your emotions. All of us need
to develop a healthy mental and spiritual outlook on life. It is
but natural that Christian old people should be happy old people
because they have a faith to live by — and die by.

"Grow old with me, the best is yet to be." Wise indeed are
the people who, by prayerfully and wisely planning for the sunset years of life, avoid the embitterment and the disillusionment
that often come in old age. This means the cultivation of good
relations to others, good communication between husband and
wife and family, widened interests, and a Christian perspective
and world view. It means looking at old age as the fulfillment

years of life. A rhymester has caught the meaning of a healthy outlook on the part of older citizens in these words:

> Do you read or write or knit,
> Or does your mind race while you sit?
> Do you golf, or whittle birds,
> Or do you think such things absurd?
> Do you fix your hair and face,
> Or feel yourself beyond such grace?
> Do you hie to church and pray,
> Or gripe about your fate all day?
> Do you talk about old age,
> Or dismiss the thought in rage?
> To be ready for senescence,
> You must first pass adolescence.[2]

4. Spiritual Problems and Their Solution

In the summer of 1953 an International Conference on the Church and Older Persons was conducted by the National Council of Churches. It gave attention particularly to eight spiritual needs of older persons, listed in *Man and His Years,* the Report of the National Conference on Aging, 1951.[3] We shall look at these basic spiritual needs and see how the message of the Christian church helps to meet them.

1) *Assurance of God's continuing love.* Think of the many special promises of God like the words of Is. 46: 4: "Even to your old age I am He; and even to hoar hairs will I carry you: I have made and I will bear; even I will carry and will deliver you." Meditating on this verse, one of our older Christians wrote:

> Though hills and mountains be removed,
> The Word of God itself has proved
> His promises are sound and sure
> And through eternity endure.
> He needs no feeble human aid
> To help sustain the things He made;
> Yet He our deeds does not reject
> If they the love of Christ reflect.
>
> (Albert O. Ney)

Dr. Martin Luther's explanation of the three articles of the Apostles' Creed are filled with the basic truths of the Christian

---

[2] From "Growing Older," an article by Dr. Seward Hiltner in *Presbyterian Life,* March 18, 1950.

[3] Federal Security Agency Health Publications, Inc., pp. 207—210.

faith so full of comfort for all the days of our life, also the
declining years. There the Christian takes comfort from the fact
that God has created him, will preserve him and watch over
him; that he, too, has been called by the Gospel into the Holy
Christian Church, the body of Christ, and will someday be called
into the higher and greater life of the children of God in heaven.
The Scriptures are full of expressions of love and counsel which
meet this basic need of old age: the assurance of God's presence.

2) *Certainty that life is protected.* The history of God's
people in the Old Testament is a continuing illustration of God's
concern for all His people in times of affluence and in times of
distress, in the flower of youth and in the older years. We have
the great "fear not" passages of Scripture that make such a
golden chain of promises so full of comfort, giving assurance
that God will never withdraw His presence. To all God's children the Lord says: "Fear thou not; for I am with thee: be not
dismayed; for I am thy God: I will strengthen thee; yea, I will
help thee; yea, I will uphold thee with the right hand of My righteousness" (Is. 41:10). The psalter, as in fact the whole Bible, is
filled with expressions of the providence and protection of God.

3) *Relief from guilt, grief, and fear.* Even Christian people
have guilt feelings; are overcome by their losses, reverses, and
sorrows; and are disturbed by fears. Some of these feelings are
normal experiences for the closing years of life, when physical
and emotional strength is waning. We have the antidote for all
guilt in the abounding grace of Jesus, our Savior (Rom. 5:20).
We have the answer to sorrow in the hope of the resurrection
(1 Cor. 15), and we have a mighty weapon against fear in such
Scripture selections as Rom. 8 and Ps. 27. Bringing this relief
with the Gospel message in adequate pastoral care is the responsibility of the whole church, the church members as well as the
pastor.

4) *Relief from loneliness.* We may tell our old folks: "We
are never alone when Jesus is in our hearts, when we can talk
to Him as a friend sitting in the next chair, when we can meditate on His Word and daily find meanings we had not discovered
earlier in life." The loneliness of old age is overcome by the
many opportunities for Christian fellowship in the church service, in men's and women's organizations in the church, in the

Bible class for older adults, in the church's visitation program, and, in fact, in the practice of love and concern that follows wherever there is true faith in Jesus Christ.

5) *Perspective of life that embraces time and eternity.* The pagans put out their aged to die in the desert. Sometimes Christian people seem to have little concern for older members of the family. When this happens, the results can be tragic. Older folks may develop a philosophy that life, after all, is only a burden to themselves and to others. To overcome this false philosophy with a Christian view of all of life and of the usefulness of particularly the older years, is part of the teaching task of the church. Surely life is not easy. Most of us have to struggle through every year. But at sixty and seventy come days when many Americans can retire from some of the arduous tasks of life and can look forward to ten or twenty years of more care-free, leisurely living, without some of the heavy financial loads of early married life. These years may be invested in a very constructive way. Furthermore, the church must teach, "Thou shalt honor the face of the old man" (Lev. 19:32). Old folks need many expressions of appreciation and recognition in all the activities of the church. They need this sense of being appreciated to maintain the satisfaction of useful living. Most of all they need to keep their hope of heaven and its joys undimmed. The New Testament is full of Jesus' glorious promises of heaven. Thus the Christian message alone will give them a proper perspective of eternity as a life with God.

6) *Continuing spiritual growth through new experiences.* Workers with the aged insist that ongoing learning is an important part of the program for the aging and that without the windows of the mind kept open through various activities of an educational nature we cannot adequately serve the senior citizen. Surely the church will provide the incentive, guidance, and opportunities for spiritual growth through Bible reading especially adapted to the aged, study courses, church periodicals, the missionary-education program, the religious programs over radio and television, such as the "Shut-In Hour." The whole work of the whole church in all the world helps to keep broader interests alive.

7) *A satisfying status in life as a person.* Here again the

Christian religion supplies fundamental teaching. Every person is precious in the sight of God. Old age is singled out for special honor. The individual Christian belongs to the family of God. The counsels of grandfathers and grandmothers are to be solicited and used by the family and by the community. The church especially can do much to satisfy this desire for status in the mind of the older person.

8) *A feeling of continuing usefulness.* Where the Christian church has continued to work with older persons, giving them status, guiding them to new spiritual growth, giving them the proper perspective for time and eternity, relieving them of their loneliness with Christian fellowship, taking care of their emotional disturbances with spiritual messages of the Scriptures, re-emphasizing the love and protection of God, it will also be ready to use its senior members in the work of the congregation. This is very important.

Nothing disturbs older people more than the feeling that they are in the discard and can do little that is actually important in life. This is not true, of course. There are shining examples of older persons who have been bedridden and yet have scattered Christian sunshine far and wide. Articles and books dealing with the subject of old age are filled with examples of persons who are making some of their greatest contributions to the church and to society after seventy or eighty.

Two cautions are in order. The minister and his people must possess a true awareness of these spiritual needs and must meet them with more than mere words. The whole attitude and feeling of the congregation must reflect toward the aged the love of Christ and genuine honor. More is called for than the recitation of Scripture passages. It is only by action, Christian behavior, Christian planning, and specific parish activities that the aged will be truly helped. We mean to say that we must translate from the Bible (and our minds) into life the Christian teachings which meet the problems of old age.

5. The Church and the Aging Family

Putting our old folks into rest homes is now a procedure recommended chiefly for only those who need nursing or special attention. This is becoming more and more a practice for several reasons. First, because it will be practically impossible to provide enough old folks' homes to take care of persons over sixty-five, and, secondly, psychologists and social workers have discovered that old folks are much happier if they can remain in the stream of society and in the home community.

For some families and for some old persons the home for the aged may be the best solution. In that case great care should be exercised in the *kind* of nursing home or rest home that is considered.

1) *Congregations need to cultivate the proper attitude toward aging and older members.* We should avoid dating them unnecessarily, that is, emphasizing that they are in an "old-age bracket." We need to know how many of these folks we have, and we need to understand each individual's personal needs. Younger men should get an opportunity to get experience in Christian work and should not be held out of office by the old guard. On the other hand, the old guard is necessary to give counsel to the young men and to share a lifetime of experience. Old folks should not be retired from Kingdom service but should be "retreaded" for a new type of service. Congregations need regularly to show them appreciation and honor with special recognition. Older persons can become members of almost all important committees. First in importance, then, are a proper attitude toward the experience of older persons and a proper administrative policy with regard to their use.

2) *Activity and usefulness is important.* Frequently the church has thought only in terms of services to the aged. These services are indeed important; but they overlook one of the strongest cravings on the part of old folks, namely, to prove their usefulness to the end of life. This indicates that activities and projects in which older persons can take part are very important to them.

A survey of the senior citizens and their past activity and interests in life will prove to be very helpful. It can be made by the board of elders or one of the organizations of the congregation. Similarly, the needs of the parish need to be studied to find just where the aging members can be used in the fields of evangelism, education, soul-keeping, stewardship, welfare, missions, worship, in the work of the auxiliary organizations, or in congregational administration. The planning council of the local church would do well to discuss the use of these persons by comparing existing talents with existing needs. Older folks can qualify as accompanists, teachers, members of the welfare committee, visitors of the sick, representatives of the church at civic meetings. They can help with a program of reading to the blind; they can give secretarial assistance in the church office and make thousands of evangelism calls; they can be effectively used in the work of reclaiming marginal members; they can help keep records in the Sunday school. Those with musical ability can help with the musical program — start an orchestra or a band or a choir. On an individual basis they can work in the "Stamps for Missions" program, do reading, and make clippings for the pastor. In fact, there is no limit to such projects except what we ourselves impose by limiting love and imagination.

There are many things that can be done even by shut-ins, such as folding the Sunday church bulletin, correcting address lists, making telephone calls, preparing materials for the church library, cataloging things for the church files, etc. A fellowship of intercession can be developed by the use of prayer lists. Let them pray for the pastor, teachers, the educational agencies, the sick, the new members being received. They can remember birthdays. They can form a home department of the Sunday school. Give them assignments for the enlistment of others and thus increase the church's service to unchurched older adults in the community. They can keep one another informed on the world-wide program of the church. They can conduct Bible classes in homes. They can be pastors' aides in extending a ministry of comfort and spiritual help.

The need for providing projects is all the more important since thousands of persons are retiring at a much younger age than formerly. Getting them busy seems more important than simply starting another organization. The biggest need of the older person is not for services and charity but rather for an opportunity to continue to be useful and productive.

3) *Community and church clubs are valuable.* Old people do not like to be completely separated. They want to belong to the whole church family and to the community. They have something to offer the children and youth and young married people. God evidently intended that they should not be separated from the younger generation (Ps. 78:1-8).

And yet they have needs of their own, and so individual churches have profited with "golden age" clubs, as have quite a number of American cities that have given special attention to the older citizen. For instance, in Cleveland, Ohio, and Philadelphia, Pa., thousands of older persons have been rehabilitated through community clubs with varied programs which include singing, storytelling, hobbies, picnics, outings, tours, crafts, and other activities. Protestant churches have found it profitable to keep them together as a Sunday Bible class which makes applications of the lesson suited particularly to the needs of the aged.

4) *The church can increase its services to the aged* by providing transportation to church, by bringing tape-recorded sermons into the homes of shut-ins. In the past this ministry has been carried on chiefly by the pastor. Why should not the members of the congregation have a large part in serving the aged? One adult Bible class, after discussing the need, elected a service committee which regularly assigned calls to be made on older folks. Elders and their helpers will need to get definite assignments, will need to be given insights and materials, will need to be ready with suggested projects and activities. Our service to the aged has been almost completely restricted to giving them a "sermon." It need not be so limited, as the books listed at the end of this chapter so effectively illustrate.

One of the most important services, however, which the church can render is to prepare members of the family to understand aging persons and how to help them most effectively. Youth and adult classes and organizations in the church may be used to pass on insights and discuss helpful procedures. Such books as *How to Help Older People* (Arthur), *When Parents Grow Old* (Ogg), *Older People and the Church* (Maves and Cedarleaf) will supply helpful suggestions. There are many changes which have taken place in the family which make it harder and harder to take care of older persons, for instance, smaller homes, more children in these homes, working wives, and other changes resulting from the transition from a rural to an urban society.

Only the church can provide new spiritual attitudes and horizons for its people that are sixty and older. As the church takes the initiative and provides an adequate program to meet their spiritual, physical, and mental needs, the church itself will get a new lease on life.

DISCUSSION QUESTIONS

1. How many older people do you have in your congregation? Interview four or five of them and list the talents they have. What special needs did you discover?
2. Why may we speak of a "new approach" to old age today?
3. What are some of the chief physical problems which older adults experience? What are some of the solutions which need to be provided by family and community?
4. Select three of the eight basic spiritual needs of older adults and indicate what your congregation is now doing to meet those needs.
5. What adjustments should older persons make in the decade immediately preceding retirement?
6. Keeping your own congregation in mind, set up a program of action to serve the aging family more adequately, listing items according to priority.

SELECTED REFERENCES

Arthur, Julietta K. *How to Help Older People.* 500 pp. Lippincott. 1954.

National Council of Churches. *The Fulfillment Years in Christian Education.* 1953.

Ray, Marie Beynon. *The Best Years of Your Life.* Little, Brown & Co. 1952.

Breckinridge, Elizabeth. *Society's Utilization of Man's Eventide.* Welfare Bulletin. Illinois Department of Public Welfare. 1950.

Hiltner, Seward. "Growing Older." Article in *Presbyterian Life.* March 18, 1950.

Lawton, George, and Stewart, Maxwell S. *When You Grow Older.* Public Affairs Pamphlet No. 131. Second Revised Edition. Feb. 1954.

Crampton, C. Ward. *Live Long and Like It.* Public Affairs Pamphlet No. 139. 1948.

Close, Kathryn. *Getting Ready to Retire.* Public Affairs Pamphlet No. 182. 1942.

Ogg, Elizabeth. *When Parents Grow Old.* Public Affairs Pamphlet No. 208. 1954.

Lawton, George. *Aging Successfully.* New York: Columbia University Press. 1946.

Lawton, George, Ed. *New Goals for Old Age.* New York: Columbia University Press. 1943.

Maves, Paul, and Cedarleaf, J. Lennart. *Older People and the Church.* Abingdon-Cokesbury. 1949.

Chapter 27

Christian Family Week

Oscar E. Feucht

---

1. History and Value

CHRISTIAN FAMILY WEEK, as an extension of Mothers Day, has been observed in the United States since 1941. The week from the first to the second Sunday in May, inclusive, has since that time been set aside as Family Week and is observed by almost all church groups. Sometimes termed National Family Week, it has received many presidential endorsements and has become truly national in scope. Civic groups and educational societies support it with their programs. Tens of thousands of churches now observe it, and millions of families are involved in this Christian home festival. The press has given liberal space both in general and feature articles. Radio and television have opened their channels to this special emphasis on the family. From year to year Family Week has been gaining in momentum.

Also in the church year there are many special days which permit an emphasis on the Christian home; for instance, the First Sunday after Epiphany when the Gospel lesson refers to the holy family. Experience, however, has shown that incidental references in sermons and an occasional special sermon are not enough properly to equip parish or parents for the teaching function of the home. Christian education is emphasized in September with a special Religious Education Week. The Christian home, because of its significance, also deserves special emphasis; and May is a suitable time. Church leaders have long felt the need of devoting at least one Sunday to the entire family rather than restricting that day to honor mainly the mother in the household. Civic leaders have recognized that it is most wholesome for a whole nation to set aside time when it thinks constructively of its homes.

Our own church has, since 1949, observed Christian Family Week and has developed special plans in its co-ordinated church program. At the Centennial Convention it passed a comprehensive resolution on the family asking "every parish to plan a constructive program to strengthen the Christian home."[1] In its 1956 convention it said, "We encourage our congregations to observe Christian Family Week, the first to the second Sunday of May inclusive, and that local boards of education use this occasion to evaluate and strengthen the year-round program of winning and serving families for Christ."

2. Purpose of Family Week

The entire concern and program of the local church on behalf of its families is to be spearheaded by the observance of Christian Family Week. We may think of it as having a threefold purpose: (1) to focus attention on basic family needs, (2) to review the past year's program and work with families, and (3) to strengthen this program as it is to be carried out in the year that lies ahead.

Christian Family Week calls attention to a basic need. While throughout the year there is a strong enlistment of the family on behalf of the church, Christian Family Week helps to enlist the church on behalf of the family. The future of the church, as well as of the nation, is dependent on the caliber of the families that make up church and nation. History and sociology give ample verification to the fact that good order, peace, and civilization itself break down when there are serious disturbances in the home life. Juvenile delinquency in our own country has come up for attention in such a consistent manner in the last decade that it is regarded by the best authorities as a serious malady. Christian people likewise have important family needs that can best be satisfied by the church. For instance, they need a better understanding of the Christian nurture of children and young people; they need a more constructive and distinctively Christian attitude toward marriage; they need help in undergirding the entire family structure with the Christian faith and with the application of Christian virtues; they need guidance in Christian family living, husband-wife, and parent-child relation-

---

[1] *Proceedings,* 1949, p. 311, The Lutheran Church — Missouri Synod.

ships. Young people need help with a Christian interpretation of sex and an adequate preparation for marriage and home-making. All families need help with regard to family worship and fulfilling the educational function of the home. Both home and church will profit from a closer co-operation between parents and teachers.

Christian Family Week is the ideal time to review the past year's program and work with the families of the parish. To what extent have family applications been made in the total curriculum? What results in terms of better understanding and Christian behavior are discernible as a result of training for Christian family living? What are the strong points, and what are the weak points, in the existing program? How much of the ten-point program of Christian family education is being carried out? — (Thorough Christian indoctrination, family worship, home visitation, marriage counseling, educating adults for marriage, parenthood, family living, guiding children and youth in Christian family living, serving the aging family, literature for the family, planning and observing Christian Family Week.)

Every few years a congregation should examine itself to learn how many young, middle-aged, and old families make up the parish. Just what is the family complexion of the congregation? At what point is help needed most, and how can it be given? What part of the program needs emphasis during the coming year? Are all classes, groups, and agencies participating? Are they enlisted and trained for the task?

Looking at the past should, however, be only the springboard for greater efficiency in the future. And so Christian Family Week will be used to strengthen the program, making it more functional: (1) to weave it into the work done with children in the Christian day school and Sunday school and vacation Bible school; (2) to apply it in the work done with the youth through the youth societies and high school and young people's Bible classes; (3) to integrate it with the program of young adults, middle-aged adults, and older adults, whenever and wherever they meet. The planning council of the church, under the leadership of the board of education, should clearly set forth its aim for the year, agree on what should be done, suggest materials, methods, and leadership, and enlist the whole congregation in the process.

Where Christian Family Week is observed with a practical, life-related program, it will make a real impact. It is significant that the church, through the ages, has spoken of the home as the primary institution of God and as the most potent teaching agency of the church. The home is also vital for the welfare of state, nation, and world. It is significant that J. Edgar Hoover, director of the Federal Bureau of Investigation, says: "If there is any hope for the future of America, if there is to be peace and happiness in our homes, then we as a nation must return to God and the practice of family prayer. . . . A godless home is built upon sands; it is an inviting breeding ground for moral decay and crime. My hope for the future of this nation is predicated upon the faith in God which is nurtured in the family."

3. Annual Theme and Program

Family life education is related to the total parish program and should not be separated from it. Yet, because it is so vital, it is well from year to year to focus on one area at a time, making this the center of a fresh approach. How the annual theme and program contribute to this fresh approach will be seen as we review the emphases which one church has presented during the past eight years. We shall indicate the theme and some of the significant materials prepared each year.

1949 — *Theme:* Christ Our Guest. *Materials:* Information Bulletin, *A Family Life Program for the Parish.*

1950 — *Theme:* Build the Family Altar. *Materials:* Tract "Pray Together — Stay Together"; article on "Seven Patterns of Family Worship."

1951 — *Theme:* Making Home Life Christian. *Materials:* Appearance of the Christian Family Standard, entitled "Our Family."

1952 — *Theme:* Let Us Show Love at Home. *Materials:* Tract by the same title; appearance of the first of the Parent Guidance Series booklets "Your Child and You."

1953 — *Theme:* Succeeding in Marriage. *Materials:* Tract by the same title; Parent Guidance booklet No. 2 *Making Home Life Christian.*

1954 — *Theme:* Family Worship. *Materials:* Tract "Why Family Worship"; film "Faith of Our Families"; Information Bulletin, *Building Family Altars in Your Parish;* Parent Guidance booklet No. 3, *Happiness is Homemade.* (Christian Family Week initiated a year-long emphasis on home devotions.)

1955 — *Theme:* Rally the Home for Christ. *Materials:* Tract "The Home for Christ"; Parent Guidance booklet No. 4, *Teen-Agers Need Parents.* Emphasis on "Church-Home Co-operation."

1956 — *Theme:* Youth Today — Parents Tomorrow. *Materials:* Tract with same title; Parent Guidance booklet No. 5, *Guiding the Young Child.*

Each year *Parish Activities,* first appearing in 1947 as a separate annual plan book, and since 1955 as the June issue of *Advance,*[2] has carried a complete list of varied suggestions for the observance of the whole month of May as Family Month. It provides topic outlines, Bible study materials, congregational and community projects, and calls attention to books, tracts, and audio-visual aids. The suggestions always include what the church and the pastor can do and what families can do.

4. What the Pastor Can Do

The pastor alerts his congregation to the opportunities and responsibilities it has in regard to the families that make up the congregation, and to the families which constitute the neighborhood where God has placed the church. The pastor supplies the necessary background and information, giving insight particularly to the officers and teachers of the church. He works with the Sunday school superintendent and other leaders in the selection and training of persons who can give intelligent leadership to family life education. Above all, the parish looks to its pastor to give the motivation and the incentives that are founded in the Gospel of Jesus Christ. In a great many instances it will be the pastor who initiates a constructive program through the board of elders and board of education. One of the greatest contributions, however, that the pastor can make is to develop a family-centered ministry by his own teaching, preaching, missionary work, and the shepherding of his flock. As he himself ministers

---

[2] *Advance,* a Journal of Practical Church Work, The Lutheran Church — Missouri Synod.

to the entire family and helps to meet its needs, he sets the pattern for, and develops, a model which the whole congregation may follow.

5. What the Congregation Can Do

The board of elders should be interested particularly in increasing the contact of the church with the home through regular visitations on the part of the pastor, church officers, teachers, and other lay workers. Elders or deacons will want to assimilate new families into the congregation and help marginal families, strengthening those that need spiritual help. The board of elders may also spearhead a definite program to increase and improve family worship, so that, not merely 25 per cent but 50 to 75 per cent of the families make fruitful use of this splendid practice.

To the board of education falls the lot of strengthening the whole program of service to the home. It may well write into its regulations the words "to help all agencies develop a service program to the Christian home through effective family life education." Planning a Christian family week, and carrying out family-life education in general, will be one of its important assignments.

Through these official boards the congregation can be led to do many constructive things. We shall list some of them:

(1) *Special church services during Family Week:* utilizing hymns, sermon, prayer, special litanies, the *Christian Family Standard* to focus attention on Christian family living.

(2) *Study groups for parents, young married couples, older adults:* set up during the Sunday school hour as a Bible class, or in connection with the congregation's program for men, women, and couples.

(3) *Family nights:* showing a film or filmstrip, discussion of a vital family topic in three separate sections (adults, young people, children), having an exhibit of materials on the family; fellowship and recreation.

(4) *Parent-teacher conferences.* These are needed in every congregation. Study materials and much helpful guidance for parents and teachers are available. Family Week supplies the incentive for greater church-home co-operation.

(5) *Integration into lessons and programs.* All teachers will

need help with weaving family-life approaches and applications
into the regular Sunday school lessons; into the program of worship, study, and service of youth, men, women, couples.

(6) *Family enlistment:* setting up a policy for reaching the
parents when the child enrolls in the church school, with a definite program to win and to serve the total family for Christ.

(7) *Family worship projects.* The booklet *Building Family
Altars in Your Parish* shows the many ways in which congregations can concretely foster family devotions.

(8) *Bible reading program.* Churches have greatly increased
Bible reading in the home with a special Bible reading schedule
(for Advent or Lent), and with the introduction of a daily Bible
reading guide such as, *Light For Your Way.*

(9) *Demonstration.* There are a number of short plays available to demonstrate family worship. Other demonstrations may
be given on marriage counseling, family visitation, etc.

(10) *Home visitation:* visiting all the families of the congregation through a group of trained workers with a special purpose
in mind, such as, introducing the *Christian Family Standard.*

(11) *Literature:* a display of books, an exhibit of tracts, placing books for the family in the church library, putting a family-
guidance tract rack in the church vestibule, using the *General
Family Packet,*[3] home visiting on the part of pastor, teachers,
elders.

(12) *Christian home magazine:* introducing one of the Christian family magazines of the church to help parents to help themselves.

(13) *Audio visuals.* There are many fine films, filmstrips,
recordings that can be introduced during Christian Family Week,
for instance, some of the "This Is the Life" films on Christian
living.

(14) *Leadership training.* Christian Family Week is a good
time to conduct a workers' institute in your own congregation
to give leaders further insights and skills for family-life education.

---

[3] Concordia Publishing House.

(15) *Home dedications.* Make available suitable materials
that can be employed in the dedication of a new home.

The congregation will work chiefly through its educational
agencies and organizations from the nursery department to the
golden-age group, and from the pulpit to the primary department.
As all teachers and workers unite in focusing on a single aim,
a lasting impact will be made. Every year the men's league, the
youth league, and the women's league focus their topics during
the month of May on some aspect of the Christian home. What
can be done in the schoolroom, the Sunday school department,
the youth league, women's league, and the men's club is limited
only by our imagination and our initiative.

One church has an annual "wedding bells" party for all those
married during the past year. Another church annually arranges
a social for young mothers. A congregation in Massachusetts
utilizes the leaders of all groups and classes with a diversified
week-long program. In the month previous the pastor fills out
a family profile of the congregation; in the previous week every
family in the church is sent the *Self-Analysis Chart for the
Home.*[4] The sermon on the first Sunday introduces the family
theme. On *Monday* evening the church council conducts a family
night to discover the needs and problems of the Christian family
and to give guidance toward solutions. On *Tuesday* evening the
ladies' guild provides a helpful discussion for the mothers of children from one to six. On *Wednesday* evening the young people's
society, in close collaboration with the youth department of the
Sunday school, discusses ways to bring about a better understanding between young people and their parents. On *Thursday*
afternoon a women's circle sets up a program for mothers of
children aged six to thirteen with regard to the Christian training in the home. On *Friday* the Sunday school staff arranges for
a family fellowship evening. On the second Sunday the congregation closes its observance with another worship service devoted
to the Family Week theme.

6. Outreach to the Community

Several Oklahoma churches have very successfully reached
all families of their own neighborhoods during Christian Family

---

[4] Concordia Publishing House.

Week through a house to house canvass with a special family packet. This packet included a friendly letter, a picture of Christ, a tract on family worship, a list of Bible readings, a devotional booklet, and a family worship covenant entitled "Our Home Shall Be a Home of Prayer," with a form for a brief home dedication on the reverse side.[5] The radio was used to present daily Family Worship Hour transcriptions.[6] In the local congregation stimulus was given with the showing of the film "Bible on the Table."

The opportunities to reach the neighborhood by means of quality radio and television programs are very great. One nationally used broadcast increased its coverage during Christian Family Week by 40 per cent simply because radio stations were more receptive to appropriate messages for National Family Week. Merchants will be willing to offer window-display space if an effective family exhibit is arranged by an individual church or by a group of churches. You will find the public library cooperative in arranging special book reviews and putting out special book exhibits that revolve about the home and homemaking. Editors of newspapers will receive not only releases with regard to Family Week observances in local churches, but in many places will be ready for feature stories.

National Family Week offers a splendid opportunity to reach beyond the four walls of the church into the homes of the community.

7. What the Family Can Do

Families should arrange to make their own home devotions especially meaningful during Family Week and to engage in spiritual conversation. Some churches have outlined different subjects for each day of the week. To develop family togetherness, the family council needs to be introduced much more widely. Most families need the opportunity of having a family meeting at least once a month. The topics of discussion should grow out of the needs of each family. They should be proposed by children as well as parents. For instance, how can all participate in family worship? How can we spend more time to-

---

[5] Broadman Press, Nashville, Tenn.

[6] Available to radio stations without cost by the Lutheran Laymen's League.

gether as a family? Are we meeting our recreational needs as
Christians should? How can we work together in remodeling
our home? What rules should apply with regard to the use of
the family car? What would be the advantages of giving an allowance to each child? How late should teen-age members of the
family be permitted to stay out? Frequently problems continue
and increase because families never take time to approach these
problems constructively and to work out some solutions.

Are our families developing a good sense of hospitality?
Do the families of the congregation visit one another, or is their
visiting restricted mainly to relatives?

New families are best assimilated as other families of the
church make them feel at home and provide the opportunity to
get better acquainted.

Families that have moved into a new home should be encouraged to conduct a home-dedication service. They may wish to
invite the pastor to read a fitting Scripture portion and to say
a special prayer, or they may wish to work out a simple service
of their own: a hymn, the responsive reading of Psalms 127
and 128, a simple prayer for God's blessings, and the reading of
the *Christian Family Standard* and the poem "Bless This House."

Families today are prone to get their entertainment outside
the home or by watching television or listening to the radio. As
a result, the old-fashioned family hymnsings are diminishing in
number. This is a serious loss, since singing songs and hymns
together does very much to weld families and relationships together. Hymnsings in the youth and adult groups should be the
patterns for hymnsings conducted in connection with family worship or on family nights at home.

While the church, of necessity, calls young people and adults
to functions in the parish house or conducts family nights, it is
equally important that the congregation encourage families to
stay at home and spend time together, not only on holidays or
on vacations but as part of the regular weekly routine of living.

8. Who Should Take the Lead?

The minister, the shepherd of the family of God; the board
of education, chosen to help fulfill Deut. 6: 6, 7; the teachers and
group leaders, who co-operate with parents; the fathers and
mothers, entrusted with children by the Lord; the husbands and

wives, pledged to sanctify their marriage and to build a Christian home.

We do not need any human resolutions to tell us what God has already indicated should be done. Almost every parish has selected a number of persons and has charged them with the development of an adequate educational program. The suggestions for Christian Family Week only remind them of things already entrusted to them and suggest means by which they can be achieved.

A celebration or public observance is never an end in itself. It is only a means to an end. Yet if nothing is said and done, how will the people get the necessary motivation and specific direction they need for building the Christian home?

It has been well said that the church has the greatest thing to be learned, the Gospel of Jesus Christ, and that the home is the most effective means for sharing this greatest good with each succeeding generation.

When Patrick Henry lay dying, he called his children around him and said: "I am about to leave you all my earthly possessions. There is one more thing which I would like to leave to you, namely, the Christian faith. If I could leave you that and nothing else, you would be rich indeed. If I could leave you everything else and not that, you would be poor indeed."

DISCUSSION QUESTIONS

1. Clip the directives and collect all materials your church has provided for the observance of Christian Family Week. Then write a one-page story on the observance in your parish. How would you improve the program?
2. How would you define the purpose of National Family Week (community sponsored)? Of Christian Family Week (church-sponsored, community-sponsored)?
3. Compare the materials made available by the church body (denomination) for the guidance of families with that made available by a single local church in its library, tract rack, study program.
4. With your own congregation in mind, which congregational project would you propose for the next three Christian family weeks?
5. What community projects should be explored during National Family Week in your town?
6. Have a panel discussion on the family council.

SELECTED REFERENCES

Board for Parish Education. *Parish Education.* March, April, May issues, 1949 to 1954.

The Lutheran Church — Missouri Synod. *Advance.* March, April, May issues, 1955, 1956.

National Council of Churches. *International Journal of Religious Education.* April 1941.

Board for Parish Education. *Parish Activities.* 1949 to 1954.

National Council of Churches. *Annual Family Week Releases* (tracts, etc.).

National Sunday School Association. *Family Week Suggestions.*

Denominational Family Week Materials.

PART VI

Materials for Family Life Education

(I) Congregational Family Profile Form

(II) What Is Your Church Doing to Prepare Its Constituency?

(III) A Check List for the Christian Family

(IV) How to Reach Fringe Families

(V) A Year's Program for a Parent-Teacher Group

(VI) Premarital Counseling Guide for Pastors

(VII) A Check List for the Christian Congregation

(VIII) Selected, Annotated Bibliography

(IX) Selected, Annotated Audio Visual Aids

CONGREGATIONAL FAMILY PROFILE FORM

Form 201
Board for Parish Education
The Lutheran Church — Missouri Synod

INSTRUCTIONS FOR FILLING OUT FAMILY PROFILE FORM

The attached form will help you discover the family complexion of your congregation. Take your congregational list and place before the name of the head of each family the classifying number 1 to 12 that applies to that family. Notice that *most* of the families that fall into category 3 will also fall into either category 4 or 5, which are partial subdivisions of category 3. This applies also to category 8 (of which 9 and 10 are partial subdivisions).

This profile is concerned basically with *families,* and you should fill out the profile accordingly. A family is a group of *two* or more persons related by blood, marriage, or adoption, and living together. Unmarried communicants *not living in the parental home* are to be listed in categories 14 to 14b. Unchurched parents and children are to be listed in category 13 to 13b.

Note the age divisions. The age of the older spouse determines the age section into which the *entire* family will fall.

Every family and every unmarried communicant will fall into one of the categories under column "A." Notice that *some* families and some unmarried communicants will *also* be listed in some of the other columns, "B" to "E."

(This is a guide for classifying *families,* not individuals).

This profile and the whole Family Life Program of your church have been designed to help you. This profile can serve you best if it is filled out conscientiously and accurately. At a glance it provides you with a general picture of the family complexion of your congregation. The sub-categories provide a more detailed breakdown. No two congregations are exactly alike. One will have many young couples, another may have many older adults.

The chief purpose of the profile is to provide a factual basis on which to develop a service to families. *The profile will indicate largely what type of family life education is suited to your parish.*

(Note 1) To help you we give the following illustration: A congregation has 25 families with more than 1 child (3), of these families 15 have children 0—12 years (4), 22 have children 0—12 years AND 13—18 years (5). This means that there are 7 families with children 13—18 years and 3 families with children over 18.*

* (Note 2) Children in military training or college should be classified as at home and included. For the purpose of this survey the term "child" includes *unmarried* persons up to age 18; thereafter such person to be classified as an adult.

(Note 3) "Persons under Christian Instruction" here means children and adults enrolled in Sunday school or any adult class not attached to "families" in categories 1 to 12.

(Note 4) "Unmarried communicants not living in parental home," for instance, the young lady who comes from country to city and attends Grace Church but lives at YWCA.

FAMILY PROFILE FORM

ongregation: _____ Address: _____

o. of Communicants: _____ (circle one): Metropolitan Urban Suburban Rural

o. of Families: _____ If you serve several congregations, check here ☐

ate: _____

	A (Total No.)	B (Mixed Rel.)	C (H. or W. unch.)	D (Widow; Widower)	E (Divorced)
FAMILIES WITH BOTH SPOUSES UNDER 40 YEARS OLD:					
1. Husband and/or wife (no children in home)					
2. Father and/or mother with *only* 1 child in home					
3. Father and/or mother with *more* than 1 child in home					

Families with —
  4. Children age 0—12 years: _____
  5. Children age 0—12 & 13—18: _____

	A	B	C	D	E
FAMILIES WITH OLDER SPOUSE 40—65 YEARS:					
6. Husband and/or wife (no children in home)					
7. Father and/or mother with *only* 1 child in home					
8. Father and/or mother with *more* than 1 child in home					

Families with —
  9. Children age 0—12 years: _____
  10. Children age 0—12 & 13—18: _____

	A	B	C	D	E
FAMILIES WITH OLDER SPOUSE OVER 65 YEARS:					
11. Husband and/or wife living alone					
12. Husband and/or wife living with children or others					
TOTALS					

INDIVIDUALS NOT INCLUDED IN ANY OF THE ABOVE CATEGORIES

	A	B	C	D	E
13. Persons under instruction from unchurched homes					

   13a. Children (up to 18), No. of families

   13b. Adults (18 up), No. of families _____

	A	B	C	D	E
14. Unmarried communicants not living in parental home		✕✕	✕✕		

   14a. Adults under 40, No. of families _____
   14b. Adults over 40, No. of families _____

THE FAMILIES OF _____

CONGREGATION

This bar graph form indicates how you may visualize for your congregation its family complexion. Combine totals of 2 and 3 and again of 7 and 8. Reduce figures to percentages. Using the percentage scale at left fill (shade) in the bars or columns.

O. E. F.

"Other" Individuals
- (14) Unmarried communicants not living "at home"
- (13) Children and adults unchurched

Families "over 65"
- (12) Living with children or others
- (11) Husband & wife only

Families "40 to 65"
- (7) & (8) Having children
- (6) Husband & wife only

Families "under 40"
- (2) & (3) Having children
- (1) Husband & Wife only

Percent

100
95
90
85
80
75
70
65
60
55
50
45
40
35
30
25
20
15
10
5

(What types of Family Life Service in your parish are indicated by this survey?)

Form 201-A (Alternate)

FAMILY PROFILE FORM

Congregation: _____ Address: _____

No. of Communicants: _____ (circle one): Metropolitan   Urban   Suburban   Rural

No. of Families: _____ If you serve several congregations, check here ☐

Date: _____

FAMILIES WITH BOTH SPOUSES
Under 40 years old:

Having NO children	
Having children	
Total	

FAMILIES WITH OLDER SPOUSE
40—65 years old:

Having NO children	
Having children	
Total	

FAMILIES WITH OLDER SPOUSE
Over 65 years old:

Living alone	
Living with others	
Total	

TOTAL NUMBER OF FAMILIES WITH Children and youth at home	
TOTAL NUMBER OF FAMILIES Having no children at home	

NOTE: This alternate form is submitted for those who do not have adequate records or the secretarial help needed to fill out the more complete profile form. It will yield quick results but is not a complete substitute for the larger form. For definition of terms see the larger form.

WHAT IS YOUR CHURCH DOING

to prepare its constituency? *

Please check or fill blanks where blanks are found.

1. Training for marriage and family life in this church:

    _____ Is given no consideration

    _____ Is entirely incidental

    _____ Is taught in courses with this specific purpose

    __✓__ Is given some attention in general courses

2. If you do have definite courses for this training, they were begun about the year _____, and because the need was felt by:

    _____ Denominational   _____ Church leaders

    leaders   _____ Parents

    _____ Pastors   _____ Youth

3. The approximate per cent of the following groups are receiving this training:

    _____ Children   _____ Youth   _____ Parents

4. This training includes such topics as are checked:

    _____ Premarital education   _____ Parent and child relation-

    _____ Sex education   ships

    _____ Marriage adjustment   _____ Child training and care

    _____ Church and the home   _____ Culture and art in the

    _____ Family finance   home

    _____ Vocational guidance   _____ Leisure and recreation

    _____ Building friendships   _____ Others

5. The avenues of approach are those checked:

    _____ Sunday school classes   _____ Short courses

    _____ Youth and adult   _____ Lecture series

    Bible classes   _____ Young people's

    _____ Special clubs   leagues

    _____ Vacation schools   _____ Summer assemblies

    _____ Group conferences   _____ Others

---

* Prepared by a university student in family-life education course.

6. For this training we use leaders:

   _____ Untrained   _____ Religious education
   _____ Locally trained   directors
   _____ Pastors   _____ Others
   _____ Specialists

7. In this church the work is:

   _____ Independent
   _____ In co-operation with other churches of this denomination
   _____ In co-operation with other denominations
   _____ In co-operation with community agencies and public schools

8. Training more of an incidental nature is provided through the methods checked:

   _____ Specialists' occasional   _____ Guided reading courses
          lectures   _____ Family night programs
   _____ Series of sermons or   _____ Boy Scouts
          "Fireside Talks"   _____ Girl Scouts
   _____ Treated in general   _____ Others
          training courses

9. Teaching materials for these courses are:

   _____ Prepared by local leaders
   _____ Sent out from demoninational headquarters
   _____ Selected from various sources

10. Reading materials are provided in the following ways:

    _____ Circulated through church library
    _____ Co-operating public library
    _____ Church giving pamphlet literature
    _____ Pastor's lending shelf
    _____ Others

11. To create appreciation for the home we foster and observe:

    _____ Home dedication   _____ Fellowship evenings in
    _____ Home visitation week   church
    _____ Home arts week   _____ Dedication of parents
    _____ Family go-to-church   _____ Infant Baptism
           weeks   _____ Others
    _____ Christian Family Week

12. Outside agencies with which we co-operate in this work are:

   _____ Parent-teacher   _____ Institute of family rela-
        association   tions
   _____ Juvenile court   _____ Court of domestic rela-
   _____ YMCA   tions
   _____ Council of Churches   _____ YWCA
                                            _____ Others

13. This field of training seems to have the following effects on the regular program of the church:

   _____ No effect
   _____ Decreased time for other vital work
   _____ Decreased interest in other work
   _____ Increased interest of parents _____ of youth
   _____ Unified home and church
   _____ Broadened service of church to community
   _____ Increased interest of community in church
   _____ Developed more stable constituency
   _____ Brought all the family into the church program
   _____ Others

14. Judging from the types of marriage and home life today, what opinion have you of:

   A. Need for training for marriage and family life through the church? _____

   _____

   B. Efficiency of the training the churches are giving in this field? _____

   _____

15. May your church families have consultation on problems of the home through:

   _____ Co-operating agencies   _____ Referred to public profes-
   _____ Church-employed   sional agencies
        counselors   _____ Pastor
                                            _____ Others

16. The pastor employs the following means for preparing the betrothed for marriage:

_____ None

_____ 1—5 hours counseling

_____ Parents' knowledge of wedding

_____ Courses in premarital training _____ (number of weeks)

_____ Require physical examination certificates

_____ Publishing intention to wed

_____ Others

17. Books you recommend for betrothed and newlyweds:

(III)

A CHECK LIST
for
THE CHRISTIAN FAMILY

For Husband and Wife
Father and Mother
Children and Young People
Other Adults in Family

I. The Church in the Home

If it were not for the church, there would be no Christian homes. Check your home on:

1) _____ Table prayers are used regularly
2) _____ Bible stories to children
3) _____ Help given with Bible lessons
4) _____ Family devotions held regularly
5) _____ Prayers include family needs specifically
6) _____ Prayers for nation, peace, armed forces
7) _____ Each member says own evening prayers
8) _____ Each member does private Bible reading
9) _____ We practice Christian love (forbearance, kindness)

II. The Church-Going Family

The church preserves and gives to us the Bible. The Bible gives us God and security, Christ and salvation. The church blesses our children, shelters our youth, solemnizes marriage and home life, keeps us with Christ. Helps us conquer evil, meet life's emergencies and problems. Stands by our loved ones in war and peace. Through the church Christ gives us peace, hope, comfort, wisdom, character, purpose. Check your family on:

1) Church attendance as a family is _____ weekly, _____ bi-weekly, _____ spasmodic, _____ seasonal?
2) _____ Every adult goes to church regularly
3) _____ The children attend worship services regularly
4) _____ We are helping to preserve Sunday for study and worship
5) _____ Going to church is a profitable, joyful experience

III. The Whole Family in God's School

Christian education is a lifelong process. No one is truly educated who does not know his Bible. The Sunday school is not to be a children's school but the whole church at school. Confirmation should not be the end of real study. Check your family on:

1) ...... Children regularly in Sunday school
2) ...... Eligible children in weekday classes (day school, released time)
3) ...... Use vacation Bible school
4) ...... High school young people in Bible class
5) ...... Young people in Bible class
6) ...... Adults in Bible class

IV. The Family as Kingdom Workers

Faith must be put into practice. Christians are the only witnesses Christ has on earth. The Kingdom of God will be built if, under God's blessings, we will build it. Check your family on:

1) ...... Assuming the Goal of Souls as our part in winning others for Christ.
2) ...... Christian influence in your community
3) ...... Adults of family in church work
4) ...... Youth of family working in the church
5) ...... We give children projects to train them for service to Jesus
6) ...... We have concern for our congregation as "the Family of God"
7) ...... We are interested in the work of our church throughout the world

V. The Family and Christian Living

In the home Christian faith, hope, and love should find expression first. A religion that is lived at home will be lived everywhere. The Christian home is the nursery of Christian character. Check your family on:

1) ...... Reverence and respect for God
2) ...... Respect for parents, church, government

3) .... Wholesome relations between parents and children

4) .... Christian example given in all matters

5) .... Language used in the home is reverent and chaste

6) .... Christian ideals maintained in reading, recreation, entertainment, associations

7) .... Attention to character training continuous

8) .... Faith regarded as a living relationship to Jesus

9) .... Life itself regarded as a trusteeship from God

10) .... General spirit of the home is Christian

VI. The Christian Family and the World

The church gives us converted people. The church is to be the salt of the earth. Ninety per cent of the moral and spiritual power of a city comes from the church. Do you recognize the value of the church:

1) .... For your personal character and moral life?

2) .... For your success in business or work?

3) .... For the well-being of our nation?

4) .... For world peace? (A lasting peace must have a spiritual basis)

5) .... For your preservation in the true faith?

HOME VISITATION
CALVARY LUTHERAN CHURCH
Kansas City, Missouri

(IV)
HOW TO REACH "FRINGE FAMILIES"

By "fringe families" the marginal or inactive families of the local church are meant. Every church has a considerable number of these.

One pastor analyzes his large church of 1,600 communicant members as follows:

Nuclear (dynamic Christians)	3 per cent
Modal (faithful followers)	37 per cent
Marginal (indifferent or inactive)	50 per cent
Dormant (disinterested)	10 per cent

This is confirmed by another church of 1,550 communicant members, of which only 860 are considered active (55.5 per cent).

One family workshop (summer 1955) made the following suggestions toward a constructive program. It is recommended that church boards begin their discussion with these points and develop a constructive and practical program of service to the weaker family.

I. Right Attitudes and Genuine Concern

1. A brotherly attitude and constructive approach (Romans 14; 1 Thess. 5:14; Heb. 12:12, 13); evangelical helpfulness.
2. A family-centered ministry. A sense of mission to the home. Evangelizing the whole family.
3. Giving priority to the spiritually weak with regard to pastoral care. Frequently the physically ill get more attention than the spiritually ill.

II. Better Contact and Service

4. Good record keeping and soul-accounting. Up-to-date lists and addresses. Reporting absences, illness, births, deaths, crises. Prompt follow-up calls.
5. Use a twofold approach where there are children. Go to the parents to enroll the children and enlist parental help with lessons. Ask the children to enlist parents for church and Sunday school and lesson help.
6. Regular elder visitation. Organization of parish into zones

with one elder and assisting deacons in charge of each zone. (One large church arranges for a monthly visit!)

7. Pastoral contact is essential. His insights are usually needed to reach marginal and dormant families. Here deeper problems must be dealt with.

8. An active family sponsors an inactive family — to maintain closer contact, establish needs, and give helpful service.

9. An organized home visitation at least once a year with trained volunteer workers reaching all families; definite purpose, materials for each visit. For instance: How to establish or improve family worship.

10. Consistent, intercessory prayer for such families by pastor, elders, sponsors, members; remembering the special needs of each family.

11. Teachers and workers should assume the responsibility of helping members of such families to meet life's problems through personal counseling.

12. Workers trained to emphasize Christian discipleship rather than church membership and the collection of money; the glories, joys, and privileges of the Christian calling, rather than admonition without the Gospel.

13. Help these people rediscover the security, peace, hope, purpose we have through faith in Christ; the values of faith for everyday living, for life's crises, for eternal life. This can be done privately or in cottage meetings.

14. Interpret the church as a fellowship of believers, mutually helpful to one another (the church is people!), building the Kingdom of God in the hearts of men. Christians *are* the salt of the earth.

15. Help families overcome their grievances by the application of Christ's love, the spirit of forgiveness, fitting Scripture passages. Grievances can be overcome!

16. Help the family with its problems, such as, religious differences, marital discord, problem children, etc. Use materials in the General Family Packet to give such help.

17. Strengthen your program of presentation: An effective Christian growth program for youth (being used!), an effective adult education program (that reaches also marginal families).

III. A Positive Program for Teaching the Practical Skills After Reception into the Church

The workshop felt that most congregations need to give better attention to the assimilation of new members into Christian life, and that frequently the new member is not sufficiently helped with the development of the practices, habits, and skills of Christian discipleship. These were listed as follows —

Skills and Practices to Be Developed

Understanding of, and participation in, public worship
Personal Bible use on a regular basis
Spiritual consecration and witnessing for Christ
Personal prayer habits and skills
Group Bible study "to grow up into Christ"
Ability to make family worship fruitful
Participation in the functions of congregation and Synod
Acquaintance with, and reading of, church periodicals
Developing a growing sense of the stewardship life.

(V)

A YEAR'S PROGRAM FOR A PARENT-TEACHER GROUP

September: Teaching Our Children to Pray
    (*Advance,* June 1956, September Topic)
    Scene I — Class Demonstration
    Scene II — Home Demonstration

October: Building Christian Attitudes
    (*Parent Guidance Book* No. 5)
    A panel discussion: pastor, teacher, a father, a mother

November: The Teaching Parent
    Book Review and Discussion: *The Modern Parent and the Teaching Church* by Wesner Fallaw, followed by buzz groups on "Why is the home so important?" etc.

December: Keeping Christ in Home, School, Church
    Topic Discussion: When and how do we teach *evangelically* in church, home, school?

January: Teaching Missions to Our Children
    (*Advance,* June 1956, January Topic)
    (*Parent Guidance Book* No. 3)
    Missionary play by children, followed by a panel discussion.

February: Fundamental Needs of Every Child
    (*Parent Guidance Books* No. 1 and No. 5)
    Invite a Christian psychologist for a lecture or interview.

March: How the Child Grows Toward God
    (*Parent Guidance Book* No. 5)
    Three sectional meetings, each taking up same topic:
        (1) Parents of preschool children
        (2) Parents of children 6—11
        (3) Parents of children 12 and up — also parents of high school youth

April: Youth Today — Parents Tomorrow
    (Tract with same title)
    Invite a pastor, educator, judge to discuss topic, or use panel.

May: Talent Night
    Tableau by school or Sunday school class. Children, teachers, parents selected who have special talent to demonstrate.

PREMARITAL COUNSELING GUIDE FOR PASTORS

Prepared by Granger E. Westberg
Chaplain, Augustana Hospital, Chicago, Ill.

(This can be used by pastors in their premarital counseling, with the pastor giving the couple a copy after the session is over; or it can be used as a score sheet for young people to use in evaluating and predicting marriage success with the person with whom they are now going.)

Do not be too rigid in scoring this guide. For example, in question 8, on engagement, if couple has been engaged one month, score 0; if two months, score 5; if three months, score 10. Use similar discretion in all other questions. The counselor will find himself using a sliding scale, depending upon his knowledge of the couple and his interpretation of the answers given.

THE SCORE IS NOT IMPORTANT. The purpose of this guide is to help the counselor in getting the couple to express themselves, to insure coverage of all important subjects and to eliminate the lecture form of premarital counseling. Low scores on many of the questions do not necessarily mean future unhappiness. This guide serves merely to ALERT THE COUPLE BEFORE MARRIAGE TO POSSIBLE POINTS OF FRICTION which can be overcome by mature love and Christian understanding.

	None	One	Two or more
1. How many brothers and sisters do you have? Man	(0)	(10)	(15)
Woman	(0)	(10)	(15)

	Same	Fairly Similar	Very Dissimilar
2. Comparative nationalistic and cultural background:	(20)	(10)	(0)

	Each the same	Man more than woman	Woman more
3. Comparative amount of education:	(15)	(10)	(0)

4. Comparative ages: **Similar**   **Very**
                                                    Dissimilar
                              (15)   (5)

5. Comparative occupations: **Both   Fairly   Very**
                             same   similar   dissimilar
                             type
                             (10)   (5)   (0)

6. Work Record: **Regularly**   **Irregularly**
                             employed   **employed**
                   Man   (20)   (0)
                 Woman   (10)   (5)

7. How long have you known each other?
   (Based on frequent association)
   6 months or less (0)   **6 months to a year** (5)
   1 year to 3 years (10)   **3 years or more** (20)

8. How long have you been engaged? (Based on frequent association — two or more times a week)
   1 to 3 months (0)   **3 months to 1 year** (15)   **1 to 2 years** (10)
   2 years or more (5)

9. Number of social organizations to which you both now belong:
   None (0)   **One** (10)   **Two or more** (15)

10. Present amount of religious activity (attendance at church,
    etc.)*

	Man	**Woman**
Member, but no attendance at church	(0)	(0)
Not a member, and no attendance	(5)	(5)
Attend no more than once a month	(10)	(10)
Attend two or three times a month	(25)	(20)
Attend four or more times a month	(30)	(25)

11. Will you both attend the   **Yes   No, but both   One**
    same church?   **Protestant   Catholic**
                                (50)   (25)   (0)

12. Is either person a non-believer?   **Yes** (0)   **No** (50)

---

* Some questions were inspired by *Predicting Success or Failure in Marriage,* Prentice-Hall, Inc. New York 11, N. Y.

13. Until what age did you regularly attend Sunday school?
    Man:
    10 or under (0)   14 or under (10)   19 or under (20)
    Woman:
    10 or under (0)   14 or under (10)   19 or under (20)

14. How would you rate your parents' marriage?
    Man:
    Happy (20)   Average (10)   Unhappy (5)   Divorced (0)
    Woman:
    Happy (20)   Average (10)   Unhappy (5)   Divorced (0)

15. Do your parents favor your proposed marriage?   **Yes   No**
    Man   (10)   (5)
    Woman   (15)   (0)

16. How do you get along with your affianced's parents?
    Man:
    Very well (20)   Not too well (10)   Dislike them (0)
    Unacquainted (5)
    Woman:
    Very well (20)   Not too well (10)   Dislike them (0)
    Unacquainted (5)

17. Do you double-date with other couples? **Yes** (10)
    Occasionally (5)   **No** (0)

18. What hobbies do you have in common?
    None (0)   **One** (5)   **Two** (10)   **Three or more** (15)

19. How have you handled disagreements during your courtship?
    Have had none (0)   **One gives in** (10)   **Talk it through** (15)

20. Does the wife plan to work (out of the home) after marriage?
    Yes (0)   **No** (5)

21. Who will be in charge of family finances in your home?
    Husband (0)   **Wife** (0)   **Co-operatively** (10)

22. How many children do you hope to have?
    One (5)   **Two** (10)   **Three plus** (15)   **None** (0)

23. Will you live with either of your parents during the first year
    or two?   **Yes** (0)   **No** (20)

24. What books ** have you read on the subject of physical adjustment in marriage? **None** (0)   **One or two** (10)

25. Has either person been married before?   **Yes** (0)   **No** (25)

26. Why did you come to a pastor to be married?
    Custom (0)   **Parents did** (0)   **We desire God's blessing on our new home** (10)

27. Do you plan to have grace at meals and daily family devotions? **Both** (20)   **Neither** (0)   **Grace** (10)

28. Do you ever use prayer to solve any of your problems?
    Man:
         Frequently (20)   Occasionally (10)   Never (0)
    Woman:
         Frequently (20)   Occasionally (10)   Never (0)

29. Would you like to have the pastor who married you call on you in your new home? **Yes** (5)   **No** (0)

THE SCORING

To score this guide correctly, you must have three (3) columns: **Man, Woman, Both**. In a question like No. 1, the **Man** could receive a possible 15 points, and the **Woman** a possible 15 points. But in question No. 2, and those similar, the highest possible number of points (20) goes in the **Both** column.

Example:	Man	Woman	Both
Question No. 1	15	15	
Question No. 2			20
Etc.			
Total Highest Possible Score on all 29 questions	155	145	370

** Suggested Books

Wood, L. F. Harmony in Marriage. Round Table Press, New York City.
Butterfield, O. M. Marriage and Sexual Harmony. Emerson Books, New York City.
Stone, Hannah and Abraham. A Marriage Manual. Simon and Schuster, New York City.
Burkhart, Roy. A Guide for a Man and Woman Looking Toward Marriage. Hearthside Press, Flushing, N. Y.
Duvall and Hill. When You Marry. Association Press, 347 Madison Ave., New York City.
Duvall, Sylvanus M. Before You Marry. Association Press, New York City.
Kelly, G. Lombard. Sex Manual. Southern Medical Supply Co., Augusta, Ga.
Geiseman, O. A. Make Yours a Happy Marriage. Concordia Publishing House. Saint Louis, Mo.

Now add these three scores together and you arrive at a total of 670. But don't expect your score to be anywhere near that high.

When one person takes the test, he must always have a "possible" marriage partner in mind, whose score must be included in the total.

Highest Possible Score	670
Excellent Score	Above 575
Good Score	452 to 575
Fair Score	325 to 425
Questionable Score	Below 325

EDITOR's NOTE: This Premarital Counseling Guide for Pastors is available in pamphlet form from Augustana Book Concern, Rock Island, Ill.

VII

A CHECK LIST FOR THE CHRISTIAN CONGREGATION

STRENGTHENING CHRISTIAN HOMES

A Check List of Things Churches Can Do
★ star those things you would like to do
√ check the things you are doing now

1. ___ Observe Christian Family Week annually to stimulate whole year's program. (First Sunday to second Sunday of May inclusive.)

2. ___ Recognize the primary place of the family in the whole church curriculum.

3. ___ Keep families with children in mind in planning church service, sermon.

4. ___ Serve families in health and sickness, success and failure, birth to death.

5. ___ Provide families with a Christian family standard ("Our Family").

6. ___ Have church meetings for the entire family (family night at church).

7. ___ Conduct a home visitation on family devotions.

8. ___ Enlist whole families in the Sunday school (parents in adult classes).

9. ___ Avoid drawing father and mother out of the home too often.

10. ___ Encourage families to dedicate their homes to God (dedication service).

11. ___ Serve other homes in community with radio program, tracts.

12. ___ Return parental duties to the home (don't substitute for parents).

13. ___ Feature the families of the church often in the church bulletin.

14. ___ Emphasize worshiping together as a family in the family pew.

15. ____ Help every new family feel at home and participate in work of parish.

16. ____ Help families establish satisfying family worship (dramatic demonstration).

17. ____ Supply specific guidance for family worship at various stages of family's growth.

18. ____ Suggest ways to improve mealtime prayers and conversation.

19. ____ Get the "Family Worship Hour" on your radio station.

20. ____ Get "This Is the Life" on your TV station.

21. ____ Help bride and groom with premarital counseling.

22. ____ Help families solve their problems with a family counseling program.

23. ____ Discuss church's program for youth with parents of catechumens.

24. ____ Make the wedding service distinctively Christian and personal.

25. ____ Train families to talk things over in kindness and love.

26. ____ Give guidance in using the "family council" as an educational experience.

27. ____ Help families introduce more Christian reading (Bible, Christian periodicals).

28. ____ Set up a tract service (rack) to meet various family problems and needs. (For items see General Family Packet.)

29. ____ Prepare reading lists for parents (day school, Sunday school, Parent-Teacher Ass'n.).

30. ____ Provide and publicize books on the Christian family (church library).

31. ____ Develop a nursery department and a program to aid young parents.

32. ____ Give a course in child training for parents once a year (discipline, etc.).

33. ____ See to it that your program for women includes Christian homemaking.

34. ____ Put more emphasis on the family in the men's program.

35. ____ Include "preparation for marriage" in your youth program.

36. ____ Use existing adult organizations to help parents, husbands, wives.

37. ____ Have a "Family Forum" or "Family Relations Clinic" in your church.

38. ____ Use Bible class for such courses as "Our Home," "Train Up a Child," "Parents are Teachers."

39. ____ Start a Young Married Peoples' Class, Couples' Class (with Sunday and weekday program).

40. ____ Charge parents with Christian nurture at baptism of children.

41. ____ Have a Home Department in your Sunday school.

42. ____ Conduct open house for parents (day school, Sunday school) . . . (exhibits).

43. ____ Set up Parent-Teacher meetings which help parents teach religion.

44. ____ Use films, filmstrips, and other visual aids in your family education.

45. ____ Use recordings to help present topics on marriage and family.

46. ____ Have a Sunday school home Visitation Day (teachers visit in homes of pupils).

47. ____ Have parent-teacher conferences (day school, Sunday school).

48. ____ Work with courts and judges in reclaiming homes that are "breaking up."

49. ____ Use "Christian home appeals" when you make evangelism calls.

50. ____ Help also the aging family (visiting shut-ins, Golden Age Club).

Prepared by the Family Life Committee of the Board for Parish Education. The Lutheran Church — Missouri Synod, 210 N. Broadway, St. Louis, Missouri

VIII

SELECTED, ANNOTATED BIBLIOGRAPHY

on

CHRISTIAN FAMILY LIFE

WALTER F. WOLBRECHT

A bibliography on Christian family-life materials for a publication like this should not try to be exhaustive. Yet, in order to present some of the better-known works, it has been necessary to include more than two hundred titles. This indicates how extensive the materials are in this field.

Though the combination for the purpose of this bibliography is new, very few of the items listed are untried. Obviously, a list like this cannot be permanent; in fact, it is in constant danger of being obsolescent, because new books in this field are appearing on the market every month.

Inclusion in this list does not mean that any single book is thereby unqualifiably recommended or in any sense of the term officially endorsed. We believe, however, that it will prove to be genuinely helpful at one or more points to the Christian leader. For this reason it has been included.

Those persons who have assisted us in the selection of the bibliography have uniformly felt that mature Christian judgment should take the place of any attempt, however fruitless it might be, to weed out, so to speak, those items which are not 100 per cent acceptable or 100 per cent usable. Rather it was felt that the pastor and the intelligent church worker should be in a position to evaluate as he reads and to get insights for his work in the local congregation.

An attempt has been made to list the various books accurately by author, title, publisher, date, and in most cases to give the number of pages. To aid the church worker, a brief evaluation of content has been added. An attempt to include the price was abandoned because of the extremely fluctuating situation in the book market. Many of the items herein listed should be available in a well-stocked public library and in most college libraries.

Those who are interested in the purchase of individual books for personal, church, or school library will find the services of

Concordia Publishing House or the Board for Parish Education very helpful.

The Family Life Committee annually produces a shorter selected book list of fifty to sixty volumes, which also is annotated; and some books are starred to indicate those which should come first on your purchase list in setting up a church library. This shorter list is available without charge to those who will write for it.

To facilitate practical use, the books have been classified under seven categories. The use of any such category involves a certain amount of arbitrariness, but the attempt has been made to be reasonably faithful. The various categories and a brief explanation of what they include follows.

1. General Materials on Family Life

Such books and pamphlets as, in general, treat marriage, the home, and the family, or cut across the divisions below to give guidance on several areas.

2. Helping Youth Prepare for Marriage

Materials on sex, marriage, family for ages fifteen to twenty-four. Covers social relations between sexes from friendship through courtship to marriage, premarital guidance as regards those to be married, problems of young people regarding personality and adjustments to others. In this group high school and college texts on marriage and family living are also placed.

3. Making a Success of Marriage

Books and pamphlets for those who are married or about to be married; helping husband and wife make proper adjustments toward a happy Christian marriage; also parenthood; home management; mental, physical, social, spiritual aspects of married life.

4. Child Guidance and Training in the Home

Everything related to the guidance and training of the pre-school child, the school-age child, and the high school youth (birth to eighteen), directed especially to parents. Parent-education study topics, courses; materials which deal specifically with parent-child relationships and family living. In this category are also placed materials for the child and the youth related to guidance and training.

5. Helping Families Worship Together

Guidance materials in regard to the methods of conducting fruitful private and family devotions adapted to the age levels of children and the needs of members of the family. Also Bible story books, devotional aids (for all ages), and prayer books. Also literature on worship in the church from the standpoint of home motivation.

6. The Church Helping Families

Books and other resource materials for leaders in the church, both professional and volunteer, to give insight and guidance for developing and administering family-centered education and building a family-centered church. Includes: leading parents' groups, planning courses in family life, methods of counseling, guidance and care of the aging family.

7. Miscellaneous Materials

Includes such materials as cannot be easily classified in the categories above, for instance, special problems, sex-education literature that does not fit in elsewhere.

BIBLIOGRAPHY

I. GENERAL MATERIALS ON THE FAMILY

Adult Education. Handbook of Adult Education in the United States. Institute of Adult Education, 1948.
Sections on "Education for Family Living" and "Protestant Adult Education."

Althaus, Paul. Von Liebe und Ehe. Verlag, Vandenhoeck u. Ruprecht, Goettingen, Germany, about 1950.

Baber, R. E. Marriage and the Family. McGraw-Hill, 1939. 656 pages.
A standard text using research outcomes to the publication date.

Bailey, Derrick Sherwin. The Mystery of Love and Marriage. Harper, 1952. 145 pages.
Basic theological thinking on love and the concept of "one flesh."

Bowman, Henry A. Marriage for Moderns. McGraw-Hill, 1942. Revised 1948. 468 pages.
One of the texts which grew out of the popular Stephens College course designed to build a curriculum on the life needs of its alumni.

Burgess, Ernest W. and Locke, Harvey J. The Family: From Institution to Companionship. American Book Co., 1945. 800 pages.
Heavy sociological orientation which views the family as a unit of interesting personalities.

East Asia Seminar, edited by Rajah Manikam and Irma Highbaugh. The Christian Family in Changing East Asia. Philippine Federation of Christian Churches, 1955.
Church leaders of East Asia met with Christian leaders of America. The findings are worthy of note, especially for family-life education in the mission fields abroad.

Feucht, Oscar E. Building the Christian Home. Concordia Publishing House. 32 pages.
Basic principles of Christian marriage and homemaking.

Foster, Robert G. Marriage and Family Relationship. Macmillan, 1941. 214 pages.
A good case-study approach for adolescents in senior high school or junior college.

Groves, Ernest. Christianity and the Family. Macmillan, 1942. 229 pages.
Groves, who was always solid, toward the close of his career turned out one of his finest books.

Kerr, Clarence W. God's Pattern for the Home. Cowman, 1953. 147 pages.
Strikingly down-to-earth and Biblical. God's blueprint for marriage, husband, wives, parents, children, in-laws, lovers.

Kildahl, Harold B. Family Affairs. Augsburg, 1948. 102 pages.
Helpful to laymen, background material for pastor, and informative for teacher.

Leavell, Martha Boone. Building a Christian Home. Sunday School Board, Southern Baptist Convention, 1936. 172 pages.
Study manual for adult groups. Weaves Scripture into daily family living.

Lenski, Gerhard. Marriage in the Lutheran Church. Lutheran Book Concern, 1936. 377 pages.
Historical study of the doctrine and the practices of the Lutheran Church concerning marriage.

Nimkoff, Meyer F. Marriage and the Family. Houghton Mifflin, 1947.
Comprehensive college text by an eminent sociologist.

Sheatsley, Joseph. The Bible in Religious Education. Wartburg, ? (out of print).
Outstanding chapter on the home.

Thompson, W. Taliaferro. An Adventure in Love. John Knox Press, 1956. 155 pages.
A Gospel-centered book on Christian family living, hammered out on the anvil of experience. Warm and practical. Good source material for study topics.

Trueblood, Elton and Pauline. The Recovery of Family Life. Harper, 1953. 127 pages.
A serious call to family rehabilitation.

Weidenschilling, John M. Our Home. Concordia Publishing House, 1946. 112 pages.
Study manual for youth or adult groups on Biblical relationships and responsibilities of family members.

Wieman, Regina Westcott. **The Modern Family and the Church.** Harper, 1937. 407 pages.
A comprehensive survey of family-life education trends in the churches of America. Basic for college instructors. (A new edition uses the author's maiden name, Regina Westcott.)

Wieman, Regina Westcott. **The Family Lives Its Religion.** Harper, 1941. 236 pages.
Using religion in a broad sense, gives valuable insights to leaders.

Wolbrecht, Walter F., Editor. **The Christian Family in the Modern World.** Fifth Yearbook of the Lutheran Education Association, 1948. 97 pages.
Sees the Christian family as a living force making its impact on society. Contains a chapter on preparing for happy Christian marriage.

Wood, Leland F. and Mullen, J. W. **What the American Family Faces.** Eugene Hugh Publishers, 1943. 254 pages.
A stimulating war-time symposium that indicates the scope of family life education.

Wynn, John C. **Sermons on Marriage and Family Life.** Abingdon, 1956. 173 pages.
These are not textual sermons, but supply some very helpful ideas for Christian preaching on the family.

II. HELPING YOUTH PREPARE FOR MARRIAGE

Amstutz, H. Clair. **So You're Going to Be Married.** Herald Press, 1952. 82 pages.
A Christian physician presents the nature, growth, and fruits of love in marriage.

Brink, Frederick W. **This Man and This Woman.** Association, 1948. 79 pages.
For young folks contemplating marriage.

Burgess, E. W. and Fishbein, Morris. **Successful Marriage.** Doubleday & Co., 1948.
Many excellent chapters by specialists, who join the famous editors in a new composite text.

Burkhart, Roy. **From Friendship to Marriage.** Harper & Bros., 1937. 161 pages.
Handbook of help for adolescents getting ready for marriage.

Capper, W. Melville and Williams, H. Morgan. **Heirs Together.** Inter-Varsity Press (Chicago), 7th reprint in 1956. 118 pages.
A Christian and discreet approach to the privileges and responsibilities of sex. Excellent.

Derstine, Clayton. **Manual of Sex Education.** Zondervan. 120 pages.
Sex education by levels in the spirit of Christian chastity.

Dickerson, Roy E. **So Youth May Know.** Association Press, 1930.
Very popular in attempts to impart scientific sex information in a wholesome way.

Duvall, Evelyn Millis. **Facts of Life and Love for Teenagers.** Association, 1950. 360 pages. Popular Library Edition, 1955. 254 pages.
A discussion of sexual maturation, dating, loving and being loved, and getting ready for marriage. It answers youth's questions frankly, honestly, and in language that is morally clean.

Duvall, Evelyn Millis. **Family Living.** Macmillan, 1951. 410 pages.
A high school text prepared by one of the best writers in the field of family life.

Eckert, Ralph G. **So You Think It's Love!** Public Affairs Pamphlet No. 161. 32 pages.
A helpful pamphlet that asks for standards in boy-girl relationships.

Harman, Carl and Marquardt, E. W. **Vital Facts of Life.** Concordia Publishing House, 1949. 126 pages.
A minister and a physician collaborate to answer some of youth's questions.

Heintzen, E. G. **With This Ring.** Concordia Publishing House. 10 pages.
Devotions for the first week together, to be presented to the bride and groom.

Hulme, William E. **Face Your Life with Confidence** (Counsels for Youth). Prentice-Hall, Inc., 1954. 232 pages.
The best book we've seen to put into the hands of young people. Wholesome, Christian, realistic, effective, 51 chapters, 10 on "You and the Other Sex."

Hustad, Alice. **Strictly Confidential.** Augsburg, 1944. 102 pages.
    For high school and college girls about themselves as young Christians.

Jesse, Richard A. **Friendship.** 32 pages.
    A tract for all to whom making and keeping and growing with friends are problems.

Kirkendall, Lester A. **Too Young to Marry?** Public Affairs Pamphlet No. 236, 1956.
    28 pages.
    A factual, constructive, sound presentation every teen-ager who feels he is in love
    and wants to marry and all parents should read. Make it available in your church.

Landis, Judson T. and Mary G. **Personal Adjustment, Marriage, and Family Living.**
    Prentice-Hall, Inc., 1950. 392 pages.
    A high school text with chapters on "Religion and Marriage," "What About Quar-
    reling?" "Family Understanding," "The Successful Home."

Landis, Paul E. and Bond, Helen. **Your Marriage and Family Living.** McGraw-Hill,
    1946. 372 pages.
    One of the better high school texts. Well illustrated. Gives factual background of
    marriage and family.

Mayer, Fred E. **To Sign or Not to Sign.** Concordia Publishing House, 1946. 23 pages.
    Shows the Catholic prenuptial contract to be unfair, unscriptural, unchristian.

Murray, Alfred L. **Youth's Marriage Problems.** Zondervan, 1947. 182 pages.
    Written from a Christian point of view.

Nash, Arnold S., Editor. **Education for Christian Marriage.** Macmillan, 1940. 304 pages.
    Most unfortunately, out of print but worth looking for to read, to own, and to share.

Overton, Grace Sloan. **Living with Parents.** Broadman, 1954. 138 pages.
    Deals with tensions that develop between youth and their parents.

Peterson, James A. **Education for Marriage.** Scribners, 1956. 429 pages.
    An excellent and frank discussion of what people should know before marriage.

Pike, James A. **If You Marry Outside Your Faith.** Harpers, 1954. 191 pages.
    Best book on subject; with case histories; guidance in dealing with interfaith
    marriages.

Prange, Rudolph. **Steps to the Marriage Altar.** Concordia Publishing House. 16 pages.
    Tract to help youth prepare for marriage.

Reuss, Carl F. and Burntvedt, Gloria. **Proceedings of the Workshop for Teachers of
    Marriage and the Family in Midwestern Lutheran Colleges, 1949.** Eleven-page
    mimeographed report. American Lutheran Church.

Schmieding, Alfred. **Sex in Childhood and Youth.** Concordia Publishing House, 1953.
    157 pages.
    Brings together home, church, and school in a reliable discussion of sex education.

Shultz, Gladys Denny. **It's Time You Knew.** Lippincott, 1955. 221 pages.
    Attention, all parents! One of the most wholesome books on the market in language
    a teen-age girl will read (and boys, too).

Wood, Leland Foster. **Speaking of Love.** Federal Council of Churches, 1950. 31 pages.
    How it happens, how to recognize it, what to do about it — in a fine pamphlet.

Wood, Leland Foster. **Youth, Sex and Marriage.** Hearthside Press, 1945.
    A pamphlet which states the case for premarital continence.

III. MAKING A SUCCESS OF MARRIAGE

Adams, Theodore F. **Making Your Marriage Succeed.** Harper, 1953. 156 pages.
    A mine of practical helps for pastor, church worker, and married couple on the
    sanctity of love from youth to old age; check lists and illustrations from life.

Bossard, James H. S., Editor. **Toward Family Stability.** The Annals of the American
    Academy of Political and Social Science, November, 1950 (Philadelphia). 315
    pages.
    A comprehensive symposium in which leading sociologists deal with family dis-
    organization. A "must" for students in the field of marriage and divorce.

Bracher, Marjory Louise. **Love Is No Luxury.** Muhlenberg, 1951. 122 pages.
Easily read book full of insights and helps; discusses forces threatening the Christian family, value of love, little things that help marriage succeed, Christian view of sex.

Buhre, Gunnar. **Du und Ich von der Ehe.** Verlag, Kirche u. Mann, Guetersloh, Germany, — 1955?
Marriage problems as a German pastor deals with them.

Duvall, Evelyn Millis. **Building Your Marriage.** Public Affairs Pamphlet No. 113, 1946. 31 pages.
Lucid presentation of marriage as an achievement in co-operation.

Duvall, Evelyn Millis. **In-Laws: Pro and Con.** Association, 1954. 400 pages.
A comprehensive study of the problem; a sociological, psychological treatment.

Duvall, Evelyn Millis and Sylvanus. **Saving Your Marriage.** Public Affairs Pamphlet No. 213.
Deals helpfully with adjusting differences.

Duvall, Evelyn M. and Hill, Reuben. **When You Marry.** Association, 1953. 466 pages.
Well-documented, comprehensive, readable, college-level text, supplying facts from the social sciences on dating, courtship, engagement, marriage relations, family living, child training.

Duvall, Sylvanus M. and Duvall, Evelyn Millis. **Marriage Is What You Make It.** Abingdon, 1942. 32 pages.
A study course for groups by the famous couple and teaching team.

Elmer, M. C. **The Sociology of the Family.** Ginn, 1945.
Chapter on adjustments in time of crises.

Frenk, Erdmann W. **Staying Married.** Concordia Publishing House, 1948. 48 pages.
One of Concordia's better tracts.

Geiseman, Otto A. **Make Yours A Happy Marriage.** Concordia Publishing House, 1946. 74 pages.
Very popular as a wedding gift to Christian couples; simple, practical, spiritual.

Groves, Ernest. **Conserving Marriage and the Family.** Macmillan, 1946.
The emphasis is on divorce prevention.

Landis, Judson T. and Landis, Mary G. **The Marriage Handbook.** Prentice-Hall, Inc., 1949. 513 pages.
Another college text with considerable detail, for instance, on mixed marriages.

Landis, Judson T. and Landis, Mary G. **Building a Successful Marriage.** Prentice-Hall, 1948. 539 pages.
A comprehensive college course.

Landis, Paul H. **Making the Most of Marriage.** Appleton-Century-Crofts, 1955. 542 pages.
The 59 graphs and 17 tables help to make this an up-to-date book on marriage, with attention also to child-training.

Levy, John and Monroe, Ruth. **The Happy Family.** Alfred A. Knopf. 311 pages.
A classic reference, not necessarily a Christian orientation.

Popenoe, Paul. **Modern Marriage.** Macmillan, 1947. 299 pages.
Addressed primarily to young men.

Stone, Abraham, and Stone, Hannah. **A Marriage Manual.** Simon & Schuster.
Questions answered by two famous doctors and marriage counselors (secular).

Thorman, George. **Broken Homes.** Public Affairs Pamphlet No. 135, 1947. 28 pages.
Excellent study guide for this problem and its causes.

Wood, Leland Foster. **Harmony in Marriage.** Round Table Press, 1949. Revised. 122 pages.
Widely presented by ministers to couples just married.

Wood, Leland Foster. **How Love Grows in Marriage.** Macmillan, 1954. 183 pages.
How love matures and marriage succeeds. A book for husbands and wives, pastors and counselors.

IV. CHILD GUIDANCE AND TRAINING IN THE HOME

American Council on Education. **Helping Teachers Understand Children.** Commission on Teacher Education, 1945.
Does the same for parents.

Athy, Marian Poppen. **In the Nursery.** Castle Press, 1933.
Very practical guidance for teachers of three-year-olds. Manual for use of "Little Visits with Jesus."

Breckenridge, Marion and Vincent, E. Lee. **Child Development.** Saunders, 1949. 592 pages.
A nutritionist and a psychologist supply a sound, comprehensive, helpful text on how children develop physically, mentally, socially, morally. Role of home, church, school, community.

Brennemann, Helen Good. **Meditations for the New Mother.** Herald, 1953. 78 pages.
Choice Scriptural meditations to magnify parenthood and the high calling of mothers.

Children's Bureau Publication No. 30. **Your Child from One to Six.** Children's Bureau, 1945. 147 pages.
Best available for the money (20¢).

Children's Bureau Publication No. 324. **Your Child from Six to Twelve.** Children's Bureau, 1949. 141 pages.
Best available for the money (20¢).

Children's Bureau Publication No. 4. **Prenatal Care.** Children's Bureau, 1949. 80 pages.
Reliable, basic information (15¢).

Children's Bureau Publication No. 8. **Infant Care.** Children's Bureau, 1945. 126 pages.
Tested guidelines for mothers (15¢).

Children's Bureau Publication No. 347. **The Adolescent in Your Family.** Children's Bureau, 1955. 110 pages.
Gives insights to parents on guiding teen-agers (20¢).

de Schweinitz, Karl. **Growing Up.** Macmillan, 1932. 111 pages.
Well received. Sex education; 10-year-old child and parent may read together.

Doederlein, Gertrude. **Living with Our Children.** Augsburg, 1941.
How mothers and fathers can lead small children in various types of growth. Most useful with art packets.

Duvall, Evelyn Millis. **Keeping Up with Teen-Agers.** Public Affairs Committee, 1947.
Good counsel to parents in dealing with adolescents.

Eavey, C. B. **Principles of Personality Building for Christian Parents.** Zondervan, 1952. 321 pages.
The psychology of developing a Christian personality.

Fakkema, Mark. **How to Teach Obedience.** National Association of Christian Schools (Chicago), 1947. 31 pages.
Principles teaching obedience on the basis of God-given authority.

Ferguson, Rowena. **Teen-Agers, Their Days and Ways.** National Council of Christian Churches, 1952. 48 pages.
Helps parents understand teen-agers.

Feucht, Oscar E. **So You Are Parents.** Concordia Publishing House. 16 pages.
Functional, with highest motivation.

Gesell, Arnold. **First Five Years of Life.** National Education Association, Personal Growth Leaflet 181 (one of a series).
A pamphlet summary of the author's famous larger child-development studies.

Gesell, Arnold and Ilg, Frances, and Ames, Louise. **Youth (The Years from 10 to 16).** Harper, 1956.
Based on latest firsthand studies of normal adolescents.

Haentzschel, Ad. **Learning to Know the Child.** Concordia Publishing House, 1941. 86 pages.
A short, simple, and solid introduction to child psychology for parents and volunteer church workers.

Havighurst, Robert J. **Developmental Tasks and Education.** Longmans, Green, 1954. 100 pages.
　　An authority in psychology suggests education's task for the development of child, youth, adult at different stages in life.

Ilg, Frances and Ames, Louise Bates. **Child Behavior.** Harper, 1955. 364 pages.
　　Authentic clinical data on children up to age 10, by authorities in the field.

Jahsmann, Allan Hart. **Leading Children into the Bible.** Concordia Publishing House, 1948. 92 pages.
　　Shows the importance of leading the child to a meaningful use of the Bible.

Kardatzke, Carl. **The Home Christian.** Warner, 1951. 111 pages.
　　A 13-lesson course for parents. Helpful reference.

Landis, Paul H. **Coming of Age.** Public Affairs Pamphlet No. 234. 28 pages.
　　Problems of teen-agers (for parents and youth).

Levine, Milton I. and Seligman, Jean H. **A Baby Is Born.** Simon & Schuster, 1949.
　　Simply illustrated, dignified narrative for 6-10-year-olds.

Ligon, Ernest M. **Their Future Is Now.** Macmillan, 1947. 369 pages.
　　Describes the growth and development of Christian personality.

Lutheran Education Association (A Symposium). **Christian Preschool Education.** 1945. 95 pages.
　　Individual chapters on the family and social change — as an educational agency, parent training, and church programs.

Manwell, Elizabeth and Fahs, Sophia. **Consider the Children — How They Grow.** Beacon Press, 1940. 261 pages.
　　For all who have and love "kindergarteners."

Ojemann, Ralph H. and McNiel, Bessie. **Discipline.** Child Welfare Pamphlet No. 11, University of Iowa, 1948.
　　Asks for consideration of cause of disobedience.

Parent Guidance Series Booklets, Concordia; prepared under the direction of the Family Life Committee, The Lutheran Church — Missouri Synod: — Appear annually (June). No. 1: **Your Child and You** (various authors). 32 pages.
　　Deals with children's basic needs, building right attitudes, constructive discipline, spiritual growth, sex education, enlisting the home.

No. 2: **Making Home Life Christian** (various authors). 44 pages.
　　Eight studies treating the application of the Christian Family Standard.

No. 3: **Happiness Is Homemade** (A. J. Bueltmann). 44 pages.
　　Studies in homemaking, sound marriage, training for happiness, parental example, Christian education, Bible uses, television (ally or menace), child and missions.

No. 4: **Teen-Agers Need Parents** (A. J. Bueltmann). 48 pages.
　　Eight chapters to guide Christian parents in dealing constructively with high-school youth.

No. 5: **Guiding the Young Child** (Ellen K. Jagow). 44 pages.
　　Eight studies to help parents with the physical, mental, social, and spiritual growth of the preschool child.

Puner, Helen W. **Helping Brothers and Sisters Get Along.** Science Research Associates (Chicago), 1952. 48 pages.
　　Deals with children's quarrels and how to handle them. (One of the series of *Better Living Booklets* for parents and teachers.)

Ridenour, Nina. **Some Special Problems of Children (2 to 5).** National Mental Health Foundation, 1949. 72 pages.
　　Widely recommended, reliable guide.

Schmieding, Alfred. **Parent-Child Relationships in the Christian Home.** Concordia Publishing House. 22 pages.
　　Based on clinical experiences and research.

Shields, Elizabeth. **Guiding the Little Child.** Broadman, 1936.
　　A teacher-training text.

Spock, Benjamin J. **Baby and Child Care.** Pocket Edition.
    Tested guidebook, widely recommended.
Staples, Ethlyne B. and Staples, Edward D. **Children in a Christian Home.** Abingdon,
    1948. 128 pages.
    Six helpful chapters on child guidance.
Strain, Frances Bruce. **Being Born.** D. Appleton-Century Co. 1936. 144 pages.
    For joint use by parents and children (8 years and up).
Strang, Ruth. **A Study of Young Children.** Abingdon, 1944.
    Helpful to parent and teacher.
Taylor, Katherine Whiteside. **Parents Relax.** Child Welfare Pamphlet No. 78, University
    of Iowa, 1947.
    A fine introduction to this uniformly serviceable series of pamphlets.
Trent, Robbie. **Your Child and God.** Willett, Clark, 1941.
    Emphasizes the parents' importance in early religious training.
Wolf, Anna W. M. **The Parents Manual.** Simon & Schuster, 1941. 331 pages.
    Helpful, nontechnical, solid.
Wood, Leland Foster. **Growing Together in the Family.** Abingdon-Cokesbury, 1935.
    128 pages.
    Marriage as partnership with God.
Wynn, John Charles. **How Christian Parents Face Family Problems.** Westminster,
    1955. 144 pages.
    Encourages careful thinking with regard to such things as family conflicts, discipline,
    interpreting sex, mixed marriages.

V. HELPING FAMILIES WORSHIP TOGETHER

Armstrong, Oscar Vance. **Prayer Poems.** Abingdon-Cokesbury, 1952. 256 pages.
    An anthology for almost any occasion.
Bertermann, E. R. **Day by Day with Jesus Calendar.** Kaufmann, Annual.
    Daily devotions with appealing life stories and thoughts for the day.
Collects and Prayers. Muhlenberg Press, 1935. 265 pages.
    While designed for use in church, excellent in scope for private and family
    devotions.
Daily Light for the Daily Path. Oxford. 700 pages.
    Well-selected readings from the Bible, two for each day. A classic devotional
    manual.
Doerffler, Alfred. **Treasures of Hope.** Concordia Publishing House, 1945. 280 pages.
    Designed especially for older folks.
Doerffler, Alfred. **The Burden Made Light.** Concordia Publishing House, 1937. 103
    pages.
    Book of Christian comfort for the sick and burdened.
Doerffler, Alfred. **The Mind at Ease.** Concordia Publishing House, 1955. 136 pages.
    Sixty-seven messages from the Psalms for the troubled soul.
Egermeier, Elsie. **Bible Story Book.** Warner Press, Revised edition 1955. 640 pages.
    Ever-new and reliable standard.
Egermeier, Elsie. **Bible Picture ABC Book.** Warner Press, 1952. 61 pages.
    A story in simplified Bible language for each letter of the alphabet.
England, Herbert. **Listen My Children.** Fleming Revell Co.
    In the circle of the calendar year, Bible stories are combined with sharp modern
    illustrations for children in junior high-school years.
Fox, Selina Fitzheilat. **A Chain of Prayer Across the Ages.** Murray (London), 1933.
    307 pages.
    Select prayers from every age of the New Testament church.

Gebhard, Edward W. and Gebhard, Anna Laura. **Guideposts to Creative Family Worship.** Abingdon.
Many ways of meeting spiritual needs through less formal religious talks and experiences in the home.

Gross, Arthur W. **A Child's Garden of Bible Stories.** Concordia Publishing House, 1948. 146 pages.
Sixty Bible stories, simply told, to unfold the relationship of man to God.

Hegland, Martin. **For His Name's Sake.** Augsburg, 1947. 481 pages.
Simplified King James text is used in 365 New Testament readings with simple but excellent prayers.

Herzberger, F. W. **The Family Altar.** Concordia Publishing House, revised issue, 1956. 375 pages.
Old, but still one of the best daily devotionals for family use.

Hoh, Paul. **Two Minutes with God.** Abingdon, 1940. 175 pages.
Two minutes in sprightly, conversational style.

Jahsmann, A. H. and Simon, M. P. **Little Visits with God.** Concordia Publishing House, 1957. 250 pages.
Book of life-related devotions for small children.

Kunkle, Howard R. **Paul and Dorothy Go to God's House.** Concordia Publishing House, 20 pages.
A fine aid to parents in explaining public worship to small children.

Laache, N. J. **Book of Family Prayers.** Augsburg. 626 pages.
Daily Biblical meditations in church-year sequence.

Light for Your Way. Board for Parish Education, quarterly. 16 pages.
A daily Bible reading and prayer guide; pocket size.

Lochner, William. **The Good Shepherd.** Concordia Publishing House, 1929. 320 pages.
Following the scheme of Biblical chronology, stories of Scripture are explained and applied, also in prayer and song.

My Counsellor. Oxford. 768 pages.
Holy Scripture arranged topically for morning and evening meditations to feed the soul.

Nystrom, Daniel. **God in Our Home.** Augustana, 1936. 384 pages.
Fine choice for whole family use, suggesting Bible reading, key Bible verse.

Nystrom, Daniel. **Today with God.** Augustana.
Interests of boys and girls are not forgotten.

One Hundred Bible Stories. Concordia Publishing House. 214 pages, 100 pictures; age level: 9 to 12.
Using Scripture language, each story is briefly explained, traditionally illustrated, and followed by brief prayer, single stanza, or memory verse.

Portals of Prayer. Concordia Publishing House.
The permanent title of Concordia's devotional booklet series. Understandably, not every issue is particularly designed for family or children's use.

Rieke, Marcus. **Sincerely in Him.** Wartburg. 140 pages.
Intimate devotional chats on topics vital to young people.

Saleska, E. J. **A Child's Garden of Prayers.** Concordia Publishing House, 1948.
Varied short and learnable prayers embedded in good art work.

Schramm, Edward W. **At Jesus' Feet.** Wartburg. 736 pages.
Devotions written with children in mind.

Simon, Martin P. **Bible Reading for the Family Hour.** Moody, 1954. 368 pages.
A devotion for each day of the year on the child's level; Bible story, questions, related prayer.

Steiner, M. and Scott, P. **Day by Day We Magnify Thee.** 448 pages.
Daily meditations of beauty and power, selected from Luther's writings.

Sweet, Herman. **Opening the Door for God.** Westminster, 1944. 153 pages.
A help for families who want to learn to build their own worship times and skills.

Traver, Amos J. **The Deacon and Worship.** Muhlenberg, 1941. 64 pages.
  An excellent 10-lesson course on Lutheran worship.
Youngdahl, Reuben K. **Going God's Way.** 376 pages.
  Three hundred and sixty-six meditations, with suggested table talk suited especially
  to homes with young people.

VI. THE CHURCH HELPING FAMILIES

Anderson, Stanley E. **Every Pastor a Counselor.** Van Kampen, 1952. 111 pages.
  Reviews modern literature on the subject in light of the Gospel.
Annual Proceedings of the Associated Lutheran Charities Social Work Institutes.
  Almost everyone of these reports has something helpful for those who seek to
  help families, particularly unusual, problem, or delinquent families. Example: 1955
  Proceedings contains eight articles dealing with the family, four of them on serving
  the aged. (Write Department of Social Welfare, The Lutheran Church — Missouri
  Synod, 210 N. Broadway, St. Louis 2, Mo.)
Arthur, Julietta K. **How to Help Older People.** Lippincott, 1954. 500 pages.
  Subtitled: A Guide for You and Your Family.
Berner, Carl W. **Spiritual Power for Your Church.** Concordia Publishing House, 1956.
  101 pages.
  Chapter on the development of the home altar.
Blackwood, Andrew. **Pastoral Leadership.** Abingdon, 1949. 272 pages.
  A good book with regard to the pastor as administrator of a well-rounded local
  church program.
Bonnell, John Sutherland. **Psychology for Pastor and People.** Harper, 1948.
  Practical counseling for ministers in a psychiatric framework.
Burton, Joe W. **The Church and Family Life.** Sunday School Board, Southern Baptist
  Convention. 32 pages.
  A family program for the local church.
Carrier, Blanche, Editor. **Church Education for Family Life.** Harper, 1937.
  Though out of print, still available. One of the best.
Carter, Jean. **Parents in Perplexity.** American Association Adult Education, 1938.
  143 pages.
  A survey of parent education in the U. S. A.
Close, Kathryn. **Getting Ready to Retire.** Public Affairs Pamphlet No. 182. 28 pages.
  Helps you retire to something, not merely from something.
Crampton, C. Ward. **Live Long and Like It.** Public Affairs Pamphlet No. 139. 28 pages.
  Develops wholesome attitudes toward old age.
Division of Education. **Planning for Young Adults in the Church.** National Council of
  Churches, 1952. 32 pages.
  Indicates new trends and emphases.
Duvall, Sylvanus and Duvall, Evelyn Millis. **Leading Parents Groups.** Abingdon-Cokes-
  bury, 1946. 128 pages.
  Gives helpful insights to those planning a group-approach to Christian family life
  education.
Elledge, Caroline H. **The Rehabilitation of the Patient.** Lippincott, 1948. 112 pages.
  Describes emotional and social problems in illness.
Fallaw, Wesner. **The Modern Parent and the Teaching Church.** Macmillan, 1946. 228
  pages.
  The best available functional analysis of home-church co-operation — problems and
  possibilities. A "must" for leaders.
Feucht, Oscar E. **Building Family Altars in Your Parish.** Board for Parish Education.
  14 pages.
  How a congregation can help its families establish and improve the valuable practice
  of family worship.

Feucht, Oscar E. **Parish Activities,** 1947 to 1954; since 1955 June issue of *Advance* magazine. Concordia Publishing House.
   Integrated suggestions for pre-planning in the parishes, including an annual family life emphasis throughout the parish.

Feucht, Oscar E. **A Family Life Program for the Parish.** Board for Parish Education. 16 pages.
   Outlines the need for, and the aims of, a constructive program of family life education in the parish.

Fritze, Edwin J. **Bible Reading Practices.** Concordia Publishing House, 1955. 97 pages.
   New insights on family worship and Bible reading at home.

General Family Packet. Concordia Publishing House.
   Service package for pastor and church worker containing 10 large tracts, 5 shorter tracts, 4 large pieces of literature, useful in family visitation.

Gleason, George. **Single Young Adults in the Church.** Association, 1952. 120 pages.
   How to develop a basic program that meets the needs of unmarried young adults in the church.

Gleason, George. **Church Group Activities for Young Married People.** Association, 1949. 166 pages.
   Very helpful to all who wish to meet the needs of church-related couples.

Gockel, H. W. **What Jesus Means to Me.** Concordia Publishing House, 1948. 144 pages.
   Excellent for personal mission work.

Goldstein, Sidney E. **Marriage and Family Counseling.** McGraw-Hill, 1947.
   A manual for ministers, lawyers, teachers, social workers.

Green, Bryan. **The Practice of Evangelism.** Scribner's, 1951. 258 pages.
   One of the best books in the field. Can be helpful in family evangelism.

Groves, Ernest and Groves, Gladys H. **The Contemporary American Family.** Lippincott, 1947. 838 pages.
   Deals with current thinking on marriage and family living.

Guidance in Christian Home Making. (Leader's Guide for Course 420B, Revised 1948. Protestant Evangelical Forces of the U. S. and Canada, through the Department of Leadership Education, the International Council of Religious Education, 203 N. Wabash Ave., Chicago, Ill.)

Harner, Nevin C. **Youth Work in the Church.** Abingdon-Cokesbury, 1942. 222 pages.
   Good introduction to an adequate youth program.

Hart, W. Neill. **Home and Church Working Together.** Abingdon, 1951. 157 pages. Paper cover.
   A leadership training course: "How the Church Can Help Families."

Hulme, William E. **How to Start Counseling.** Abingdon, 1955. 157 pages.
   A Wartburg Seminary professor supplies valuable guidance.

Jahsmann, A. H. **Teaching Little Amalee Jane.** Concordia Publishing House, 1954. 117 pages.
   A guide to those who teach the Christian faith to little children.

Knubel, Frederick R. **Pastoral Counseling.** Muhlenberg, 1952. 102 pages.
   What shall the pastor say when someone comes with a problem?

Koss, J. Arthur, Editor. **Parish-School-Home Co-operation.** Lutheran Education Association, 1952 Yearbook.
   Suggestions regarding principles, programs, practices, possibilities.

LeBar, Mary. **Patty Goes to the Nursery Class.** Scripture Press, 1945.
   For parents when children start going to Sunday school.

Lane, Bess B. **Your Part in Your Child's Education.** Dutton, 1948. 252 pages.
   One of the few books dealing directly with organized parent education.

Lawton, George. **Aging Successfully.** N. Y. University Press, 1946.

Lawton, George. **New Goals for Old Age.** N. Y. University Press, 1943.
   A leader in the field gives new insights.

Maves, Paul and Lennart, C. J. **Older People and the Church.** Abingdon, 1949.
The congregation sees the needs of the aging and meets them.

Maves, Paul B. **The Best Is Yet to Be.** Westminster, 1951. 96 pages.
Written for Christian older persons.

Miller, Arthur L. **Lutheran Parent-Teacher Organizations.** Board for Parish Education.
8 pages.
Eight pages of plans for serving parents of the Sunday school and the Christian day
school through regular meetings.

Mixon, John L. and Hiltner, Seward. **Community Helps on Pastoral Problems.** National
Council of Churches (pamphlet).
How to use community resources effectively.

Mueller, Arnold C. **Organizing the Nursery Roll.** Board for Parish Education. 12 pages.
Guidelines for home contact through the nursery department of the Sunday school.

Mueller, Arnold C. **Growing Up with Jesus.** Concordia Publishing House, 1948. 166
pages.
For parents and church workers with nursery-level children.

National Council of Churches. **Premarital Counseling.** 1948. 40 pages.
A specialized counseling manual for ministers.

Oates, Wayne E. **The Bible and Pastoral Care.** Westminster, 1953. 127 pages.
Some very helpful chapters on the pastoral (not legalistic) use of Scriptures in
counseling.

Ogg, Elizabeth. **When Parents Grow Old.** Public Affairs Pamphlet No. 208. 28 pages.
Evaluates several means of taking care of older people.

Parent Education and Christian Family Life in the Local Church. Department of Adult
Work, Presbyterian Church in the U. S. A. 44 pages.
Especially helpful on integration of home and Sunday school.

Parent Teacher Materials Packet. National Lutheran Parent Teacher League, annually.
Packet of program helps, directives to officers and committees, study materials, book-
tract-film lists for church-related parent-teacher groups.

Popenoe, Paul. **Whom Shall I Marry?** American Institute of Family Relations, Los
Angeles.
Good example of the type of pamphlets put out by this famous family counselor.
Secular.

Presbyterian Woman's Workbook, 1956.
Year's program for women of parish, built around the theme "Christian Family Life,"
including topics, Bible study, circle program.

Ray, Marie Beynon. **The Best Years of Your Life.** Little, Brown & Co., 1952.
One of the most popular books on using the later years.

Rumpf, Oscar J. **Church and Home.** Board of Christian Education, Evangelical &
Reformed Church, 1948.
A study course for adult church members.

Schindler, Carl J. **The Pastor as a Personal Counselor.** Muhlenberg Press, 1942. 148
pages.
A balanced orientation for beginners in systematic counseling.

Simon, Martin P. **The Christian Parent Magazine.** Highland, Ill.
Monthly topics, children's devotions, helps for leaders and parents.

Smart, James D. **The Teaching Ministry of the Church.** Westminster, 1954. 207 pages.
Basic principles of Christian education re-examined, also with regard to the Christian home.

Staples, Edward D. **The Church and Families.** Board of Education, Methodist Church
(Nashville, Tenn.). 87 pages.
One denomination's suggestions for the local church.

Stelzner, E. **Methods for Workers with Nursery Children.** United Lutheran Church of
America, 1949.
New manual for volunteer church workers, the best of whom are likey to be parents.

Stern, Edith M. and Ross, Mabel. **You and Your Aging Parents.** A. A. Wyn, Inc., 1952. 212 pages.
Written to give better understanding to members of the family.

Stroup, Herbert H. **Social Work, an Introduction to the Field.** American, 1948. 659 pages.
A college text showing the nature of social work today.

Walther League. **The ABC of Youth Work.** Handbook on all phases of youth work.

Wick, Ruth C. **Toward Understanding Youth.** Augustana, 1948.
A manual for counselors of church youth groups.

Wickenden, Elizabeth. **The Needs of Older People.** American Public Welfare Association (Chicago), 1953. 146 pages.
A careful examination into needs.

Wood, Leland Foster. **Making a Home.** Abingdon, 1938. 138 pages (paper cover).
A study course for a young people's class. Teachers, note!

Wood, Leland Foster. **Pastoral Counseling in Family Relationships.** Federal Council of Churches. 96 pages.
A fine introduction to this phase of pastoral care.

Wood, Leland Foster. **Growing Together in the Family.** Abingdon, 1935. 127 pages (paper cover).
A six-lesson course for married couples on marriage and family living.

Young Adult Committee. **Young Adults in the Church.** The United Church of Canada (Toronto).
One of the best handbooks, with tested programs in Christian fellowship, study and action — in church, home, community.

Your Church Library. Methodist Publishing House, 1949.
Very useful for those whose family-life-education plans include making literature in this field available to individuals, families, and study groups.

VII. MISCELLANEOUS MATERIALS

Beers, Clifford. **The Mind That Found Itself.** Doubleday, 1953. 394 pages.
Should be read by all who deal with emotional and mental disturbances.

Board of Christian Education. **Happily Unmarried.** Bethany Press, 1946.
Almost unique in treating with candor and sympathy an increasingly prevalent problem in personal adjustment which most of the literature overlooks or tones down. Unfortunately, uses illustrations of women only.

Doyle, Kathleen. **When Mental Illness Strikes Your Family.** Public Affairs Pamphlet No. 172. 32 pages.
What you should know and what you should do.

Duvall, Sylvanus. **Men, Women, and Morals.** Association, 1952. 336 pages.
Deals comprehensively with morals and sex, and proves the wisdom of God's commandment.

Family Life, a Selected Book List. National Council of Churches, 1950. 32 pages.
A comprehensive annotated bibliography covering nine areas of family life with 28 subheadings.

Graebner, Theodore. **Borderland of Right and Wrong.** Concordia Publishing House, 1938. 122 pages.
Unraveling puzzles of conscience in many areas.

Hegland, Martin. **Problems of Young Christians.** Augsburg, 1932. 185 pages.
Good, though pietistic in spots.

Hiltner, Seward. **Religion and Health.** Macmillan, 1943.
Supplies insights into relation between the two.

Orr, William R. Scripture Press (Christian Life and Young People's Series). **Love, Courtship, and Marriage.** 32 pages. **Your Christian Wedding.** 32 pages.

Seven Rules for a Happy Christian Home. 32 pages. What the Bible Says about Divorce. 32 pages.
Written from the viewpoint of Reformed, fundamentalist theology, yet helpful to the discriminating pastor.

Overstreet, Harry. The Mature Mind. W. W. Norton, 1949. 295 pages.
Supplies helpful background for all who work with people.

Piper, Otto A. The Christian Interpretation of Sex. Scribner's 1941. 233 pages.
Supplies a constructive, basically Christian view of the gift of sex. Scholarly work.

Polier, Justine Wise. Back to What Woodshed? Public Affairs Pamphlet No. 232. 28 pages.
A provocative treatise on the "cure" of juvenile delinquency.

Preston, George. The Substance of Mental Health. Rinehart & Co., 1943. 147 pages.
Easy to read for background in the foundations of good mental health.

Rice, Thurman B. Sex Education. Five guidebooks issued by the American Medical Association, 535 North Dearborn, Chicago, Ill.
Christian element must be supplied.

PERIODICALS

Advance. Journal of practical church work, with articles on family life education. The Lutheran Church — Missouri Synod, 210 N. Broadway, St. Louis 2, Mo.

The Christian Home. Articles on parents' problems. One of the best family magazines, with topics, devotions for families. Issued by the Methodist Church, 810 Broadway, Nashville, Tenn.

The Christian Parent. Down-to-earth articles, topics, and children's devotions make this magazine very helpful. Edited by M. P. Simon, Highland, Ill.

Family Life. Twelve page, monthly bulletin, of American Institute of Family Relations, edited by Paul Popenoe, 5287 Sunset Blvd., Los Angeles 27, Calif.

Home Life. The family magazine of the Southern Baptist Convention. Issued by the Sunday School Board, 161 Eighth Street N., Nashville, Tenn.

Marriage and Family Living. Quarterly Journal of National Council on Family Relations, chief professional magazine in the field, with scholarly articles, 5757 South Drexel Ave., Chicago 37, Ill. (100 pages.)

Mature Years. Methodist quarterly magazine for older folks, with daily Bible readings and special articles, 810 Broadway, Nashville, Tenn.

National Parent-Teacher. Well-edited magazine of the National Congress of Parents and Teachers (public schools), 700 N. Rush Street, Chicago 11, Ill.

Nurture. Quarterly newsletter of the National Lutheran Parent-Teacher League, 7400 Augusta, River Forest, Ill.

This Day. General home magazine, with inspirational articles and pictures, for the whole family. Concordia Publishing House, 3558 S. Jefferson Ave., St. Louis 18, Mo.

(IX)

SELECTED, ANNOTATED AUDIO-VISUAL AIDS

A resource for pastors, teachers, leaders, and program committees
* Items starred selected for the Family-Life Training Program

A. General Materials on Family Life

Christian Homes, Churchcraft. Sale $5.00 — filmstrip with script.
Shows positive attitudes toward the home, the church, and the community, reinforced by Scripture.

* Family on Trial, filmstrips and records. Sale $10.00; rental $2.50; 12 minutes.
Produced by Methodist Church. Contrasts the influence of two homes, one genuinely Christian, the other only nominally Christian.

The Christian Family, 40-frame filmstrip with guide. Sale $3.00. Churchscreen.
Applying Christian principles to typical problems of family life.

* Families First, 17-min. film; rental $3.00. A social study.
Happy, well-disciplined family contrasted with one disturbed by friction. Discussion starter.

B. The Church Helping Families

* The Church Serves the Family, filmstrip with recording, with guide. Sale $8.00; rental $2.50.
Produced by the Methodist Church. Shows how church (1) prepares youth for homemaking, (2) guides parents, (3) develops home-church co-operation.

C. Helping Families Worship Together

* At Home with God, filmstrip with records, 20 min. Rental $3.00. 70 frames.
Presents the values of family worship; shows how to get started; answers the usual objections.

* Faith of Our Families, 40-min. film. B & W. Rental $11.50, with discussion guide.
A down-to-earth film of engaging interest showing how five families hold their devotions. Received awards for educational value.

Bible on the Table, 30 min. B & W film. Rental $8.00.
How one family was changed through daily home devotions; features young people.

The Family Altar, 30 min. B & W film. Rental $9.00.
A neighbor is saved from despair by the strength received in the Fisher family devotions.

D. Helping Youth Prepare for Marriage and Family Living

* Dating Do's and Don't's, 14 min. Coronet Films. Rental $1.50.
Whom to choose for a date. What to do on a date. Raises questions for discussion.

Boy Dates Girl, 40 frames, B & W filmstrip, script. Sale $3.00.
When, how, where to date; for teen-agers; useful for guided discussion. Highly recommended.

* You and Your Family (YMCA), 11 min. Rental $1.50.
To help audiences discuss the problems of young people and their parents.

* You and Your Parents (Coronet), 15 min. Rental $1.50.
Shows natural process of growing away from the family and how parents and children should understand one another.

* **Preparation for Marriage** Series of 5 filmstrips with long-playing records, prepared by Methodist Church. Sale: Series $35.00; sale per unit $8.50.

> (1) **Junior High Friendships,** 49 frames. Classroom discussion on boys meeting girls.
>
> * (2) **How About a Date?** — 54 frames. The problems of dating for senior high school age.
>
> * (3) **Is This One for Me?** — 53 frames. Best of series. Shows what to consider in choosing a life's mate: respect, knowing other person well, emotional maturity, parental approval, religion. Highly recommended.
>
> * (4) **The Meaning of Engagement,** 49 frames. Value and place of counseling. Don't rush into marriage!
>
> * (5) **Helping Youth Prepare for Marriage,** 69 frames. How one family did a superb job in guiding its children. Very good.

* **And With This Ring,** 64-frame filmstrip with recording. Ev. Lutheran Church. Sale $8.75; rental $2.50.

> A teen-age Protestant receives a proposal from a Roman Catholic. Sound Christian counsel. Background for discussion.

E. Making a Success of Marriage

As for Me and My House, 30 min. B & W film. Rental $9.00.
> Common faith in Christ is the best basis for marital harmony and happiness. Very effective.

Second Chance, 70 min. B & W film. Rental $15.00.
> Huband and wife in pursuit of careers and social standing drift away from church. Awakened to their loss, they recommit themselves to Christ.

The Jealous Heart, 30 min. B & W film. Rental $9.00.
> True-to-life story of worldly ambitions nearly wrecking a marriage. It is saved by the timely visit of the understanding pastor.

* **In Time of Trouble,** 14-min. film, B & W. McGraw-Hill, Rental $5.00.
> Woman with drinking husband comes to the pastor for help and indirectly discovers she may be partly the cause. Marital counseling technique.

* **Marriage and Divorce,** 15 min. B & W, March of Time film, Rental $2.50.
> Realistic presentation of problems in marriage today. Every church worker should see it — and use it.

* **The American Family — Can Religion Hold it Together?** ("This Is the Life" episode No. 426), 30 min. B & W film. Rental $9.00.
> Panel discussion on divorce and family stability. Points up 4 basic factors in Christian family life.

* **Marriage Today,** 22 min. B & W film. Rental $6.00. (McGraw-Hill)
> How two couples achieve success in marriage by working at it; being solid, responsible persons; caring first of all for their children.

* **Till Death Us Do Part,** a 10-min. recording, Episode No. 1 of "Happiness is Made at Home," Upper Room, Family Week Series, 1908 Grand, Nashville 4, Tenn.
> Value of premarital counseling. Importance of a staunch committal to God.

F. Parent Education and Co-operation

* **That We May Work Together,** 60-frame filmstrip with script. Rental $1.50.
> Very effectively shows the value of church and home co-operating in Christian training.

My Brother, 30 min. B & W film. Rental $9.00.
> The Christian answer to race prejudice. Story revolves around Filipino widow and her 8-year-old son.

The Higher Pardon, 30 min. B & W film. Rental $9.00.
The place of forgiveness in good family relations.

The Rolling Stones, 28 min. B & W film. Rental $8.00.
Families need to settle down and find roots in the community and church.

G. Child Guidance and Training in the Home

A Chance to Grow, 30 min. B & W film. Rental $9.00.
Teaches significant lessons to parents on supplying children opportunities to grow and practice religion in the home. How to train children in assuming responsibility.

Honor Thy Family, 30 min. B & W film. Rental $8.00.
Skillfully used by a wise leader, this film can lead to a new appreciation of parents.

The Way He Should Go, 30 min. B & W film. Rental $9.00.
Contrasts two patterns of child training, showing the advantages of the Christian way.

As the Twig is Bent, 30 min. B & W film. Rental $9.00.
Nourishing souls of children is as important as feeding and clothing bodies.

* **For the Record,** 82-frame filmstrip with records in Family Life Audio Visual Series of National Council. Cartoon type.
Mr. and Mrs. Perry neglect the spiritual care of Billy and get wholesome advice from their pastor based on Deut. 6:5-7.

Harvest from Holidays, 74-frame filmstrip, with record from same series.
Shows how incidentals and ordinary experiences of the family can be used to build spiritual strength. Needs adaptation.

The Beginning of the Rainbow, 30 min. B & W film. Rental $9.00.
Christian teaching pays off in home happiness and contentment.

Torn Between These Two, 26 min. B & W film. Rental $8.00.
How selfishness was overcome when a mother learned what sharing Christian love really means.

Getting Along with Your Parents, 38-frame filmstrip with guide. Sale $3.00. Church-screen.
Six positive things a teen-ager can do to get along better with parents.

H. Study Courses

* **Know Your Child,** series of 8 color filmstrips; with manual only. Rental $1.50, with 45 r. p. m. records, rental $3.00 each.

1. Sources of Truth	5. Similarities in Growth
2. The Dynamics of Growth	6. Differences in Growth
3. The Stages of Growth (early)	7. Freedom and Discipline in Growth
4. The Stages of Growth (later)	8. The Challenge

Produced by Moody Bible Institute. Well received by Lutheran educators. Available from Concordia Publishing House.

Successful Teaching, series of 8 color filmstrips; with manual $1.50, with tape recording $2.50, with 45 r. p. m. records $3.00 each.

1. The Teacher
2. The Pupil
3. The Language
4. The Lesson
5. The Teaching Process
6. The Learning Process
7. Review and Application
8. The Final Test

Produced by Moody Bible Institute. Recommended by Lutheran educators. Available from Concordia Publishing House.

Teaching the Bible Series: Each 75 frames, two 78 r. p. m. records, leader's guide, 15 min. B & W. Sale $12.00 each; rental $2.50 each.

* Teaching the Bible to the Preschool Child
   How to use and teach the Bible to the small child at home and at church.

Teaching the Bible to Children 6 to 11
   Shows parents and teachers how to lead school-age children to a fruitful use of God's Word.

Teaching the Bible to High School Youth
   Dramatic story of a teacher's experience in teaching and applying the Bible to teen-age youth.

Marriage for Moderns, McGraw-Hill *series* of films to be used with college groups and Bowman's book *Marriage for Moderns.*

(1) This Charming Couple   (4) It Takes All Kinds
(2) Marriage Today   (5) Who's Boss
(3) Choosing for Happiness

   Recommended for Christian groups with reservations. Needs a Christian interpreter using the approach: What can we learn? How can we adapt? Are these principles Christian and Biblical?

Preparation for Marriage Series (for adolescents)
   (Described above under: D)

I. Serving the Aging Family

Such a Busy Day Tomorrow, 55-min. film, free from U. S. Social Security Office.
   An old man, without family, living in a boarding house, has his life changed from despair to happiness and usefulness through a center for older people.

Life With Grandpa, film produced by March of Time, Ideal Films, 207 E. 37th St., New York City 16. Rental $4.00.
   Gives an overview of the problems of old age and how to meet them.

Adventures in Maturity, 22-min. film. Free from libraries, local or state health depts.
   How a woman, resigned to a rocking-chair existence, finds a new life for herself.

   NOTE: All these are available through the Audio Visual Service of Concordia Publishing House, 3558 S. Jefferson Ave., St. Louis 18, Mo.